The Third Force
in Missions

The Third Force in Missions

A Pentecostal Contribution to
Contemporary Mission Theology

Paul A. Pomerville

The Third Force in Missions:
A Pentecostal Contribution to Contemporary Mission Theology

© 1985, 2016 Hendrickson Publishers Marketing, LLC
P. O. Box 3473
Peabody, Massachusetts 01961-3473

ISBN 978-1-61970-768-9

Printed in the United States of America

First Printing Revised Edition—July 2016

All Scripture quotations, unless otherwise indicated, are taken from the Holy Bible, New International Version®, NIV®. Copyright © 1973, 1978, 1984, 2011 by Biblica, Inc.™ Used by permission of Zondervan. All rights reserved worldwide. www.zondervan.com. The "NIV" and "New International Version" are trademarks registered in the United States Patent and Trademark Office by Biblica, Inc.™

Library of Congress Cataloging-in-Publication Data

Names: Pomerville, Paul Anthony, 1937- author.
Title: The third force in missions : a Pentecostal contribution to
    contemporary mission theology / Paul A. Pomerville.
Description: Peabody, MA : Hendrickson Publishers, 2016. | Originally
    published: Peabody, Mass. : Hendrickson Publishers, c1985. | Includes
    bibliographical references and index.
Identifiers: LCCN 2016012774 | ISBN 9781619707689 (alk. paper)
Subjects: LCSH: Pentecostal churches--Missions. | Missions--Theory.
Classification: LCC BV2565 .P66 2016 | DDC 266/.994--dc23 LC record
    available at http://lccn.loc.gov/2016012774

CONTENTS

FOREWORD BY
ARTHUR F. GLASSER (1985)

The appearance of this long-awaited volume on the distinct contribution of the Pentecostal movement to contemporary mission theology is an occasion for rejoicing. Dr. Paul A. Pomerville is uniquely qualified to produce this study. He has fruitfully served the American Church, has been an effective field missionary in Indonesia, and has through diligent study acquired a solid grasp of the complexity—in theory, praxis, and theology—of the cross-cultural communication of the Christian faith.

Pentecostals are often described as evangelicals with a plus. By the plus is meant a dynamic and joyful experience of God that is deep and ongoing and which heightens one's sense of Christ's Lordship and the Spirit's leading. Along with this is the claim that the Scriptures become Spirit-taught, that prayer attains new levels of edification, and that personal holiness is reinforced in every way. Moreover, one's witness to the living Christ becomes more spontaneous and it is tangibly confirmed in the minds of those who hear it.

All this is true. Many evangelicals have been challenged by the immediacy and reality of God that Pentecostals reflect along with their freedom and unabashed willingness to confess openly their allegiance to Christ. The achievements of their churches are equally impressive, reflecting their settled conviction that the full experience of the Holy Spirit will not only move the church closer to Jesus at its center, but at the same time, press the church to move out into the world in mission.

However, because this plus is almost totally in the realm of experiential religion, there are those who would question whether the Pentecostal movement has any substantive contribution to make to the church's understanding of the theology of her worldwide mission. They would contend that the basic building blocks of a Trinitarian theology of mission existed long before Pentecostals appeared on the scene: the sovereign electing grace of God the Father, the universal sufficiency of the gospel of God the Son, and the calling into being and empowering of the church to make disciples of all peoples by God the Holy Spirit. And yet, when one places this study by Pomerville alongside the classical form of Protestant mission theology, it soon becomes apparent that concepts and themes have been supplied from the Pentecostal frame of reference that add both comprehensiveness and strength to the older framework.

As you peruse this study you will find yourself not only increasingly appreciating and respecting the Pentecostal movement worldwide for its devotion to Christ and its missionary obedience. You will also become increasingly grateful for its significant contribution to the evangelical understanding of the missionary calling and increasingly grateful to God for the provision of his Holy Spirit to enable the church to rise more fully to its demands.

I rejoice in the privilege of commending this book to the Christian public. My prayer is that it will help many to attain a deeper sense of the significance of the Pentecostal movement. God has truly raised up this "Third Force" in the twentieth century to "hasten the coming" of his day through accelerating the missionary obedience of his church.

ARTHUR F. GLASSER
DEAN EMERITUS AND SENIOR
PROFESSOR OF THEOLOGY AND
EAST ASIAN STUDIES
SCHOOL OF WORLD MISSION
FULLER THEOLOGICAL SEMINARY

FOREWORD BY WILLIAM W. MENZIES (1985)

A conspicuous feature of the modern Pentecostal movement from its beginnings at the turn of the century has been a passion for evangelism and missions. Sensing the urgency of reaching the lost before the imminent return of Christ, Spirit-baptized believers scattered to remote places with the gospel. These pioneers, often lacking adequate academic preparation and material resources, regularly established strong national churches in areas that seemed to others to be almost impervious to significant Christian penetration. Particularly in animistic cultures that were deeply conscious of the world of spirits and demons, Pentecostals frequently secured unusual response. Has such church growth been the result of sheer expenditure of physical energy? Did these people stumble onto some particularly effective technique? Or, is it possible that underlying the experience and the practice of the Pentecostals there is a theology which merits exploration?

Paul Pomerville, Assemblies of God missiologist, has attempted to probe the theological implications underlying the unusual contribution of Pentecostal missions to the modern Christian church. In this volume, the author has demonstrated convincingly that Pentecostals, although deeply indebted to conservative, orthodox evangelicalism, nonetheless have a distinctive theological contribution to make. Drawing upon his considerable knowledge of historical theology, Pomerville makes the point clear that from the age of the Enlightenment, scholastic Protestantism has extended its influence on modern evangelicalism. This influence is disclosed in an uneasiness with the supernatural manifestations of God's power, in an eagerness to ascribe as "superstition" a serious belief in the demonic. Pentecostals, conscious of God's power to take authority over evil spirits and satanic power, at this point are not quite identical to their evangelical "cousins."

This book is important for several reasons. First, it is a serious call to Pentecostals to articulate their theology, not just as an apologetic for parochial consumption, but as a contribution to evangelical missiology. What Pentecostals have sought to emphasize, perhaps almost intuitively, now needs to be expressed with clarity and skill. Pomerville points out, incidentally, that Pentecostals run the risk of missing this opportunity by default should they permit evangelicalism to dictate the hermeneutical and theological agenda for them.

Second, this study is a penetrating analysis of the development of evangelical theology. Pomerville is gently suggesting to his dear evangelical colleagues an important reason for the disparity in penetration of animistic cultures between rationalistic-oriented fundamentalism and Spirit-oriented Pentecostalism. The historical roots of fundamentalism may need to be examined afresh, so that new directions may be explored that will occasion a fresh breath from the Spirit of God.

When Paul Pomerville asked me to read his manuscript, I became aware that he was writing a volume of unusual significance. He has issued a useful challenge to Pentecostals, who should be articulating their theology with greater clarity, and a challenge to evangelicals to consider new ways to make room for the empowering of the Spirit. In this way, Pomerville places missiology in a new light, with a consequent bright impact on a dark world. This book should be read thoughtfully by every earnest Christian who is concerned about reaching his generation for Christ. I suspect that this study will become one of the most provocative essays to emerge in the field of mission theology in this decade.

WILLIAM W. MENZIES
VICE PRESIDENT OF ACADEMIC AFFAIRS
CALIFORNIA THEOLOGICAL SEMINARY
FRESNO, CALIFORNIA

PREFACE TO THE FIRST
EDITION (1985)

As the third force in Christianity, Pentecostalism has a significant contribution to make to contemporary missions. The purpose
of this book is to state what that contribution is. Hopefully, others
will be stimulated to further theological reflection in the pursuit of
a Pentecostal theology of mission.

The phrase "third force" was coined midway through the twentieth century when the phenomenal vitality and growth of the Pentecostal movement became evident. Perceptive churchmen saw that,
along with Roman Catholicism and Protestantism, Pentecostalism
made up a "third corner" or "third force" in contemporary Christianity. However, this phrase was not only used to refer to the movement's statistics or size. It was applied to Pentecostalism because
the movement revived a dimension of the Christian faith which had
almost been eclipsed in the Western world—the experience of the
Holy Spirit. The demise of the experiential dimension of Christianity, therefore, is the backdrop for Pentecostalism's contribution to
contemporary missions. This theology and experience of the Spirit
must be used to solve contemporary mission problems.

A chief value of my approach to Pentecostalism's contribution is that the methodology is not polemical in nature. The fact
that the author is a missiologist within the Pentecostal movement
does have its advantages. However, both mainline Protestant and
Roman Catholic theologians are the chief sources for affirming
the neglected doctrine of pneumatology in the common Christian
tradition and its bearing on the issues of contemporary mission

theology. Our effort is to enrich a Pentecostal theology of mission from the common Christian tradition, but at the same time to develop fresh Pentecostal insights into contemporary mission issues. This somewhat "ecumenical" focus in this approach also includes the Pentecostal movement in the non-Western world. A major context of contemporary mission issues concerns the African Independent Church movement. The notion that the African Independent Churches, for the most part, represent indigenous Pentecostal movements highlights a major issue of mission theology—the contextualization of the gospel in non-Western cultures. The inclusion of these "hidden Pentecostals" in the worldwide Pentecostal movement gives the Western church numerous case studies of the incarnation of the gospel in African culture.

I am indebted to Dr. Arthur F. Glasser of Fuller Theological Seminary's School of World Mission for direction and advice in researching Pentecostalism's contribution to contemporary mission theology. Special appreciation is also extended to Dr. William W. Menzies for reading the manuscript, offering invaluable advice, and encouraging me to publish my findings, and to Dr. Ben Aker for his editorial contribution.

PREFACE TO THE SECOND EDITION (2015)

Why would a book written thirty years ago be published in a second edition? For the reason that the book's subject matter is still current, is still of interest and value, and has some enduring quality. The worldwide Pentecostal-charismatic movement was the subject matter of the first edition of *The Third Force in Missions* in 1985. The book proposed that Pentecostals were a third force in missions and that, alongside Protestant and Roman Catholic missions, they had a contribution to make to the church's mission in the world. Pentecostal-charismatic movements are not only still with us and of primary interest in Christianity, but in the last thirty years they have proliferated and become a major factor in the expansion of the Christian faith in the world, especially in the Southern Hemisphere. Today, it is not even reasonable to speak of "global Christianity" without a reference to Pentecostalism. In global Christianity, the Pentecostal-charismatic movement has taken center stage today and it has an enduring message for the church and its mission. Our view is that Pentecostal movements across the globe today are *renewals of Jesus' universal gospel of the kingdom of God*; the charismatic phenomenon that Christians experience today was the normative Christian experience of the New Testament.

The spontaneous expansion of the Pentecostal-charismatic movement for the past thirty years has caused the majority population of global Christianity to shift from the Northern to the Southern Hemisphere. Today that part of the globe accounts for two-thirds of the world's Pentecostal-charismatic Christians. The most recent "wave" of the Pentecostal-charismatic movement began to gain momentum in the Southern Hemisphere at the beginning of the twenty-first century. In some countries it has not only become the dominant form of the Christian faith, but in some cases Pentecostal-charismatic Christians have become a majority of the Christian population. Whether the Pentecostal-charismatic movement has a contribution to make to Christian missions *today* is a moot point.

Thirty years ago, however, I was preparing a doctoral dissertation for Fuller Theological Seminary's School of World Mission titled "Pentecostalism and Missions: Distortion or Correction? The Pentecostal Contribution to Contemporary Mission Theology" (published by Hendrickson Publishers as *The Third Force in Missions*). At the time, most evangelicals considered Pentecostalism to be a "distortion." In the 1980s there were some evangelical theologians saying the Pentecostal-charismatic movement *was* a "correction" to an overly rational view of the Christian faith. My dissertation took this tack, primarily using non-Pentecostal theologians to support my thesis. Also, I had information of my own on the contextualization of Western theology from a previous thesis at Seattle Pacific University, "A Case Study in the Contextualization of Theology: A Critique of the Reformed View of Scripture in the Post-Reformation Period," that pointed to a distortion in *evangelical* theology.

At the time of writing the first edition of *The Third Force in Missions*, the suggestion that the Pentecostal-charismatic movement was a "third force" in Christian missions was "a stretch" in the view of evangelicals. Many considered the claim to be presumptuous. For them, the subject of the worldwide Pentecostal-charismatic movement was a somewhat esoteric one, because there was an "information gap" as to its size and importance in the evangelical community. Even after the first two waves of the Pentecostal-charismatic movement (classical Pentecostals at the beginning of the twentieth century, and the charismatic movement midway through the century), there was *still* a statistical "information gap" about the worldwide movement among evangelicals.

I realized something was wrong. The absence of a statistical picture of the worldwide movement just did not add up. Though technology then was not what it is today, it was sufficient to create statistics on the worldwide movement. At the time, there was a great interest among evangelicals for presenting a statistical picture of the un-evangelized peoples of the world, and this was done with success, even documenting the unfinished mission in unreached tribes. The continuing obscurity of the worldwide Pentecostal-charismatic movement among evangelicals, however, was a puzzle. Fortunately, there was David Barrett's newly released *World Christian Encyclopedia* (1982) that was sympathetic to Pentecostalism and provided statistics on the worldwide movement, including statistics on the African Independent Church Movement that he considered a valid part of the worldwide Pentecostal-charismatic movement.

My attempt to give "a reliable estimate" of the number of classical Pentecostals, charismatics in mainline churches, and the "new Pentecostals" in the independent churches of the developing world was fraught with difficulties. I found that the "information gap" was not technological in nature but an ecclesiastical-theological bias among evangelicals against Pentecostalism. The "information gap" appeared to be due to: (1) bias or prejudice against Pentecostalism; (2) denominational and theological bias against "charismatics" and their experience with the Spirit in their mainline church communities; (3) ethnocentrism with regard to non-Western Pentecostal-charismatic movements in the developing world (the *new* Pentecostals); and (4) faulty reporting by classical Pentecostals (e.g., differentiating between "members" and "adherents" in counting Pentecostals, which significantly lowered the total statistics). All of the above factors caused an underreported and understated picture of the worldwide movement. Nevertheless, *The Third Force in Missions* showed that the worldwide Pentecostal-charismatic movement in 1985 was not only an important force in the church's mission, but actually represented a statistical one-third of "committed, born-again Christians worldwide"—an actual "third force" in Christian missions.

Unfortunately, *the same difficulties are present today—three decades later*—for obtaining a reliable estimate of the worldwide Pentecostal-charismatic movement. This is why I felt it important to publish a second edition of my original book. Today, in spite of three historic "waves" of the Pentecostal-charismatic renewal there *still appears to be a hesitancy* to report worldwide statistics of the movement clearly, and it appears that the statistics are *still understated* for the same reasons as in 1985. Ironically, this is *still* the case even after the explosive growth of the "third wave" in the Southern Hemisphere in the twenty-first century. There is *still* no major reflection among evangelicals on this unprecedented Pentecostal-charismatic growth of the Christian faith, along with an accurate statistical picture of the global movement. After thirty years of astounding growth of Pentecostal-charismatic movements, it is ironic that any kind of "information gap" remains—but it does, especially in the Southern Hemisphere. Therefore, we must *again* focus on what we formerly called the "hidden Pentecostals"—the contextualization of the Christian faith, in its "Pentecostal form," in the many cultures and nations of the Southern Hemisphere.

The somewhat aggressive manner in which this book pursues accurate information on Pentecostal-charismatic movements in the Southern Hemisphere, challenging contemporary statistics, is not sectarian in nature, representing Pentecostal triumphalism. It is to preserve the Pentecostal experience of the Spirit as a contribution for world missions, which was the subject of the 1985 edition. After thirty years and three waves of Pentecostal-charismatic renewal, however, we now state clearly that this contemporary historical evidence of renewals *shows the Pentecostal experience with the Spirit to be normative New Testament Christian experience.* In other words, we view the easily distinguishable historic three waves of Pentecostal-charismatic movements in the twentieth and twenty-first centuries as *renewals of Jesus' gospel of the kingdom of God.*

This New Testament view of the gospel precludes the traditional evangelical bifurcation of the work of Christ and of the Spirit (Yong, 2005, p. 37; Tan-Chow, 2007, p. 34). Both are part-and-parcel of *Jesus' theology of the kingdom*; there is no need for Southern Hemisphere theologians to struggle with rational, analytically-oriented Western categories of systematic theology (soteriology and pneumatology) in articulating indigenous theologies. They need not be described in an awkward way as "pneumatological soteriology." The biblical theology of the gospel of the kingdom of God inherently includes both of these categories of systematic theology; in fact, it incorporates *all of its categories.*

Rather than being sectarian in pointing to the true impact and size of the worldwide Pentecostal-charismatic movement, our purpose is to uphold and defend that twofold "good news of the kingdom of God"—the redemptive death of Jesus Christ for the sin of humanity and the gift of the Spirit. This is not an arbitrary description of the "good news," attempting to justify the Pentecostal distinctive; nor is it an attempt to delineate all the good things in the gospel (e.g., "fourfold" or "fivefold" gospels). It is Jesus' description of the gospel and the apostles' perception of the gospel they declared throughout the New Testament. Jesus' theology of the kingdom in the New Testament is also a biblical theme of the Old Testament (Bright, 1953; Pomerville, 2009, pp. 104–14), and it is the *foundation for a Pentecostal theology*—a biblical theology as opposed to a systematic theology.

While the first edition of *The Third Force in Missions* showed that the influence of post-Reformation rationalistic culture and theology reduced the experience of the Holy Spirit in the evangelical view of the gospel, there was a sense in which the 1985 study was incomplete. The negative influence of *dispensational theology* that distorted the gospel and hindered a true Pentecostal theology of mission was mentioned in the first edition; I showed that it was detrimental both to Pentecostal theology and the reporting of the Pentecostalism, but its danger to the gospel message and the ongoing Christian mission was not developed. Ironically, this unorthodox theology—which contradicts Reformation theology, a Trinitarian theology of mission, and Jesus' gospel of the kingdom of God—undermines the very core of the Pentecostal-charismatic movement and *continues* to influence evangelicals *and Pentecostals* thirty years later.

Could the "third wave" of Pentecostal-charismatic renewal in the Southern Hemisphere today, where two-thirds of the Christian community is Pentecostal-charismatic and there are indigenous theologies of mission emerging, *still* be telling us something about the deficiency of *both* evangelical and Pentecostal theology in the North? The *Third Force in Missions'* discussion of the kingdom of

God motif in the New Testament lays the foundation for a Pentecostal, biblical theology that contradicts and corrects dispensational theology. The kingdom of God theme in the first edition was seen to be the basis for a true Pentecostal theology, and examples of that contention were given in the discussion on contemporary mission theology; but the urgent necessity for developing a biblical theology to replace so-called "biblical" dispensational theology was not pursued.

The thirty-year interim provided further opportunity to investigate dispensational theology's influence among evangelicals and Pentecostals. In preparing and writing my books since then (*Culture Blind Evangelicals and the Good News of the Kingdom of God*, 2009; *Rediscovering the Gospel: Its Eclipse in American Culture*, 2010; and *The New Testament Case against Christian Zionism: A Christian View of the Israeli-Palestinian Conflict*, 2014), it became apparent that dispensational theology has been largely instrumental in preventing evangelicals from seriously considering the size of the Pentecostal-charismatic movement (the "information gap"), as well as obscuring the Pentecostal experience as a real option for evangelicals to believe.

Today, the influence of dispensational theology among both evangelicals and Pentecostals continues to obscure the worldwide Pentecostal-charismatic movement, and it continues to prevent evangelicals from seeing the movements as renewals of the normative New Testament gospel of the kingdom in Christian experience. The core of each of the above books speaks to the need for seeing *Jesus' theology of the gospel of the kingdom* and his apostles' expression of that theology as a "biblical theology" in the New Testament that would replace the damaging influence of an Israel-focused dispensational theology. On "dispensational" grounds, it denies the presence of this powerful "gospel of the kingdom" today, the church as the empowered new people of God who mediate that gospel to the world, and the very age of the Spirit itself. It is a system of theology that contradicts the basic tenets of Reformation theology and supplants Jesus' role at the midpoint of salvation history with an Israel-focused theology. My book *The New Testament Case against Christian Zionism* exposes Christian Zionism's use of this unorthodox theology, its erosion of the truth of the gospel, and the chaos and contradictions it causes in the evangelical-Pentecostal community. The first edition's discussion of mission theology and biblical theology put the failure and inadequacy of dispensational theology in bold relief. In this second edition, I provide further commentary and examples from contextualization of the gospel in the Southern Hemisphere (indigenous theologies) that addresses dispensational theology's failure with regard to the church's ongoing mission and its obscuring the "good news of the kingdom of God" in the world today; its excessive focus on an eschatological kingdom marginalizes Christ's immediate presence in the "already" kingdom of God and his readiness to meet their needs. However, a complete refutation of dispensational theology is not possible in this second edition of *The Third Force in Missions*; for this, the reader should refer to *The New Testament Case against Christian Zionism: A Christian View of the Israeli-Palestinian Conflict.*

✶ ✶ ✶

At the same time of the "two waves" of Pentecostal-like renewals at the beginning of the twentieth century in the Azusa Street revivals, as well as the charismatic movement in mainline Protestant churches midway through the century in America, corresponding and simultaneous outpourings of the Spirit took place in the churches of the Southern Hemisphere, some that had no historical connection with the movements in the Northern Hemisphere. In 1985, many evangelicals denied these "independent" movements were "Christian," stating they were merely "nativistic movements." A more subtle form of this denial of the validity of Pentecostal-charismatic movements in the Southern Hemisphere remains today. Then, some of the movements were only loosely connected with other non-Pentecostal "mission churches," yet they were experiencing a renewal of first-century Pentecostal phenomena. My first edition argued for their "place" in the Pentecostal-charismatic renewal. Now, over thirty years later, it is necessary to bring attention once again to these "hidden Pentecostals"—although they are not so hidden today, they are *still* statistically underreported and *still* viewed with suspicion. This is ironic because this Pentecostal renewal in the Southern Hemisphere—the third wave—may well have created the "first force" in twenty-first century Christian missions. However, this notion is obscure in the West, due to the underreporting of what have been called "neo-Pentecostal," "renewalist," and "independent" movements in the Southern Hemisphere.

The first edition of *The Third Force in Missions* showed that the Scriptures were central in the independent church movements in the "developing world;" these churches were people of "the Book," and they believed Jesus to be the Lord and Savior of all. They did not place specific emphasis on the gift of the Spirit or a "Pentecostal baptism of the Spirit" in their churches; they were just people responding in faith to Jesus and his message of "the good news of the kingdom of God" in the New Testament (Luke 4:43; Matt. 4:17, 23; 9:35)—without the restricting, rational worldview and rational gospel that were so prominent in the Northern Hemisphere. To the contrary, their indigenous worldview was naturally open to the supernatural phenomena of the New Testament world. Ironically, they were faulted for this. Furthermore, many had thrown off association with Western missions' churches, and in their newfound freedom were seeking a new identity—as Christians—contextualizing the gospel of the kingdom of God in their own cultures in a post-colonial world.

Now, with thirty-year hindsight, we see that in the beginning of the twenty-first century the churches of the Southern Hemisphere had matured in their indigenous non-Western cultural settings, growing in the word of God and witnessing to the power of the gospel of the kingdom of God among neighboring countries—among cultures similar to theirs. What amounted to "assaults on their cultures" by Western missionaries in imposing a Western-oriented gospel and theology in colonial and post-colonial times had now faded into the historical past. They no longer had to contend with foreign concepts and forms of worship in developing their own cultural expression of the Christian faith, and their efforts to witness to neighboring areas and cultures did not involve a "cross-cultural" missionary effort of the magnitude that Western missionaries had faced. Their "mission fields" were "culturally near" neighbors, and the spread of the faith was natural and spontaneous among the poor communities of the Southern Hemisphere, just as it was in the history of the early church in New Testament times.

Under these "ordinary circumstances" of believing and proclaiming the "twofold gospel"—Jesus as Lord and Savior of all, and his gift of the indwelling Spirit with outward charismatic manifestations of the Spirit—there has been a rapid and deep expansion of the Christian faith in the cultures and nations of the Southern Hemisphere in the twenty-first century. This gospel of the kingdom naturally resonates with the poor who readily respond to its hopeful message (Matt. 5:3). I give this brief description of the "third wave" of the Pentecostal-charismatic renewal—what is happening "down south"—as the power of Jesus' gospel of the kingdom of God being unleashed among responsive peoples in a spontaneous expansion of the Christian faith. The third wave of the Pentecostal-charismatic movement in the Southern Hemisphere confirms that such movements are "renewals" of the powerful "gospel of the kingdom of God." But there is also the sense that a new, fresh, and effective paradigm of the Christian faith is emerging for world evangelization.

Not only has the center of Christianity shifted to the global south, but the church's future mission to the world has shifted there as well. In the *next* thirty-five years (in 2050), according to some predictions, the world will be dominated by 2,918,070,000 Christians and 2,761,480,000 Muslims. Some in the "North" see this as an omen of conflict and warfare between these two religions (dispensational theology's influence). However, it is not necessary to succumb to "dispensational" pessimism or the disastrous result of dispensational theology's pseudo-apocalyptic eschatology that attempts to "help God" with the coming of Armageddon. To the contrary, there is reason to believe that such a situation may represent an unprecedented period of missions for the proclamation of the universal and powerful "good news of the kingdom of God," as well as an occasion for the Christian faith to expand spontaneously in the world prior to the Lord's return (Matt. 24:14).

In this "new Pentecostal paradigm" of the Christian faith in the South, Christians are experiencing *the norm* of New Testament spiritual experience and the power of the gospel of the kingdom of God. The context of hatred between the West and Islam that is so prevalent in the Northern Hemisphere, which is exacerbated by Christian Zionism and its dispensational theology's excessive and ill-founded Israel-influence, is not a major part of the equation there. Therefore, the churches of the Southern Hemisphere may well be the answer to *reaching the world of Islam*—that is in their very midst—with the universal "good news" of the kingdom of God. In this second edition, I want to confirm the size and vitality of the Pentecostal-charismatic movement in the Southern Hemisphere and to draw attention to this mission to Islam as well. The Southern Hemisphere, with its Christians' cultural affinity with the New Testament and its gospel of the kingdom of God, portends a major movement in the future of Christian missions—a literal "first force" in missions.

PAUL A. POMERVILLE
BALI, INDONESIA, 2015

INTRODUCTION: MISSIONS FROM A PENTECOSTAL PERSPECTIVE

This book draws attention to the Pentecostal contribution to contemporary missions. The notion of a contribution involves not only a worldwide Pentecostal movement representing phenomenal growth but also a deficiency in contemporary missions. An inordinate "silence on the Holy Spirit" is part of the Protestant mission heritage. The Pentecostal movement addresses that silence in a significant way. The value of this book for contemporary missions concerns the degree to which that silence affects God's ongoing mission in the world today—from the Pentecostal perspective that pneumatological silence is a critical problem in the church's response to God's mission today.

Contemporary theologies of mission neglect the role of the Holy Spirit. Max Warren refers to the neglect of the Spirit when he speaks of Pentecostalism and the charismatic movement as "protest" movements. He states that the movements protest the neglect of the role of the Holy Spirit and that they are a healthy correction to the torpidity of church life (1976, p. 126). Michael Green also speaks of the neglect as a "domestication" of the Spirit in the West (1975, p. 12). The "silence on the Holy Spirit," though, is not restricted to Western mission theologies. William Menzies speaks of a "practical subordinationism" of the Spirit in Christian theology due to the contextual focus of eighteenth- and nineteenth-century theologies (1979, pp. 68, 71). The creedal statements of the church in those periods testify to the low profile of the Holy Spirit in Western theology, and the root of the "silence" concerns the contextualization of the Christian faith in Western culture.

In Harry Boer's definitive study on the significance of Pentecost for missions, he expresses surprise over the paucity of theological attention devoted to this subject (1961, p. 12). David Bosch also states that pneumatology, in terms of the Spirit's out-directed ministry, began to be neglected as early as the second century. He states that the missionary dimension of pneumatology was rediscovered in the eighteenth century but that it played no significant role in Protestant theology (1980, pp. 241–42).

While pneumatology often took the place of an appendage to theology in the above-mentioned periods, its absence in contemporary mission theology is especially conspicuous. Early in the twentieth century Roland Allen stated, "Missionary work as an expression of the Holy Spirit has received such slight and casual attention that it might almost escape the notice of the hasty reader" (1960, p. 21). In the last quarter of the twentieth century Allen's observation, at least in terms of the missionary role of the Holy Spirit, still holds true. Relatively little has been written on the crucial significance of the Holy Spirit in connection with the missionary witness of the church, a subject that Allen spoke of as "one whole hemisphere of the Spirit" (1960, p. 21). Lindsell (1949), along with Allen (1960) and Boer (1961), supports the thesis that the role of the Holy Spirit in modern missions and mission theology is greatly neglected.

Pentecostals are quick to recognize the neglect of pneumatology but slow to articulate it. However, Melvin Hodges, a classical Pentecostal missiologist, is specific in describing the neglect. He describes the "silence on the Holy Spirit" as a neglect of an indispensable qualification for missions—the enduing of Pentecostal power (1977a, p. 149). He links the relative success of Pentecostal missions directly with the "place" that Pentecostals give to the Holy Spirit, a place similar to that which New Testament believers gave to the Spirit (p. 35). The phenomenal growth of the Pentecostal movement and its dynamic missionary thrust are behind Hodges's claim. Such evidence should be worthy of the attention of the evangelical world.

The value of the first edition of the book for Pentecostals was that it was an effort to articulate the Pentecostal contribution to contemporary issues of mission theology. It helped to fill in the tremendous gap that existed with respect to Pentecostal-oriented missiological literature. The missiological information gap may have been due to the tendency of Pentecostals toward activism; they are "task theologians" (their theological focus being on the specific encounters of mission). Or, it may have been due to the want of academic training in the field of missiology (or the failure to appreciate its importance for mission in the modern world). Nevertheless, the articulation of a Pentecostal theology of mission *is* crucial for the Pentecostal movement. Pentecostals are frequently not aware that mission theory lays the necessary theological foundation for guiding mission practice. But mission theology provides a biblical criterion for evaluating mission activity in the light of the contemporary problems of mission. In examining Pentecostal mission theology in this study, the perspective is limited to the somewhat representative classical Pentecostal viewpoint and, of course, my own specific theological viewpoint.

AN EVANGELICAL-PENTECOSTAL PERSPECTIVE

I will attempt to define my own evangelical-Pentecostal perspective in this introduction. It may be surprising for some evangelicals to see that the Pentecostal perspective differs little from the rest of evangelicalism in matters of basic Christian belief. However, it will become clear that the Pentecostal perspective has an "edge" when it confronts the experiential dimension of the Christian faith. This perspective is also crucial for exposing a fundamental distortion that the Western worldview has brought to the Christian faith— its intellectualization, or rationalization. It is a definite asset when assessing the worldwide Pentecostal movement. A sympathetic approach to Pentecostalism is crucial when non-Western expressions of the phenomenon are evaluated (e.g., African Independent Churches).

I view my Pentecostal-evangelical perspective as an asset to the study of Pentecostalism and missions. My Pentecostal experience, education (in part), ordination, and ministry took place within the context of the Assemblies of God fellowship. As a participating Pentecostal, I have been identified with classical Pentecostalism's missionary enterprise, its presuppositions, and its norms and values. In other words, I represent an insider's perspective with respect to the Pentecostal worldview and the movement's missions efforts. This intuitive understanding of the movement affords the opportunity to make a critical evaluation from the perspective of a sympathetic participant. Often, new religious movements such as Pentecostalism are not described with objectivity by outside observers. Numerous illustrations of this are found throughout this study. Especially poignant are those that emerge from observations of Pentecostalism in non-Western cultures. From the standpoint of critics, the movements often "serve as spiritual ink blots, reports of the movements tell us more about the observers than about the observed" (Needleman, 1978, p. 142). My inside perspective, therefore, is crucial for articulating the Pentecostal contribution to contemporary missions.

An awareness of the value of one's classical Pentecostal worldview does not mean the study will be excessively biased or doctrinaire in nature. On the contrary, such awareness allows for the control of bias. Research is always an interpretation. Bias is inevitable; pure objectivity is an illusion. However, one's bias can be gauged when it is explicit. Rather than a supposed "presupposition-less" approach, objectivity involves the elimination of "unconscious" presuppositions, values, and desires. "Scientific" objectivity concerns the recognition of possible bias and the implementation of means to control it. This study is approached with a consciousness of the impact that my Pentecostal worldview brings to the task. Worldview is recognized as a context that impinges on interpretation.

WHO IS AN "EVANGELICAL"?

The term "evangelical" is as problematic as the term "Pentecostal." What does the connection of the two terms with a hyphen (evangelical-Pentecostal) mean? In the first place, it intends to communicate that Pentecostals are part of contemporary evangelicalism.

But this still needs clarification, for who is an "evangelical"? David Bosch notes that Pentecostal-charismatics make up one of six distinguishable evangelical groupings: the new evangelicals, the separatist fundamentalists, confessional evangelicals, the Pentecostal and charismatic movements, the radical evangelicals, and ecumenical evangelicals (1980, p. 30). This non-Pentecostal recognition of the Pentecostals as an evangelical group identifies my perspective as evangelical. However, my evangelical-Pentecostal perspective is closer to the "new evangelical" group listed above than the "separatist fundamentalist" group. The theological distance between these two groups represents, somewhat, my own theological pilgrimage. Such a pilgrimage involves a more informed understanding of Scripture, theology, and the contemporary Christian movement. But it also involves a holding onto and continued appreciation of what is basic to one's evangelical faith and experience. At least, Bosch's groupings above show evangelicalism to be anything but a monolithic block!

In his article "The Split-Up Evangelicals," Billy Graham says he would have a hard time defining what evangelicalism is today (Woodward, 1982, p. 89). The "split" the article refers to concerns the fundamentalist evangelical group, whose leader the article states is Jerry Falwell, and the more moderate middle of evangelicalism (the new evangelicals), who "shook off the separatist tendencies inherent in fundamentalism" (p. 89). The article attributes the leadership of the latter group, at least symbolically, to Billy Graham. However, the identification of evangelicalism with particular persons only confuses the issue. This article does attempt to define and identify "evangelical" when it states that a generation ago an evangelical was a Protestant who emphasized: (1) personal commitment to Jesus (usually a "born again" experience), (2) biblical authority, and (3) a "preoccupation" with making converts (p. 89). Rather than what divides evangelicals, the key to their identification and definition is what they hold in common.

The definition of "evangelical" properly concerns an identification of principles that can be found in the central Christian tradition, principles that are impulses from the "evangel" in the New Testament. Some have called these principles the "evangelical impulse." According to the threefold Reformation emphasis, the evangelical impulse concerned: (1) the authority of Scripture, (2) salvation by faith, and (3) the universal priesthood of believers (Webber & Bloesch, 1978, pp. 46–47). However, a description of the evangelical impulse by which we may approximate the meaning of evangelicalism must reach beyond the fundamentalist phenomenon and work of nineteenth-century scholastic theologians!

Seven principles that have been identified with the evangelical impulse in history are: (1) the authority of the word of God, (2) orthodoxy (correct belief), (3) personal salvation by grace, (4) dedication and commitment, (5) evangelism and missions, (6) ecumenism *(koinōnia)*, and (7) social concern (Ramm, 1973; Inch, 1978; Quebedeaux, 1974 and 1978; Webber & Bloesch, 1978; Bloesch, 1973; Dayton, 1976). An evangelical, therefore, is a Christian who identifies with this particular configuration of belief and practice. Evangelicalism represents this "impulse," which spans not only the history of the church from Pentecost to the present, but also the full ecclesiastical spectrum of the Christian faith in the contemporary world. No particular group is in focus, therefore, when one speaks of "an evangelical"; rather, the focus is on the principles of belief and practice. They are drawn from the New Testament and illustrated in the central tradition of the Christian church.

Pentecostalism's distinctive experience with the Holy Spirit brings a fresh sharpness to the term "evangelical." This distinctive experience with the Spirit causes the Pentecostal to reach back beyond the nineteenth-century fundamentalist phenomenon, and the Reformation itself, to the "evangel" as described by the early church in the New Testament. As a renewal movement, Pentecostalism represents a renewal of first-century Christian experience. But it has more to contribute to contemporary evangelicalism than a specific New Testament reference point (the day of Pentecost). It brings a dimension of the Christian faith to light that has all but been eclipsed in Western Christianity—the experiential dimension.

Pentecostalism adds an "eighth principle" to the evangelical impulse described above: the principle of the dynamic nature of the Christian faith. Actually it is not an additional principle, but an inherent part—the dynamic core—of the whole evangelical impulse.

It is spoken of as an additional principle here because of its demise in the history of Western Christianity. Pentecostalism represents the restoration of the dynamic Spirit-dimension to each of the seven principles of the evangelical impulse. The eighth principle involves the *activity of God* in contemporary Christian experience, in terms of the ministry of the Holy Spirit.

Each of the principles of the evangelical impulse could be, and often is, held in an intellectual and static way, not at all reflecting the activity of God in them. The principle of the authority of the word of God in evangelicalism is static and devoid of the activity of the Holy Spirit. Its *locus* is held to be the text of Scripture rather than the witness of the Spirit in the believer's heart as the Reformers believed. The criterion of biblical scholarship is frequently confused with the ministry of the Holy Spirit in this matter. The *principle of orthodoxy* is likewise held in a static manner, which is referred to as an unchangeable doctrinal deposit handed down from either the sixteenth or nineteenth century. The rationalization of the Christian faith is especially evident here. The assumption is that the results of the contextualization of the Christian faith in a specific period of the history of the church are absolute, normative, and perennial. This view of orthodoxy presents problems for the contextualization of the faith in non-Western cultures in contemporary times. The chaos that this distortion brings to the developing world by means of Western missionary efforts is illustrated both by the failure to contextualize the Christian faith and the resulting "reactionary" independent movements in that part of the world. The *principle of salvation by grace* has often been intellectualized until conversion is interpreted as intellectual acceptance of correct doctrine alone, and faith is considered to be an "evidence-less" affair (apart from Scripture, that is) in evangelicalism. An expectation of the activity of God beyond the conversion experience is considered a *lack* of faith! Further, the last two chapters of this book show how the *principles of evangelism and missions* are distorted when the mediated activity of the Holy Spirit through the church is eliminated in mission thinking. The terms are redefined until conversion, evangelism, and Great Commission mission disappear in the church's mission to the contemporary world. So it continues with each of the evangelical principles—each can be merely a static concept and thereby distorted when the dynamic dimension of pneumatology is neglected.

When the "eighth principle" of the evangelical impulse is taken into consideration, however, the Christian faith involves a dynamic, living experience with God the Holy Spirit. God the Holy Spirit is active in connection with his written word (the principle of the authority of the word of God). Its authority concerns the witness of the Spirit confirming the word in the hearts of men and women. Also, God the Holy Spirit is active in the contextualization of the gospel, in fresh applications of the word to the life of faith in society (the principle of orthodoxy). Theology is seen to be a dynamic, biblical, contemporary process, serving the church in its contemporary life of faith. The inordinate fear of syncretism so frequently shown by Western theologians toward developing world theologies would be dissipated if the dynamic dimension of these first two principles were in focus. God the Holy Spirit is also active in conversion missions today; the dimensions of the salvation experience are central to mission theology (the principle of personal salvation by grace). Therefore, the motivation, nature, and execution of missions principally involve the evangelistic mandate under the active supervision of God the Holy Spirit (the principle of evangelism and missions). God the Holy Spirit is active, as he was in the first century, in the areas of piety and worship (the principle of dedication and commitment). In the Pentecostal-charismatic movement, God the Holy Spirit is active in bringing into being an ecumenism born of the Spirit (the principle of ecumenism). God the Holy Spirit is active in the church in meeting the world's total need (the principle of social concern). By means of the mediated activity of the Holy Spirit, God works through the people of God in the world to bring about justice and righteousness. His immediate presence and activity in this cause is a reality.

The seven evangelical principles mentioned here, especially in the context of the "eighth Pentecostal principle"—the activity of God the Holy Spirit—make up the general agenda of contemporary mission theology. This in itself is an indication of the potential Pentecostal contribution to mission theology. Pentecostalism involves the assumption of God's continuing activity in the world today, and this assumption addresses a major dimension of contemporary mission theology.

The Pentecostal perspective brings fresh insights on how God is active by means of the inward and outward ministry of the Holy Spirit. It is concerned with the "ontic" principle of theology and Christian experience. This refers to a view of the faith in which the Christian is seen to confront not only Scripture but also the Holy Spirit. The theological process and Christian experience have the character of presence, the "there-ness," the immediacy of God. This process and experience represent a confrontation with the reality of God the Holy Spirit and the living word. Because the neglect of the Spirit pervades the various areas of mission theology, it is beyond the scope of this book to articulate all of the various implications of a common denominator such as pneumatology. The Pentecostal contribution presented in this study is selective in that only the major implications of the Pentecostal perspective for contemporary mission theology are discussed.

The connection of "Pentecostal" with "evangelical" by means of a hyphen (evangelical-Pentecostal) also indicates that, from the Pentecostal's viewpoint, his or her distinctive experience with the Holy Spirit is part of the "evangelical impulse." The assumption of a valid, contemporary Pentecostal experience, not unlike that recorded in the New Testament, is based on both the contemporary, empirical Pentecostal movement and the description of that experience in the New Testament. Its contemporaneity as a *renewal* of New Testament Christian experience rests on biblical theology—Jesus' gospel of the kingdom of God. It concerns the interpretation of salvation history in which this contemporary period of the church is viewed as continuous with that of the New Testament. This interpretation is based on the "present" kingdom of God motif in the New Testament and the ministry of the Holy Spirit in "the time between the times" (Ladd, 1974, pp. 42, 139, 271; Blauw, 1962, pp. 73, 79; Bright, 1953, pp. 197, 216–19, 232; Filson, 1950, pp. 75–76; Bosch, 1980, pp. 66, 236; Cullmann, 1964, p. 144; Montague, 1976, p. 367). It is in this assumption of God's continuing activity in the world today through the gospel of the kingdom of God that the Pentecostal contribution to contemporary mission theology emerges.

WHO IS A "PENTECOSTAL"?

The question of who is a "Pentecostal" is even more problematic than who is an "evangelical." An attempt to define the modern
Pentecostal movement is beset with numerous difficulties. Some of
the major ones are: (1) its origin and manifestation among diverse
Christian traditions; (2) its penetration and expression in diverse
cultural contexts around the world; (3) its very nature, involving a
personal spiritual experience; (4) the historic controversy as to its
biblical foundations; and (5) the great diversity of theological explanations concerning the nature of the Pentecostal experience and
the movement itself. The term "Pentecostal" is used in this study
to designate the wider renewal of the charismatic work of the Holy
Spirit in all forms of Christianity. However, three major streams of
Pentecostalism usually recognized are: (1) classical Pentecostalism,
(2) neo-Pentecostalism, and (3) Catholic charismatics (Sandidge,
1976, p. 6; Hummel, 1978, p. 39).

"Classical Pentecostalism" refers to those Pentecostal churches
that broke away from the historic churches of Protestantism in the
early part of the past century. The issue that occasioned this break
was the belief that the event on the day of Pentecost mentioned
in Acts 2:4 refers to an experience available to Christians of all
ages. The "baptism of the Holy Spirit" was believed to be evidenced
by the accompanying sign of "speaking with other tongues as the
Spirit gives utterance" (Menzies, 1971, p. 9). The issue of glossolalia
caused the historic churches to ostracize the "tongues speakers." It
also became the prime unifying factor among early Pentecostals
who came from diverse Christian traditions. Hollenweger emphasizes the common factor among Pentecostals as "all the groups
who profess at least two religious crisis experiences (1. Baptism or
rebirth; 2. The baptism of the Spirit), the second being subsequent
to and different from the first one, and the second usually, but
not always, being associated with speaking in tongues" (1972, p.
xix). Hollenweger leaves the option open for the evidence of the
Pentecostal experience to include other charismatic signs besides
glossolalia. Often the term "Pentecostal movement" is confined to
that group of sects within the Christian church that are comprised

of classical Pentecostals, and it is therefore a reference to "the Pentecostal denominations."

The term "neo-Pentecostalism" refers to that movement of the Holy Spirit in the late 1950s in the historic *Protestant* churches that emphasized the baptism of the Holy Spirit and charismatic gifts and graces of the Spirit (Sandidge, 1976, p. 8). (Note: In 2015, the term "neo-Pentecostals" was set aside for those "new" Pentecostals of the third wave in the Southern Hemisphere.) A difference between classical Pentecostals and neo-Pentecostals (or charismatics as they are often called) is that those who have had the latter Pentecostal experience have not left their own churches. Therefore, the "charismatic movement," or "charismatic Renewal," refers to a manifestation of Pentecostal life *within* various traditions of Protestant Christianity. This is not to infer, however, that their theological explanation of the Pentecostal experience is identical to that of classical Pentecostalism.

The designation "Catholic charismatics," or "Catholic charismatic renewal," refers to the Pentecostal movement within the *Roman Catholic* Church. This movement also involves a "baptism of the Holy Spirit" and manifestations of the gifts of the Holy Spirit. However, Roman Catholics prefer the term "renewal" to "movement." Such preference is connected with the view of the baptism of the Holy Spirit as an actualization of what was already received at baptism and confirmation. The baptism of the Holy Spirit is conceived, therefore, as a "release" of the Spirit rather than an "incoming" of the Spirit. The Catholic viewpoint emphasizes important characteristics of the Pentecostal experience in a personal and sacramental sense as "renewal" (an experience with the Holy Spirit who is "already there"). From a historical perspective, the Pentecostal movement *is* a *renewal* (Sandidge, 1976, pp. 11–12). Sandidge states concerning the term "renewal": "Charismatic Renewal" properly is a broad term, referring to all forms of Christianity including Roman Catholicism, the Orthodox churches, mainline Protestantism and Evangelicalism" (p. 11).

There is an advantage in speaking of the theological diversity represented by the above three classifications as a Pentecostal unity. This has been challenged, unsuccessfully, recently in the proliferation of Pentecostalism in the Philippines (Synan & Yong, 2014).

This case illustrates the necessity for giving priority to the *theological center* of the movements over against sociological theories of causation and proliferation when dealing with a "Christian" movement founded in biblical revelation (see chapters 1 and 2 in *Third Force in Missions* for further examples in the African context). The focus of the Pentecostal-charismatic movements as "renewals" of the normative gospel of the kingdom of God in the New Testament precludes erroneous claims, such as those in the Philippines case where the author states that Pentecostal-charismatic Christianity is declining, but in actuality the movements are flourishing (Burgess & van der Maas, 2003, pp. 201–7). Not seeing the movements as a Pentecostal unity, questioning the distinctive of the Pentecostal experience without reference to New Testament biblical data exacerbates the identity problem. The objections to the term "Pentecostal" in the Philippines (if indeed this is true) appear to be rooted in the "name game" regarding the movements in a diverse ecclesial context, without the guiding theological core of the Pentecostal experience. Furthermore, the use of sociological research without reference to the movements' theological core compounds the author's political bias against "Pentecostalism" in the Philippines, due to recent elections (Synan & Yong, 2014, e-book location 4472–86).

The theological unity of Pentecostal-charismatic movements is found in their consideration as "renewal movements," a renewal of the experience of the Holy Spirit like that recorded in the history of the early church. The common denominator in all the theological diversity of the movements, which is considerable even among classical Pentecostals (not to mention charismatics!), is an experience with the Holy Spirit not unlike that experienced by first-century Christians. Such an experience of the Spirit has punctuated the entire history of the church. The "Pentecostal movement" in the sense of a renewal movement, therefore, reaches back to the work of the Holy Spirit with the church that began on the day of Pentecost and continues throughout the "last days" until Jesus Christ returns for his church.

I must add to this description of renewal the resurgence of the charismatic experience of the Holy Spirit among the independent churches of the developing world. This movement of the Holy Spirit, however, does not require further classification in terms of Pentecostalism. The movements only need to be mentioned as to their location and given a designation that differentiates them from the above three movements (classical Pentecostals, neo-Pentecostals [Protestant churches], and Catholic charismatics). Including these "new" Pentecostals is an important distinction for gauging the extent of the worldwide Pentecostal movement.

My claim is that these renewal movements in the developing world are Pentecostal and are part of a worldwide Pentecostal-charismatic renewal. For various reasons that will be stated in the coming chapters, I have called this stream of renewal in the developing world the "hidden Pentecostals." The three main streams of Pentecostalism, both in the Western and non-Western world, have various "tributaries" that can be identified. For instance, within the neo-Pentecostal and Catholic charismatic streams one can differentiate between the following: Roman Catholic Pentecostals, Orthodox Pentecostals, Anglican Pentecostals, non-Roman Apostolic-type Pentecostals (Irvingites), and Black neo-Pentecostals. All of the various tributaries of the charismatic/neo-Pentecostal and classical Pentecostal streams are found in non-Western cultures also. This is clear in the discussion of David Barrett's findings in chapter 1 (see also Barrett, 1982, pp. 782–83).

The Pentecostal movement among the African Independent Church Movement (AICM), for instance, involves both the classical Pentecostal-type "come out" churches described above; e.g., the Aladura societies among the Yoruba churches (Peel, 1968, pp. 73, 109). There are 5,000 separatist churches in the AICM, virtually all of which were at one time movements within the mission churches (Barrett, 1979, p. 63). A movement that in 1980 represented a Christian community of approximately *thirty million people*, being largely Pentecostal in nature, must not be missed in describing the worldwide Pentecostal movement; to miss this segment of the renewal is to understate the size of the worldwide movement. I focus on this segment of the Pentecostal-charismatic renewal when I determine a reasonable estimate for the worldwide movement today.

In this second edition of this book, I have incorporated the "hidden Pentecostals" of the first edition as a Pentecostal-charismatic movement in the developing world, calling them "neo-Pentecostal-charismatics." (Other terms used in works on the Pentecostal-charismatic movement in the Southern Hemisphere are: "neo-Pentecostals," "renewalists," and "independent church movements.") From this contemporary perspective, then, I have combined the charismatic renewal among Protestant and Catholic churches into the one designation of "charismatic movement," referring to it as the "second wave" of Pentecostal-charismatic renewal. This leaves the "neo-Pentecostal" term for the "hidden Pentecostals" in the recent Pentecostal-charismatic renewal in the Southern Hemisphere (the developing world), or the "third wave."

It is necessary to give a short missions' historical background to the neo-Pentecostal churches in the Southern Hemisphere before addressing Pentecostalism in America. The American ecclesial history (the first and second waves of Pentecostal-charismatic renewal) produces confusion when there is an attempt to apply that American paradigm of Pentecostalism to the Pentecostal-charismatic movement in the Southern Hemisphere, especially in terms of ecclesial definitions and doctrine. Rather, our verifying touchstone is Jesus' gospel of the kingdom of God that the apostles articulated in the New Testament. This speaks to the biblical and theological core of the Pentecostal experience and eliminates much confusion.

A New Paradigm: Global Christianity

In Ralph Winter's book *The Twenty-Five Unbelievable Years, 1945–1969*, he notes the historical fact that prior to 1945, 99.5 percent of the non-Western world was under colonial domination, and at the end of 1969, 99.5 percent of the non-Western world was independent (Winter, 1973, pp. 1–3). This dramatic change in the developing world took place in a short twenty-five-year period when four hundred years of colonial domination were rolled back to zero. Most Americans could hardly keep up with the name changes of countries on the map, let alone understand the pressing issues of the new independent nations. Nevertheless, for Americans today, the developing world in the Southern Hemisphere is but a small blip on their radar; furthermore, American Christians are also unaware of an unprecedented surge in the growth of Christianity in the developing world. A new paradigm of "global Christianity" has emerged of which, for the most part, Northern Christians are unaware (Jenkins, 2002, pp. 4–6; Pomerville, 2009, p. 18).

Midway through the twentieth century, the "mission churches" that were the result of Western missionary efforts were under the domination of Western culture. They mirrored Western culture in terms of doctrine, ethics, and style of worship; they looked like the "old paradigm" of Western Christianity. The importance of local culture and customs had long been a "benign insinuation" of new Christians in these churches, but for the most part missionaries were either unaware of their pleas or ignored them. While missionaries were aware that the churches had to be "indigenous" (which means "of the soil," or in other words, adapted to local culture) in terms of being self-governing, self-supporting, and self-propagating, attempts of local Christians to implement local cultural customs in worship, or establish an identity with local culture, were met with warnings of "syncretism"—the mixing of "pagan" culture with the gospel.

When the developing nations became free from Western colonial domination (toward the end of the "twenty-five unbelievable years"), the churches began serious efforts to express that freedom and to gain cultural identity as Christians by implementing local cultural customs in faith and practice. These efforts were not received well by Western missionaries. Western missions' organizations rejected churches that broke away from the "mother churches" over the issue of cultural identity. In Africa, these breakaway "independent churches" that implemented local cultural customs to express their Christian faith numbered in the hundreds of millions and were located in regions of the fastest population growth (Jenkins, 2002, pp. 7–8). However, they were labeled "nativistic movements" by Western "old paradigm" ethnocentric Christianity, which denied their Christian validity. Today, these churches are at least viewed as valid Christian churches, but their experience with the Spirit is still suspect in the eyes of some evangelicals and Pentecostals, due to their cultural and spiritual identity.

After several decades of phenomenal growth, the issue of culture has become acute in the identity of the churches of the Southern Hemisphere. The "new paradigm of global Christianity" is expressed in a variety of different cultural contexts. In addition, midway through the twentieth century, these independent churches that had received their political freedom from the West *also* experienced an outpouring of the Holy Spirit, just as Western Christianity did during the second wave of the charismatic movement. However, the charismatic phenomena in the Southern Hemisphere were interpreted as "nativism" by Western churchmen. This rapidly growing "cultural mosaic" of the Christian faith, therefore, became a challenge to the "old paradigm of Western culture" as a norm for the expression of the faith. The mission churches were not only a challenge to the *Western form* of the Christian faith, but they were also a challenge to the *spirituality* of Western Christianity, because the churches of the Southern Hemisphere "looked like" and "acted like" the churches of the *New Testament*.

THE NEW PARADIGM IS A CORRECTION OF THE OLD

The churches planted by Christian mission efforts in the Southern Hemisphere have exploded in growth, multiplying through independent "break-away" churches, until the numbers of Christians in Asia, Africa, and Latin America today outnumber those in the Western world. When we speak of a "Global Christianity," we must understand that the majority of the Christian world is now in the Southern Hemisphere (Jenkins, 2002, pp. 2–3). However, the new churches of the Southern Hemisphere do not "look like" the churches of the Northern Hemisphere. They are firmly rooted in the cultures of the developing world, expressing the Christian faith in terms of their own cultural customs and their own style of worship. For some ethnocentric evangelicals and Pentecostals, this is a problem.

Due to the phenomenal growth of Christianity in the Southern Hemisphere, the old paradigm of "Western Christianity" has shifted to a new paradigm: "global Christianity." Global Christianity means a *"multicultural* Christianity"; furthermore, it is biblical. Jesus' gospel of the kingdom of God is universal and can be contextualized in any culture. The conflict between the gospel and Judaism in the early church—a major theme of the New Testament—proved the gospel of the kingdom of God to be *universal.* Classical Pentecostals cannot afford to insist on an ecclesial "contextualized" version of Pentecostalism as a norm for export to the Southern Hemisphere or for evaluating their experience with the Spirit; the criterion for that is the New Testament, specifically Jesus' and the apostles' theology of the gospel of the kingdom of God. Rather, classical Pentecostals in the West should take a close look at the "new paradigm in the South," determine what a true contribution to these new churches might be, and even consider that these churches may be a correction to the old Western paradigm of Christianity in the Northern Hemisphere.

Using the historical circumstances of the emergence of Pentecostals in North America and Europe, along with their schisms and doctrinal controversies, may confuse the evaluation of Pentecostal-charismatic movements in the Southern Hemisphere. This leaves researchers with doubts about the new movements' validity, cynicism, or defining their "Pentecostal-ness" as hopeless task (Anderson, 2013, pp. 118, 121–22, 126, 252; Roebeck, 2011, pp. 2–3, 7–8). The "naming game"—attempting to put global Pentecostal-charismatics into a "Western ecclesial box" with a logical, exact classification, and attempting a precise "definition" of movements in the Southern Hemisphere—is a manifestation of the Western worldview itself; that worldview introduces a problem for evaluating global Pentecostalism.

It may be helpful to note that the same problem emerges when attempting to apply a rational, analytical Western worldview in interpreting the Acts of the Apostles in order to identify the Pentecostal distinctive, especially with regard to the initial evidence of the Pentecostal experience (Fee, 1976, pp. 130–31). The document was written for people with a *non-Western, holistic supernatural worldview*; a better approach for the Western interpreter would be a holistic one, especially when interpreting its references to the speaking-in-tongues events. A holistic approach should be used with a holistic document. Otherwise, we may be asking our own questions of a text that is speaking about something else.

A holistic approach would entail the construction of a "taxonomy" of Pentecostal-charismatic experience in Acts, assessing all of the events in the document according to the points Luke highlights about the receiving of the Spirit: the problem of presenting proof to the Jewish Christian leadership that the Gentiles were included in the church, the Spirit's confirming function (Acts 8 and 10), and the lack of awareness on the part of those far from Palestine that the gift of the Spirit was available and part of the gospel (Acts 19). In the end, this approach actually reveals the strategic importance of the evidence of tongues in cases of the reception of the Spirit in the early history, rather than a proof-texting approach that attempts to put the Pentecostal experience in a precise Western scholastic theological-ecclesial box, in a document that does not reveal such a worldview. We need to avoid the error of the excessive influence of one's own context in evaluating another culture or a document from another culture (see the discussion on the initial evidence for the baptism of the Holy Spirit in chapter 4).

I submit that viewing and evaluating Pentecostal-charismatic renewals in the cultures of the Southern Hemisphere should be done from the perspective that they are renewals of Jesus' gospel of the kingdom of God and the articulation of *that theology* by the apostles in the New Testament. In other words, analysis of the movements should be based primarily on New Testament biblical theology, not sociological theory or religious phenomenology. These approaches serve other purposes; they cannot serve as the primary basis for evaluating the recent movements.

While the first two decades of the twenty-first century have shown amazing developments of indigenous Pentecostal theologies in Africa, Asia, and Latin America, this does not mean that Northern Pentecostals no longer have a theological contribution to make. A Pentecostal biblical theology and hermeneutic would be a crucial contribution, at least for a while, in the Southern Hemisphere, to assist Southern theologians in avoiding errors as they contextualize and develop their own ethnic theologies. This would help them to put past evaluations of Pentecostal movements from the perspective of religious phenomenology and social analysis in biblical perspective, taking what is good and helpful and rejecting what does not apply. A theological criterion is needed for this; they rightly observe that Western systematic theology cannot and should not be the criterion. Also, a Pentecostal biblical theology would help them deal with the negative influence of dispensational theology and other unorthodox theologies that have emerged in the history of Pentecostalism in the West, as well as help them deal with the new unorthodox theologies that will surely emerge in their own countries.

The above discussion on the evaluation of Pentecostalism in the Southern Hemisphere is intentionally separated from Pentecostalism in America to avoid potential confusion. A helpful diachronic (based on historic links) and synchronic (based on denominational links, congregations, networks, and so on) treatment of Pentecostalism in the Southern Hemisphere can be found in the "Empowerment21" movement documents on Global Renewal Christianity (Synan & Yong, 2015), along with a discussion of the biblical nature of Pentecostal-charismatic movements. The following discussion is a continuation of the "Introduction to Pentecostalism in 'America'" in the first edition of *The Third Force in Missions*.

Since the Pentecostal contribution to contemporary mission theology given in this study is from the classical Pentecostal viewpoint, further distinction should be made within this somewhat diverse major stream of Pentecostalism in America concerning who is a Pentecostal. In *The American Pentecostal Movement: A Bibliographic Essay*, David Faupel suggests the following classifications of classical Pentecostalism:

1. Those denominations that hold a Keswick view of sanctification . . .
2. Those denominations that hold a Holiness view of "entire sanctification" . . .
3. Those denominations that hold a "Jesus Only" view of the Godhead. (1972, p. 12)

David Barrett adds two further classifications: Perfectionist-Pentecostals (Free Pentecostals, Deliverance-Pentecostals, Radical-Pentecostals, and Revivalist-Pentecostals), who emphasize four crisis experiences (conversion, sanctification, baptism of the Spirit, and deliverance/ ecstatic confession/prophecy/perfectionism or authority/discipling/ shepherding); and Apostolic or Pentecostal Apostolics, who stress the complex hierarchy of living apostles, prophets, or other charismatic officials (Barrett, 1982, p. 127). Barrett's classification of classical Pentecostalism is given in full in chapter 1.

For a period of some fifteen years, the Pentecostal movement in America had no distinctive doctrinal shape because its membership was drawn from various Protestant traditions, and only the Pentecostal experience held them together (Menzies, 1975, p. 83; Faupel, 1972, p. 13). However, the theological issues of sanctification and pneumatology became the primary issues that caused the above threefold division. Piepkorn states, "If salvation and the work of Jesus Christ were dominant themes of the Reformation movement that produced the Protestant denominations, then sanctification and the work of the Holy Spirit were the significant themes in the movements that resulted in the formation of Holiness and Pentecostal churches" (1979, p. xiii). That threefold division also reflects the varied theological traditions that originally influenced the Pentecostal movement: Wesleyan-Holiness and Keswickian-Reformed.

In his article "The Non-Wesleyan Origins of the Pentecostal Movement," William Menzies discusses the strong influence of Keswickian and Baptistic theologies on the Assemblies of God in its formative years (1975, pp. 86, 88, 90–93). In his history of the Assemblies of God, *Anointed to Serve*, Menzies states:

> From the Keswick wing of the Holiness movement, chiefly through the agency of the Christian and Missionary Alliance with its Missionary Training Institute at Nyack, New York, came the Bible Institute program, the ecclesiology of the Assemblies of God, the missionary vision, the emphasis on divine healing, much of its early hymnology, and even a significant portion of its early leadership. (1971, pp. 27–28)

The very title of Menzies's history, *Anointed to Serve*, illustrates the Keswickian view that the second experience, referred to as "the baptism of the Holy Spirit," was an "enduing of power" for service. This contrasted with the Wesleyan-Holiness view that it was a cleansing from sin—Wesleyan eradication-perfectionism (Menzies, 1971, p. 26).

The Assemblies of God has been recognized as a representative model of classical Pentecostalism. Concerning this claim, Menzies states that:

> It is the author's contention, after extensive interviews with Pentecostal leaders, evangelical churchmen, and representatives from the larger church world, that the Assemblies of God, largest of the American Pentecostal bodies, is indeed the most representative of the Pentecostal organizations, and can serve usefully as a microcosm of the Pentecostal movement as a whole. (1971, p. 10)

Faupel agrees with Menzies's claim:

> He [Menzies] further points out in a footnote that others such as Bloch-Hoell, Nichol and Kelsey (all non-Assemblies of God men) have made the same claim for the Assemblies of God. By this, he means all of the issues and forces which have brought to bear on any part of the Pentecostal movement have at some point affected the Assemblies of God as well. Despite initial reservations this writer has come to accept this as basically true. (1972, p. 21)

Such an observation concerning the denomination points to the representative value of my general viewpoint in describing the Pentecostal contribution to contemporary missions. Even though my perspective is that of Keswickian Pentecostalism, this particular Pentecostal viewpoint may be considered as somewhat representative for the whole of classical Pentecostalism in the West.

In the attempt to address the Pentecostal contribution to contemporary mission theology, the discussion enters areas of theological controversy for which there is no Assemblies of God or classical Pentecostal position. Therefore, the somewhat fresh theologizing in this study from the Pentecostal viewpoint is occasioned both by the underdeveloped nature of pneumatology in general and Pentecostal mission theology in particular. Of course, in these cases the viewpoint given is my own. One such case that illustrates this point is the issue of the nature of revelation in chapter 5. The Pentecostal believes that revelation is dynamic and continuous in nature. This is due to his or her experience with the gifts of the Holy Spirit today, and the activity of the Holy Spirit in connection with the written word of Scripture. Care has been taken, however, to differentiate between the continuous revelatory activity of the Spirit and that which resulted in Scripture. This is done by careful explanation concerning the latter's normative nature and by speaking of the former as revelation with a small *r*. Also, it should be noted that theologizing in these new areas is not characterized by primarily quoting Pentecostal theologians. In fact, those quoted are relatively few throughout the book. Rather, the fresh theologizing in these areas is supported by biblical exegesis and reference to mainline Protestant and Roman Catholic theologians. In other words, in this book I attempt to develop pneumatology in connection with mission theology on the basis of Scripture and the central Christian tradition.

The reader should also be aware that, due to the fact that Pentecostalism's main contribution falls within the area of the experiential dimension of the Christian faith, my emphasis on the Christian "experience" does not necessarily involve existential theology. Christianity *is* an experience with God. Chapter 3, "A Correction of a Western Distortion," discusses the distortion that the period of Protestant Scholasticism brought to the central Christian tradition. Pentecostalism provides a corrective balance to the intense intellectualization of the faith that took place in that period. That it is necessary to qualify an affirmation of the experiential dimension of the faith is a testimony to the distortion in contemporary evangelicalism. Existential theology, however, was also a reaction to that rationalization of the Christian faith. Therefore, existential theologians *do* provide some insights into the scholastic distortion of the faith. But Pentecostalism's emphasis on Christian experience is dramatically different from that of existential theology. The crucial difference is that for Pentecostals the hermeneutical horizon (the authoritative starting point) for theologizing is not human experience or a philosophical position but *Scripture*.

The reluctance of some evangelicals to pursue the experiential dimension of the Christian faith, however, goes deeper than avoiding existential theology. It involves the excessive impact of the

Western worldview and scholastic theology on evangelicalism. This thesis has been argued well in a historical study by Jack Rogers and Donald McKim, *The Authority and Interpretation of the Bible* (1979).

Some evangelicals may be content with the unhappy combination of a warm conversion experience and a cold intellectual doctrine and apologetic, but the Pentecostal cannot afford that tension. The very center of his distinctive is jeopardized: the dynamic, charismatic experience of the Spirit in the Christian life. Therefore, he must probe the depths of the experiential dimension of the Christian faith within the bounds of biblical theology for a consistent Pentecostal theology. One could say that for this reason, Pentecostalism represents an alternative to a liberal subjectivism (existential theology) and a conservative rationalistic-objectivism (scholastic-fundamentalist theology). The thesis of this book is that Pentecostalism represents a biblical, relevant contribution to contemporary Christianity.

The "evangelical-Pentecostal" perspective described here claims to be rooted in first-century Christian experience, that which was *normative in the documents of the New Testament*. The Christian faith is rooted in history, and biblical authority is a prominent evangelical principle in contemporary evangelicalism. The multiple evangelical groups mentioned previously, as well as the multiple Pentecostal groups, represent an ecclesiastical-theological entity that identifies its belief and experience with the "evangel" of the New Testament. These facts catapult the issue of hermeneutics to the center stage of evangelicalism. Billy Graham has stated that "the issue of the '80s is going to be hermeneutics, or how to interpret Scripture properly and apply it to personal and social life" (Woodward, 1982, p. 91).

A primary effort of this study is to face up to this key issue of hermeneutics and to provide fresh theological reflection concerning the issue from a Pentecostal and Reformation perspective. Part Two of this book is concerned with this crucial issue. Chapter 5 is devoted to the hermeneutical task as the idea of "mission strategy" is examined. The hermeneutical issue is also central in a discussion of contemporary mission theology. Not only do the various approaches to contemporary mission issues reflect different hermeneutical methods, but the idea of contextualizing the Christian faith in non-Western cultures and ethno-theology makes its discussion imperative.

Part One—"Pentecostalism: Distortion or Correction?"—introduces the phenomenon of the Pentecostal movement by outlining its worldwide scope, examining its historical origins, and describing its theological nature. Part Two, "Pentecostalism: A Missions Contribution," continues the examination of Pentecostal theology, focusing on its theological contribution in terms of the kingdom of God motif, the Pentecostal experience, and the nature of mission strategy. The movement's contribution to Western Christianity is viewed as a correction of a fundamental distortion that has significantly impaired contemporary mission theology and practice. Contemporary mission issues are addressed from a Pentecostal-biblical viewpoint, using the much-neglected biblical theme of the kingdom of God.

PART ONE

PENTECOSTALISM, DISTORTION OR CORRECTION?

1 An Emerging "Third Force"

The international Pentecostal movement is a modern missionary phenomenon. Pentecostal historian Vinson Synan writes that the movement in 1980 consisted of "over 50,000,000 classical Pentecostals in uncounted churches and missions in practically every nation of the world" (1980, p. ix). While referring to the impact of the Los Angeles Azusa Street revival, Synan wrote in 1980:

> By this year, there are estimates of the number of Pentecostals and charismatics in the world that approach the 75,000,000 mark. That would mean that roughly 1,000,000 persons per year have accepted the premises of the Los Angeles Pentecost in the years since 1906. (p. xxiv)

Therefore, the Pentecostal movement may be spoken of as a modern missionary phenomenon due to its rapid growth in a relatively short period of the Christian church's history, and due to its international and ecclesiastical scope. The movement has reached across a multitude of cultural frontiers in its missionary ventures. It has also penetrated all of the traditional expressions of the Christian faith.

The phenomenal growth of the movement has been cited as a major cause for a change in the attitude of Christianity toward Pentecostalism. Generally speaking, an attitude of passive toleration in the early 1920s gave way to one of acceptance midway through the twentieth century. This acceptance was due to many factors. Among them was the appearance of the neo-Pentecostal movement (charismatic movement) in the denominational churches, and classical Pentecostalism's move into what has been called the "maximum efficiency stage" of organization (Synan, 1971, pp. 223–24). Another way of referring to the latter factor would be to say that many Pentecostal "fellowships" began to be recognized as permanent Christian denominations. In comparing the modern Pentecostal movement with previous unsuccessful charismatic revivals in the history of the church, Menzies states:

> It would not be until the modern, 20th-century Pentecostal revival that such a charismatic movement would enjoy the uniqueness of *survival.* The outstanding characteristic of the modern revival is that it has endured sufficiently long to be more or less accepted within the broader confines of orthodox evangelical Christianity. This has not happened since the first century! (1971, pp. 28–29)

With regard to the Assemblies of God, such acceptance was marked by their participation in the National Association of Evangelicals. This was to the dismay, however, of separatist fundamentalist groups (Menzies, 1971, pp. 183–84).

However, the phenomenal growth of the movement, especially on the mission fields of the world, has generally attracted the attention of non-Pentecostal Christianity. Even those in disagreement with Pentecostal theology began to praise the movement's missionary success. In terms of numbers, growth, and influence, the movement was recognized to be at the heart of the international missionary movement. It was noted that "Pentecostalism and mission are almost synonymous" (Bruner, 1970, p. 32).

The factor of Pentecostalism's rapid growth and worldwide scope began to gain the attention of Christianity in a new way midway through the twentieth century. One of the earlier prophetic statements about Pentecostalism was Henry P. Van Dusen's coining of the phrase "The Third Force" when referring to the scope and potential of the movement (1958, p. 113). Van Dusen spoke of the modern Pentecostal movement as a new "Reformation": the emergence of a new, third, major type and branch of Christianity alongside Roman Catholicism and historic Protestantism (1955, p. 946). Van Dusen's statement referring to Pentecostalism as "The Third Force in Christendom" marked a change from an attitude of mere acceptance of a movement, which caused some embarrassment to the Protestant world, to a patent acknowledgement that Pentecostals had a *contribution* to make to modern Christianity. Van Dusen stated concerning that contribution:

The tendency to dismiss its Christian message as inadequate is being replaced by a chastened readiness to investigate the secrets of its mighty sweep, especially to learn if it may not have important neglected elements in a full and true Christian witness. (1958, p. 124)

In his book *The Household of God* (1954), Bishop Lesslie Newbigin identified another potential contribution by the movement. The idea of the "third force" was also inherent in Newbigin's evaluation of the movement. He suggested that the Pentecostals may contribute to a Catholic and Protestant understanding of the church in terms of its dynamic dimension in the reception of and abiding in the Holy Spirit (pp. xi, 24, 82–83). This three-cornered understanding of the church—Catholic, Protestant, and Pentecostal—echoes Van Dusen's idea of Pentecostalism as a third force in Christianity, but specifies the movement's unique contribution.

Various other non-Pentecostal theologians who examined Pentecostal theology also began to speak of the movement's contribution to Christianity. While challenging the Pentecostal doctrine of the Baptism of the Holy Spirit, James D. G. Dunn began his analysis of Pentecostal theology by noting:

The Pentecostal contribution should cause Christians in the "mainline" denominations to look afresh with critical eyes at the place they give to the Holy Spirit in doctrine and experience and in their various theologies of conversion, initiation and baptism. (1970, p. viii)

In 1976, Kilian McDonnell, a Roman Catholic charismatic, stated:

It does however seem both unrealistic and wanting in theological discernment for the non-Pentecostal world to write off the deep commitment, profound prayer life, and exceptional growth of Classical Pentecostals, from fifteen to thirty-five million people. (p. 264)

With the increased attention paid to the Pentecostal movement, due to its vitality and phenomenal growth, came a growing realization that the movement might represent a renewal of neglected elements of the Christian faith.

The rapid growth of Pentecostalism on various mission fields was somewhat indirectly publicized in missiological circles through church growth studies from the School of World Mission at Fuller

Theological Seminary, which were designed to scientifically gauge the growth of the various Protestant churches. Such scientifically prepared materials helped greatly in drawing the Christian world's attention to the Pentecostal movement as a "missionary" phenomenon. Several studies were directed specifically to examine Pentecostal church growth—especially in the areas such as Brazil where Pentecostalism was flourishing—and gave direct, reliable knowledge of the dynamics of Pentecostal growth and the extent of the movement (Read, 1965; Read, Monterosso & Johnson, 1969; McGavran, Huegel & Taylor, 1963; Montgomery, 1967; Palmer, 1974; Gaxiola 1970; Smith, 1970).

C. Peter Wagner in *Look Out! The Pentecostals Are Coming* (1973) centered attention on why Pentecostalism was experiencing phenomenal growth in Latin America. Wagner's sympathetic treatment and "church growth" analysis of Pentecostalism uncovered numerous causes for Pentecostal church growth. At the same time, his work pointed to the basic dynamic behind such growth factors: the Pentecostal experience of the Holy Spirit (pp. 29, 39, 79–80). That Wagner also believed that the Pentecostal movement provided a valuable contribution to contemporary missions is indicated by the revised title of the 1978 edition of his book, *What Are We Missing?*

Therefore, in the 1960s and 1970s it became known that the Pentecostal movement was worldwide in scope and that Pentecostal communities were the fastest growing in the world (Synan, 1971, p. 223). It was predicted that Pentecostalism was to become the major form of Christianity in the developing nations (Marty, 1975, p. 96). However, some may still question whether there is sufficient evidence to speak of the Pentecostal movement in such hyperbolic terms as the "Third Force in Christendom." These doubts may exist even in the light of the growing awareness of the impact of Pentecostalism around the world, its phenomenal growth, and therefore its apparent potential for a contribution.

AN INFORMATION GAP

It is a gross understatement to say that there was an information gap in evangelical Christianity's perception of the Pentecostal movement in 1985. It is somewhat paradoxical that a movement of such worldwide scope should have such a paucity of documentation (in the English language, that is). However, Pentecostals themselves are part of the reason for the information gap. They are not known for documenting their growth or for articulating their theology. Traditionally their whole experiential-pragmatic orientation has tended to make them neglect such endeavors. Of course, the information gap referred to here is a lack of information about the nature and scope of the movement. Especially wanting is the type of information that the non-Pentecostal Christian world would deem reliable, such as works written under scientific discipline (histories, theologies, church growth studies, and so on). On the other hand, the lack of scientific materials may also be due to the lack of conviction on the part of some Pentecostals and evangelicals as to the usefulness of such materials. This is especially true with church growth studies; even the theological ground for such studies is often questioned (McQuilkin, 1973, pp. 12–13, 39–40).

Recent histories on the Pentecostal movement in the United States, written by both Pentecostal and non-Pentecostal historians, have helped to clarify the nature and distinctive of the movement. But when the challenge of the *worldwide* Pentecostal movement's existence is addressed, in non-Western cultures especially, the proportions of the information gap are overwhelming.

Walter Hollenweger, author of the historical worldwide survey of the Pentecostal movement *The Pentecostals* (1972), is one of the most knowledgeable historians about the extent of the worldwide movement. Unfortunately, due to the rapid growth of the Pentecostal movement in some countries, the statistics as old as those found in Hollenweger's work are no longer adequate. In a subsequent article Hollenweger has stated that there is no reliable overview of the charismatic renewal in the developing world (1980, p. 68). In *The Pentecostals*, Hollenweger states concerning the worldwide spread of Pentecostalism, "I believe that the statistics are mostly too low, not because they accord to individual denominations too few members— there are a few cases of exaggeration—but because there are large Pentecostal bodies which are unknown to the Pentecostals themselves, and about the size of which they have no information" (p. 63).

Hollenweger's observation that there is an ignorance of the worldwide scope of the movement among the Pentecostals themselves is instructive. In addition to the experiential-pragmatic orientation of the Pentecostal, the general lack of appreciation for history and an active sectarianism among Pentecostals may be reasons for the information gap (1972, p. 413). Often, numerous Pentecostal groups in relatively close geographical proximity know little about one another, not to mention their ignorance of the larger Pentecostal movement in the world. This fragmentation of local Pentecostal movements, as well as the loss of perspective of a worldwide movement, can only be counterproductive with regard to the effectiveness of their missionary thrust in the world. Apart from the benefits of a unified missionary thrust, such fragmentation must be apprehended by the non-Christian world as particularly unappealing.

The reason why a worldwide phenomenon such as the Pentecostal movement has existed relatively unknown in Christianity, however, cannot be explained merely by focusing on the Pentecostal's value orientation, neglect, or shortcomings. An examination of Western Protestantism's complicity in the information gap is also necessary. There are tendencies and factors in Western theology and worldviews that shed light on the information gap. Some of the more influential of these are a latent ethnocentrism, a heritage of scholasticism, and the influence of dispensationalism. To varying degrees, each of these tendencies can be attributed to the impact of the Enlightenment on Western culture. They represent distinct liabilities for assessing the validity of Pentecostal movements, especially those in non-Western cultures.

It is in the saving activity of God in salvation history—specifically the activity of the Holy Spirit through the agency of the church—that the priority of mission is found. The priority of proclaiming the gospel, or the Great Commission mission in the power of the Spirit, dominates the church's mission in the Acts of the Apostles. The New Testament puts emphasis on the evangelistic mandate, God's "special" mission. Yet dispensational theology ignores and marginalizes the New Testament, considers the church to be a *parenthesis* in salvation history, and preempts Jesus' *present* kingdom of God by denying it and focusing on the future eschatological kingdom. This undermines the church's mission and purpose in the world, as well as the very notion of an "age of the Spirit," beginning at Pentecost and continuing on until the second coming of Christ. In terms of the subject of this book—Pentecostal-charismatic movements—the system of dispensational theology denies these outright.

A Latent Ethnocentrism

First and foremost, the Pentecostal movement's existence in a variety of non-Western cultures presents a special problem for the acceptance of such movements in Western Protestant Christianity in general. This is especially true for indigenous Christian movements that exist with no formal ties with Western mission churches, such as the "independency movements" in Africa. This aversion to foreign forms and expressions of the Christian faith is rooted in a traditional, latent ethnocentrism in Western Christianity. Such aversion to cultural-oriented expressions of the Christian faith is well documented in the histories of Western Christian missions; two examples of Western reaction to independent church movements in Africa are given below in the section "The Hidden Pentecostals."

Oosthuizen cites the cultural development of Western Christianity as the reason for the "Western approach" in African missions. He explains:

> Hemmed in by Islam, the gospel had been accommodated to the social and personal life of European peoples to such a degree that the false idea developed that a nation can be conceived of as *corpus Christianum*. This fallacy is alive in the concept of Christian civilization. The synthesis that has taken place between gospel and culture in the west has not only affected the expansion of Christianity but distorted its very depth and vitality. (1968, p. 3)

Prior to the period of Protestant missions, Protestant Christianity became "contextualized" in Western European culture due to isolation. Islam bracketed Western Europe in the South and East, and

Roman Catholic Spain and Portugal ruled the seas. It was contextualized to the point, according to Oosthuizen, where the gospel was severely impacted by Western culture, even to the point of distortion.

The particular "distortion" inherent in the idea of *corpus Christianum* ("Christendom") was that the Western political-economic-sociological structure, religiously founded, was to be expanded throughout the world. Of course, this idea of bringing "Western civilization" to the peoples of Asia and Africa was supported by the belief that Western culture and its expression of Christianity were superior. With the establishment of thriving, indigenous churches outside of Western civilization, the concept of *corpus Christianum* died (Margull, 1960, p. 147). However, the death of *corpus Christianum* did not mean that *Western ethnocentrism* died. The Christian faith was still "contextualized" in Western culture in the missions-sending countries. The idea of a propagation of Western Christian civilization died, and perhaps the idea that Western culture was superior diminished somewhat. But the idea that the Western expression of the gospel was somehow normative did not die in Western missions, nor did it die in *Western theology*. The latent ethnocentrism in the Western expression of Christianity remains a potential liability for recognizing the validity of indigenous Christian movements.

Western Scholastic Theology

There is a growing awareness today that the gospel is supracultural in nature and that all cultures are valid for the expression of the Christian faith (while granting the gospel is always intrusive, in that all cultures must be transformed and redeemed by it). But the recent history of Christian missions still shows a latent ethnocentrism in the missionary endeavor. Although the distortion of Western Christianity that Oosthuizen cites—*corpus Christianum*—is no longer a living concept in Western missions, Western theology is still highly impacted by the historical circumstances and influence of the Enlightenment. This introduces the second difficulty with respect to identifying valid Pentecostal movements in non-Western cultures: Scholasticism, or scholastic theology.

Protestant Scholasticism in the post-Reformation period produced a theology that was greatly influenced by Western culture. In the later post-Reformation period a rationalistic, static theology was influenced further by Common Sense philosophy—a highly ethnocentric view of reality (Pomerville, 1980, pp. 73–75, 78–80, 94). It is difficult, therefore, to separate the influence of scholastic theology from the discussion of a latent ethnocentrism in Western missions. The discussion of the two must blend together at this point. The notion that the theology that developed in the West is somehow normative (often it is held to be absolute and perennial) is shown by the attitude of some Western theologians and missiologists toward African, Asian, and Latin American theologies. Such endeavors are often under a cloud of suspicion in the minds of Western theologians. Generally speaking, however, they represent efforts only of non-Western peoples in theologizing from their *own* perspective of biblical revelation in the light of problems, questions, and needs in their *own* cultural context. Syncretism and heresies in Western Christianity, both present and past, are forgotten by the Western critics, or they do not seem as sinister as those alleged to emerge from non-Western cultural contexts. The same attitude often prevails when considering indigenous Christian movements in non-Western contexts.

Before the Western theologian can attempt to remove the "mote" in the expression of African or Asian Christianity, he must first recognize the "beam" in his own expression of the faith. The problem in focus is not one that merely involves a fidelity to the gospel in non-Western cultures and its distortion there. It also involves a fidelity to the gospel in *Western culture* and its distortion *there*. What distortions have resulted due to the impact of *Western* culture on the gospel? The erosion of the sense of the supernatural has to be at the top of the list, as well as the eclipse of the experiential dimension of the Christian faith. The dynamic, biblical theologizing represented in ethnic theologies is in stark contrast with a static, rationalistic, scholastically oriented systematic theology of Westerners and, therefore, it is suspect. The dynamic experiential nature of independency movements contrasts with the Western cerebral expression of the faith. The nature and shape of Western theology itself is often at the bottom of the Western aversion to both indigenous Christian theologies and indigenous Christian movements—especially those of the Pentecostal type. A latent ethnocentrism influencing Western theology and worldview has been a major factor that has contributed to the information gap on Pentecostal movements in non-Western cultures.

Dispensationalism

The third difficulty in assessing the worldwide scope of the movement, dispensationalism, is combined with two case studies in Africa below. Dispensational theology's marginalization of the New Testament in its Israel-centered, future eschatological kingdom emphasis eliminates *a priori* the validity of non-Western Pentecostal movements, giving those who espouse the theology free reign to deny their validity, and calling them "nativistic movements." The following study on the African Independent Church Movement (AICM) focuses on all of the above major difficulties in the Western approach and evaluation of such movements.

One of the clearest evidences of a latent ethnocentrism in the history of modern missions is the phenomenon of independent church movements in the developing world. Add to the previously mentioned latent ethnocentrism the factor of Pentecostal phenomena, which are prominent in the movements, and a major potential difficulty emerges for evangelicals in evaluating the worldwide Pentecostal movement. The Pentecostal nature of many of the indigenous Christian movements not only presents a problem for objective evaluation, but it has also been the occasion for the rejection of the movements in the history of missions. Therefore, the bias against Pentecostal phenomena has largely contributed to the information gap on such movements.

Whether the Westerner's difficulty with Pentecostal phenomena in non-Western indigenous movements is due to pure bias, sectarianism, or one's theological stance, such as dispensationalism (often a combination of these is the case), all of these have contributed to the information gap on the movements. Such theological attitudes and positions have created a parallel to what missiologists call "hidden peoples." In terms of world evangelization, "hidden people" are those groups (whether geographically near or far) that are isolated from hearing the gospel because of their cultural differences. These cultural differences act as an invisible cultural barrier that "hides" them, especially from those who bring the gospel to them from a diverse cultural background (Wagner & Dayton, 1978, p. 47). In a real sense, the above affective and theological biases against Pentecostal phenomena have created "hidden Pentecostals."

THE HIDDEN PENTECOSTALS

Two representative works on the African Independent Church Movements (AICMs) that show the legacy of colonial missions and the ethnocentrism of Western missionaries are examined below. These case studies illustrate the impact of Western ethnocentrism as Western missionaries view the movements in relation to Christianity in non-Western contexts. Another reason for the examination of the movements is to illustrate how the "root causation" factor of the movements—the impact of Western culture—is the same factor that tends to prevent objective evaluation of the movements *today* in the West. First, the cause and nature of the movements are briefly discussed, using both the viewpoint of a recognized authority on the AICM and the viewpoint of an African participant. Then, the two Western evaluations of the movements are discussed, one a classic evaluation from South Africa and another concerning Africa in general. An authority on the AICM, D. B. Barrett, views the phenomenon as

> representing a genuinely African response to the Christian faith. All center on the basic African concept of the people of God as a community and the legitimacy of Christianizing African traditional concepts and practices. They represent a creative response on the part of African Christianity to the turmoil and disruption that followed the breakdown of traditional patterns of life as a result of contact with the Western world. (1979, p. 63)

Barrett underlines the necessity of accepting the "contextualization phenomenon" in understanding the movements. In other words, it is necessary to recognize the imperative of the gospel being "incarnated" in African culture, even though it is impacted by that milieu. Also, it is necessary to recognize the inevitability of the impact of Western culture upon that expression of Christianity and theology. The contextualization phenomenon is in accord with an "incarnational" concept of divine revelation and it deals with a *twofold fidelity.*

First, contextualization involves a fidelity to the gospel as it is incarnated in culture. But it also involves a fidelity to the cultural context to which it comes. The incarnation is the theological model for this view of the contextualization phenomenon. Barrett states concerning the former fidelity:

> Granted the spectrum of types, ranging from the ultraorthodox to the definitely syncretistic, almost all these bodies are nevertheless characterized by a clear acceptance, often under new and original African forms, of the centrality of the historical Jesus as Lord. (1979, p. 65)

With regard to their causation, Barrett views the AICMs as a single phenomenon. He states that local causes are often emphasized, but in his analysis of the movements all over Africa there is a correlation between separatism and (1) a strong traditional African society, (2) a strong colonial impact, and (3) a strong missionary impact (1979, p. 65). He states, "The correlation suggests that the underlying cause of the whole AICM is the clash of African culture with colonial and missionary cultures" (p. 65).

In his article "Identity Crisis in the African Church," Ngoni Sengwe views the origin of the AICM as a reaction of African Christians to a Western cerebral-oriented expression of the Christian faith. Sengwe, once a member of an AICM, sees the movements as efforts of the African church to meet the felt needs of Christians in their African cultural milieu (1981, pp. 93, 95). Sengwe's theory of causation is supported by some of the best authorities on the AICM (D. B. Barrett, H. W. Turner, V. E. Hayward, and others who are both Western and non-Western in origin). The theory chiefly has to do with the neglect and, at times, the direct destruction of the African worldview and society due to its contact with Western missions (Sengwe, 1981, p. 95).

The missionary neglect involved with this particular theory of causation is not only a "passive-avoidance" neglect of African society, perhaps due to ignorance of it or prejudice against it, but it also involves the Western failure to respond *positively and biblically* to the vacuum created in African society after the Western form of Christianity displaced many of its traditional customs. Western missions failed to understand the African milieu sufficiently, and they also failed to articulate the biblical view of the supernatural so that Africans could apply it in their Christian lives. That life concerned a sociocultural milieu dominated by the spirit world. The African lacked the necessary New Testament biblical models for living and coping with his environment "as a Christian." Sengwe speaks of the effort of the AICMs in restoring the "place of the supernatural" in African Christianity by providing such a biblical model (1981, p. 95).

Both of the failures of Western missions noted here are rooted in the Western development and expression of the Christian faith. Due to the impact of the Enlightenment in Western culture, with its emphasis on a rational, word-oriented faith, this faith was ill prepared to understand and empathize with African culture. It was also ill prepared to respond to African culture biblically in presenting the supernatural as represented by New Testament theology and pneumatology. Those areas of theology were seriously underdeveloped in Western culture due to the impact of the Enlightenment. Sengwe is correct when he notes that the AICM arose out of a clash between Western culture and African culture, *not* out of a clash between the *gospel* and African culture (1981, p. 94). A primary factor in the contemporary rejection of indigenous Christian movements, therefore, is often a recurrence of the factor which caused them: a latent ethnocentrism. Sengwe gives three reasons why missions and mainline denominations have ignored the AICMs:

1. The AICMs are not in "the camp," they have no connection with mainline denominations,
2. Their structures and worship patterns are "foreign"; they may not be in line with Western Protestant tradition, and
3. Dangers of syncretism. (1981, p. 92)

The same reasons, however, could have been cited for avoiding and rejecting the early Pentecostal movement in the United States. The characteristics of the Zionist and Aladura-type churches Sengwe points out in his article are essentially the same as those that historians of the Pentecostal movement in the United States have discovered in their movement's past. The characteristics Sengwe mentions are: (1) emphasis on the Holy Spirit in healing, prophecy, and revelation; (2) legalism; (3) schism; (4) a de-emphasis on education; (5) mistrust in medicine and emphasis on healing administered by "prophets"; (6) a restoration of the "place" of the supernatural; (7) rapid growth; (8) the authority of the religious experience; and (9) the involvement of the laity or discovery of community (1981, pp. 93–97).

As early as 1963, H. W. Turner suggested that movements such as the Zionist and Aladura groups in Africa were non-Western varieties of the worldwide Pentecostal movement (1963, p. 116). Both the indigenous garb and Pentecostal nature of the movements have been reasons why they have been neglected and rejected by Western observers. In the Western treatment of the AICMs a combination of ethnocentrism, rigid scholastic-oriented theology and dispensationalism are often mixed together with an explicit bias against Pentecostal phenomena. Such treatments reveal the necessity of evaluations from a "native" perspective, both African and Pentecostal. Injecting a somewhat humorous, but instructive note in this regard, John V. Taylor refers to the developing world's response to traditional Western attempts at understanding the indigenous nature of the church in that part of the world. He states:

> On the whole the Christian leaders of Africa and Asia have been unimpressed, not only because they are reactionary or suspicious of our motives, but because they believe we are only playing at it. Their unspoken thought has been: "Have these dear idiots any idea what they are asking for?" If they met a truly indigenous worship, they might be shocked, and if they allowed us to express our understandings of Christianity in our own way they probably wouldn't recognize it. (1969, p. 171)

One of the most quoted works on the AICM, which also is considered a classic on the movements, is Bengt Sundkler's *Bantu*

Prophets in South Africa (1948). It should be noted that Sundkler's first edition represents a relatively early evaluation of Pentecostal-type independent churches (Zionist) in the problematic racial context of South Africa. The first edition of the work is a classic example of biased reporting of Pentecostal phenomena by a non-Pentecostal, encompassing all of the above cited Western prejudices. In fairness to Sundkler, however, it should be remembered that at the time of his writing the charismatic movement had not yet taken place in the denominational churches. That this evaluation of Sundkler's work is not too severe or inappropriate is indicated by Sundkler's own remarks in the 1961 edition of his work. Also, its severity is necessary in view of the continuing counter-productive influence that his work had in 1985 for an objective evaluation of the AICM. The "inkblot" principle is especially evident in Sundkler's work. His account of the Zionist church movement reveals more about his presuppositions than it does about the phenomena that were taking place in the Bantu movement. Perhaps one of the chief contemporary contributions of the work is the lesson it illustrates concerning the contextualization phenomenon in this regard. Sundkler's worldview and presuppositions were a *context* (Western worldview) that impacted his theology and perception of the target culture.

Sundkler's basic premise was that Zionist Christianity was a "bridge" leading Zulu Christians back to traditional African religion, to paganism (1961, pp. 17, 196, 240, 259–60, 262–63). He speaks of efforts of indigenization as "Bantu syncretism in the independent churches" (p. 196), and describes the movement as a "syncretistic movement of baptizers" (p. 201). The similarity of religious institutional forms and functions between Zulu traditional religion and Zulu Zionism (the African-Pentecostal expression of the Christian faith) is, for Sundkler, clear evidence of syncretism. In his estimation, this supports his "bridge to paganism" theory concerning the movements. He states, "The basic pattern from which Zulu Zionism is copied is that of diviner and witch-finder activities rather than that of the historic Christian church" (p. 242). However, the prophet-exorcist role Sundkler refers to is *also* represented in the New Testament and in contemporary Pentecostalism.

Basic to Sundkler's "bridge to paganism" theory is the out-of-hand rejection of apostolic-Pentecostal theology and a Pentecostal expression of the Christian faith (pp. 259–60, 262–63). Sundkler's theological presupposition, therefore, ruled out a Christian alternative that, if valid, brings his "bridge" theory into serious question. A Pentecostal expression of the Christian faith would allow for a "Christianizing" of the religious and social forms and functions that were so crucial to African society. It would also provide New Testament models and meanings with which to reinterpret their customs and worldview.

Pentecostal missionaries had been in South Africa since 1908, and the "separatistic church movement," as Sundkler calls it, dates as early as 1890 to 1910. The main secessions took place about 1917–1920 (Sundkler, 1961, pp. 48–49). Perhaps an indication of Sundkler's being a product of his time, especially in regard to paternalism, is his statement that the African Zionist leaders emerged due to the churches being "left in the hands of the Africans" by Pentecostal missionaries. Again, the difference in views of mission supervision of indigenous churches is evident, but the Pentecostal indigenous view here is in a pejorative context. Sundkler views Pentecostalism in the same pejorative context when he states,

> Within modern Protestantism, especially in America, most of the secessions which have arisen from time to time have been caused by different interpretations of the Holy Spirit, and it is only to be expected that some of the same difficulties will arise in such African Churches as are the outcome of missionary efforts from Western Churches of Pentecostal, Apostolic Faith and Zionist type. (1961, pp. 242–43)

In passing, it might also be noted that Sundkler's statement that "the same difficulties" might be expected in the African milieu ignores the radical difference between the Western and African milieus in which the movements occurred. Their respective societal needs in terms of gospel's application and the resultant cultural expression of Pentecostal Christianity would be quite different. The central orientation of African society and culture to the spirit world and the society's institutions for coping with that reality play a major role in the causation of the movements in the African milieu. Pentecostalism addressed a *severe* problem in the matrix of African society; it addressed the very core of African worldview and African social structure.

Of course, Sundkler's statement is directed toward the schismatic tendencies of the American Pentecostal movement, but it ignores the issue of the causation of the respective movements from the standpoint of contextual need. Sundkler *is* aware of Pentecostalism, at least from America (classical Pentecostalism) and England (Apostolic Faith, Irvingite Pentecostal tradition). Yet, in his work, Pentecostal phenomena are consistently equated with Zulu practice and only occasionally with Western Pentecostalism, and then in a pejorative sense (Sundkler, 1961, p. 221). I do not deny here the possibility of non-Christian Pentecostal-like phenomena in the African context. I merely draw attention to the direction of Sundkler's bias with regard to Pentecostal phenomena.

The second classic example of a treatment of the AICM, which exemplifies the combined factors of ethnocentrism, rigid scholastic theology, and a rejection of Pentecostalism, is G. C. Oosthuizen's *Post-Christianity in Africa: A Theological and Anthropological Study* (1968). This work also illustrates the use of Sundkler's book as a main source (twenty-seven references alone in a chapter on "The Holy Spirit Misunderstood"), with no mention of Sundkler's later repudiation of the "bridge to paganism" theory (Oosthuizen, 1968, pp. 128–29). It is evident that Oosthuizen espouses this theory throughout his work, with the difference that he speaks of it as a "bridge to *nativism*." Oosthuizen's statement that only *some* of the African Independent movements developed into "post-Christianity" is eclipsed by the book's title (p. xi), which accords with his "bridge to nativism" idea borrowed from Sundkler, and his nearly consistent reference to the movements as "nativistic movements."

Oosthuizen deals with the "independent movement" as a sociological phenomenon apart from the church. In his view, rapid social change caused African society to turn back upon its traditional worldview—prophetism (p. 30). Oosthuizen believes the factors that gave rise to independent movements are disappointment with white civilization and Western Christianity, reactions against missionary paternalism, and an injunction of "the Spirit" (pp. 60–61). He then summarizes:

> Basically, it is this: the misunderstanding by White-dominated non-indigenous Churches of the psychology, philosophy, languages, culture and traditions of the African, resulting in very little communication in depth and leading, via frustration, to *fanaticism*. (p. 61; emphasis mine)

While pointing to the traumatic, in-depth impact of Western culture on African Christianity, Oosthuizen still does not allow for truly "Christian" secessions from mission churches. He identifies the same dynamics in the origin of "nativistic" movements as that in the independent movements in Africa and, therefore, assumes that the presence of the same dynamics makes the AICM also nativistic in nature! The context in which the AICM takes place is Christian, however. The movements represent secessions from Protestant mission churches (some of them even remaining in the mission churches, e.g., the Aladura societies). The same dynamics of deprivation and revitalization also take place in *Christian* movements (Wallace, 1979, p. 423). For Oosthuizen, an effort to contextualize the gospel in African culture is equivalent to the syncretism of the gospel with traditional African religion (1968, p. xiv). Therefore, in his view, the movements are to be understood as nativistic movements, not valid Christian movements.

The dimensions of ethnocentrism and influence of a rigid scholastic theology emerge in Oosthuizen's discussion of the doctrine of the church. He does not call the movements "churches," due to their efforts to attain African identity! The indigenous nature of the church appears as a dilemma that a rigid Western-oriented ecclesiology is unable to resolve. He states, "The African personality must be offered positive development in the Church, which means the Church must discard its foreignness" (p. 21). But at the same time he asserts, "The great task of the Church is to be the Church; not an ethnic institution, but the Church of Christ" (p. 21). The result of this tension between cultural and spiritual, or human and divine, identity, is a rejection of the former. This occurs instead of accepting both identities in their biblical tension, as the incarnation illustrates. Oosthuizen's presupposition is that churches cannot be "ethno-centric" like nativistic movements. His reasoning is that "being ethno-centric, they are not churches; because the church can only be defined as the Body of Christ" (p. xiv). Oosthuizen uses the term "ethno-centric" as synonymous with "ethnic identity," which to him has the same pejorative connotation as does "ethnocentrism." He does not admit that the Western church is an expression of the Christian faith *contextualized* in Western culture, having "ethnic identity," and in turn is not the "pure" Body of Christ (his terms) devoid of cultural identity. Oosthuizen states concerning the contextualization of the Christian faith in non-Western cultures:

> Although some of the movements referred to in the analysis are *not* nativistic, they have nevertheless non-Christian elements in their bosom, as in the case of many Churches in Africa, which are easy bridges to nativism. All this shows how dangerous an emphasis on indigenisation or relevance for its own sake is for the Church, because it is easily misunderstood. (p. 79)

Oosthuizen seems little aware that Western churches also have non-Christian, Western elements in their bosom, and this fact does not necessarily lead to a defection from the Christian faith. Furthermore, missiologically speaking, "relevancy" is never merely for "its own sake," but it has to do with a people's understanding of the gospel and its vitality in society in terms of its power and spontaneous expansion. While risk is present in indigenization, it evolves into a syncretism phobia or a syndrome where the factor of the Holy Spirit is omitted in the venture.

Reflecting the typical Western "syncretism syndrome," Oosthuizen states, "Indigenisation or relevance of the church in Africa is most important, but this is a dangerous task, which should be based on sound theological judgment" (p. xiv). Of course, by "sound theological judgment" he means sound *Western* theological judgment. The subjective criterion Oosthuizen uses to judge whether a movement is a "church" or not is the traditional "where the Word is rightly preached and the sacraments rightly administered" (p. xiv). The Western theological criteria used to determine what "rightly" means are: (1) the position held on the Trinity, (2) the position of

the prophet in the movement, and (3) the function of the Holy
Spirit—a vital force, numinous power, or the Holy Spirit glorifying
Jesus Christ in men (Oosthuizen, 1968, p. xiii). If applied to classical
Pentecostals in the United States by someone prejudiced against
Pentecostal phenomena, these theological criteria would also rule
out the Christian validity of the majority of Pentecostalism (e.g.,
the Jesus Only groups and those emphasizing the gifts of healing
and prophecy)!

The most important factor to observe here, however, is not subjective criteria applied by one prejudiced against Pentecostalism.
Such a "syncretism syndrome" view of indigenization and "bridges
back to nativism" view of independent movements reveal a serious
deficiency in *pneumatology*. The domination by fear with respect
to indigenization shows a serious undervaluing of the ministry of
the Holy Spirit among a people in the venture. Indeed, the Spirit's
ministry is entirely missing from the discussion. This "silence on
the Holy Spirit" by Western theologians reveals the pneumatological bankruptcy of such scholastic-oriented Western theology. In
Oosthuizen's explanation of the rise of messianic movements in the
context of Christian missions, he says:

> In the Gospels the main theme is: "Fear Not!" The power of evil spirits
> is broken, and this makes an immense impression on the converts
> from the animistic world. But this relief creates a vacuum which is
> later filled again in times of crisis either with the old or with all kinds
> of Utopian expectations. (1968, p. 87)

With regard to utopian, messianic expectations, Peel states, "In
Africa millennialism is one of the less characteristic features of independent churches" (1968, p. 3). While Oosthuizen is correct to
mention the vacuum left in African society, his failure to mention
the New Testament alternative for filling the vacuum—the Christian doctrine concerning the ministry of the Holy Spirit—is very
conspicuous. In the power encounter Oosthuizen refers to in the
above statement, pneumatology is ignored. He repeatedly refers to
the missionary's message reacting against African tradition, creat-
ing a "vacuum" in society, and rightly so (p. 87). But he always
speaks of the people filling the vacuum by a return to traditional

African religion. Is it true that the gospel is inadequate in filling a spiritual vacuum left in an animistic African society after it turns to Christ? Is there no source of immediate contact with the presence and power of God? Or is it specifically Oosthuizen's "Western" expression of the gospel that was found to be wanting? In a statement that also illustrates the rational-static nature of scholastic theology, he states,

> The God of the missions is too remote for a system in which men's "gods" belonged to their lineage, and although far removed, could be approached through their ancestors. The God in the Christianity with which they came in contact had much to do with their souls, and with certain individuals but not with them in all spheres of life and as a whole community. (p. 119)

Surely a people coming out of mainline Protestant mission churches, possessing the Scriptures in their vernacular and particularly oriented to the spirit world, would be aware of the New Testament alternative in filling the vacuum. Also, would not the Holy Spirit among them reveal his power in their situation? True, a Western, radically reduced expression of the Christian faith could not fill the vacuum, but a Pentecostal expression *could and did* in numerous cases. Also, it is important to remember here that the Pentecostal expression of Christianity under discussion, as well as the majority of the AICMs, began in a *Christian context*, not African nativism. Hollenweger links the origins of Bantu Independent Churches of South Africa specifically with the Apostolic Faith mission and the Christian Catholic Church in Zion, Illinois—Pentecostal bodies (1972, pp. 120–21). Oosthuizen's "bridge to nativism" theory is as lacking as Sundkler's early "bridge to paganism" theory. The theory fails when the *a priori* rejection of the Holy Spirit's apostolic ministry is considered in the light of the contemporary Pentecostal movement. That expression of the faith is a valid Christian alternative for filling the vacuum in African society.

The possibility that the AICMs may represent *a bridge to New Testament Christianity in the African context,* rather than a bridge to paganism, is not considered. As previously mentioned, this alternative of a Pentecostal-type ministry manifesting itself in the

African context is supported by some of the leading authorities of the AICMs. Oosthuizen's silence on New Testament pneumatology in this respect points to a theological bias against Pentecostalism. In a direct reference to Pentecostalism, Oosthuizen states,

> The misunderstanding of the person and work of the Holy Spirit in Africa is not confined to the nativistic movements, many of the Pentecostal Churches revealing [sic] the same difficulty. These movements in Africa have been greatly influenced by Negro Baptist and Pentecostal sects from the United States. (1968, p. 120)

Oosthuizen states that the great theological problem in Africa is the confusion that exists with regard to the Holy Spirit and ancestral spirits (p. 122). Recounting some of the charges leveled against the mission churches by the African Independent Churches he states:

> Their hostility against the missions was summed up in the accusation that they had no spirit in the congregations and they maintained that, with rare exceptions, none of the missionary evangelists had it either. (p. 124)

He explains further that these missionaries did not fall in line with the ancestral cult like their (the AICM) prophets did (p. 124). Oosthuizen moves from a description of traditional African animism to a description of worship in the AICM without any discrimination whatsoever. For him, there is no difference: "The functions of the ancestor spirits have been transferred to the Holy Spirit, or simply 'the Spirit' so that in the independent post-Christian movements their 'holy spirit' is no longer the Holy Spirit of whom we learn in Scripture" (p. 129). Yet Oosthuizen rejects clear references to the operation of the spiritual gifts, such as those listed in 1 Corinthians 12 (p. 125). He not only fails to admit the insufficiency of pneumatology in Western theology in the face of the needs of the African context, but he also assumes that any spiritual manifestations on the part of the African are "ancestral spirits" and not the Holy Spirit. The question that emerges is: Who misunderstands the biblical meaning of the Holy Spirit in this case, the African or the Western theologian? Or does this situation under discussion reveal a deficiency on the part of both parties, at opposite ends of the theological continuum?

Furthermore, it is insufficient to merely point out a parallel between spirit-possession in traditional African religion and the Pentecostal phenomena in the AICM. The presence of non-Christian oracles and ecstatic religion in New Testament times and its parallel with the New Testament experience with the Holy Spirit was no proof that the early New Testament experience was pagan. In the context of the discussion here we could ask: Could it be that the parallel between pagan spiritism and Pentecostal phenomena is frequently pointed out because pneumatology in the minds of Western theologians is such an esoteric subject?

Of course, the problem could be merely a prejudice against a Pentecostal expression of the Christian faith. One wonders about Oosthuizen's awareness concerning historic occurrences of charismatic renewal, when he states concerning glossolalia, "There is no evidence of glossalaly [sic] amongst the Montanists" (p. 140). The generalizations Oosthuizen makes concerning the Holy Spirit and the AICM are reminiscent of the prejudicial charges made against early Pentecostalism in the United States. The validity of the activity of the Holy Spirit, in terms of apostolic-charismatic type ministry today, is problematic for many. It is relatively easy to attribute such activity in the African context to paganism, especially for the ethnocentric theologian. For in doing so, he is freed from the possibility of further Christian response. It also agrees with his Western theological dichotomy of the religious "upper world" and the naturalistic "lower world." It preserves the Western elimination of the "middle spirit world" and its deistic concept of the providence of God.

It will become evident in later chapters that such a view of the activity of God mentioned above is at the bottom of major missiological issues. Also, many evangelicals hold to a dispensational theology that reserves charismatic phenomena to either the past or future periods of salvation history. In other words, it is easier to fault the African worldview than it is to fault one's own Western worldview and theology when considering contemporary Pentecostal phenomena.

A Reliable Estimate of
Pentecostalism (1985)

The difficulties enumerated above about the definition of the worldwide Pentecostal movement also represent the problems involved with gathering statistics on it. The elusive nature of a definition, however, is nothing in comparison to the elusive statistical picture of the worldwide movement. The penetration of the Pentecostal phenomenon across the ecclesiastical spectrum presents a problem. This is the case with charismatic groups who do not want to leave the impression that they are a schismatic group within their own Christian tradition. Phenomenal rates of growth also add to the difficulty of obtaining current statistics; precisely accurate statistics are almost impossible on a worldwide scale. The presence of the Pentecostal phenomenon among a diversity of cultural contexts has also presented difficulties with its identification, and this diversity has impeded the statistical enumeration of the groups. The question "Who is a Christian?" becomes problematic with non-Western Pentecostal movements.

Frequently, legalistic Pentecostal groups have a large number of persons who, although they are Pentecostal in experience, are not included in the membership statistics and listed as "unaffiliated." Often the reason for this is their nonconformity to a particular social practice required for membership in American Pentecostal churches. This factor alone renders Pentecostal statistics to be less reliable. These unaffiliated adherents can number as many as the membership of a church. As of 1981, the Assemblies of God statistics for El Salvador show 43,000 baptized members and 95,000 "other believers." The Statistics for Guatemala show 43,000 baptized members and 78,015 "others believers." Brazil shows 3,350,000 baptized believers with 2,750,000 "other believers" (Division of Foreign Missions, 1981, p. 7). The fact that the Pentecostal phenomenon involves a spiritual experience that can be interpreted differently according to one's particular theological tradition and perspective also complicates the statistical task. The question "Who is Pentecostal?" then becomes problematic. Add to the above difficulties an incipient ethnocentrism toward non-Western expressions of

Pentecostalism and a prejudice against that expression of the faith, and you have a picture of the difficulty in gaining a reliable estimate of the worldwide Pentecostal movement.

Various figures concerning the scope of the movement have already been suggested by various persons quoted in this chapter. The figures thirty-five million, fifty million, and seventy-five million have already been mentioned. Are these Pentecostal claims about the movement exaggerated? Is the assessment of non-Pentecostal churchmen, theologians, and missiologists about the significance of the movement hyperbolic in nature? Does Pentecostalism deserve the accolade of "The Third Force in Christendom"? A survey of available statistics on the worldwide movement, growth rates of Pentecostal-charismatic communities, and reports of Pentecostal leaders indicate that the commonly reported statistical picture of the movement's scope is too conservative. Rather, the typical view of its scope is something like the tip of the iceberg, or to use a more appropriate metaphor, like a wisp of smoke from a rapidly spreading flame.

The title of this section, "A Reliable Estimate of Pentecostalism," was chosen due to these difficulties involved in gathering statistics on the worldwide movement. A proper statistical survey would consume a book in itself if it were comprehensive, accurate, and up-to-date. The term "reliable" refers to the effort to base the estimate on the best information available. D. B. Barrett's *World Christian Encyclopedia* (1982) represents a monumental survey of the Christian faith worldwide. Although Barrett was not Pentecostal in experience, his work is sympathetic to Pentecostalism, especially in Africa, because he wrote a doctoral dissertation on the African Independent Church Movement (AICM). His comprehensive volume presents data from which a reliable estimate can be made. Many of the problems mentioned previously are overcome in Barrett's work. The work surveys 150 major ecclesiastical traditions, 20,800 distinct Christian denominations, and the status of Christianity in 223 countries.

Barrett's information concerning Pentecostalism is significant due to his sympathetic and knowledgeable grasp of the Pentecostal movement in the non-Western world. Although some of his statistics are based on the years 1970 to 1972 (Barrett, 1982, p. 46), projections of growth are given based on growth rates up to 1985. Of course, the significance of Barrett's statistics must be measured by his methodology. Barrett used a new methodology in categorizing Christianity in that he divided his statistics into three basic categories: (1) professing Christians—those who identify themselves as Christian, or confess Christ, (2) affiliated Christians—those claimed by the churches, or the total community, and (3) practicing Christians—those faithfully involved with the institutional life of the church (Barrett, 1982, p. 47). These categories each have their advantages and disadvantages with regard to identifying the scope of Pentecostalism. ·

In the first edition of *The Third Force in Missions*, Pentecostals were classified in three major streams: (1) classical Pentecostals, (2) neo-Pentecostals, and (3) Catholic charismatics. However, there are many tributaries within these three main streams that Barrett mentions in his *World Christian Encyclopedia*. His "Global Tables" show the following *charismatic* classifications: Roman Catholic Pentecostals, neo-Pentecostals, and Catholic Pentecostals–non-Roman, apostolic-type, and Irvingites (1982, pp. 782–83). Barrett explains that the statistics on charismatics serve merely to aid in understanding the scope of charismatic renewal, because of their tendency to avoid the image of schism in the church. Barrett describes the difficulty in determining the scope of the various charismatic movements:

> In many parts of the world, new Christian movements are beginning and growing rapidly, the largest example being the global neo-pentecostal and charismatic movements within the major older denominations. Such groups have little time or opportunity for self-analysis, and usually keep neither statistics nor exact membership lists. Further, many movements exist within the structures of older denominations, value their close relations with them, and oppose the collecting of statistics as tending to artificially crystallize their identity and to appear to divide charismatics from their non-charismatic fellow-Christians. (p. 55)

Also, the statistics given for charismatics are often limited to the "practicing Christian" category.

A significant statistic Barrett gives for charismatic groups, however, is their phenomenal *rate of growth*. In Africa, for instance, in the 1980s, Catholic Pentecostals were growing at an unbelievable rate of 45 percent per year, neo-Pentecostals at 27 percent per year, and Anglican Pentecostals at 25 percent per year. Other Christian groups were reported at 2 to 5 percent growth per year. The same phenomenal rate of growth for Pentecostals held for the other continents as well (pp. 782–83). Barrett states:

> Our Tables 1 [country by country survey] envisage phenomenal growth in the number of Catholic charismatics (pentecostals [*sic*]) in South America, rising by AD 2000 to 7 million in Brazil alone. . . . This projection is based on present trends; but many observers hold it to be distinctly probable that within the next decade or two the trends may be accelerated and the leadership or even the bulk of the laity in Latin American Catholicism may become predominantly charismatic. (p. 69)

Note that in 2000, Brazil had 79,949,999 Pentecostal-charismatic Christians (Burgess & van der Maas, 2002, p. 35). "Predominantly" in this estimate of Latin American charismatics means something well over 50 percent (Barrett, 1982, p. 69). Barrett gives the total number of charismatic Christians in the above classifications worldwide in 1985 to be 14,444,830 (p. 6).

Barrett divides classical Pentecostalism into two basic, separate ecclesiastical traditions: (1) white classical Pentecostalism, and (2) non-white or black/developing world "pentecostalism" (in Barrett's work, "Pentecostal" with a capital *P* always refers to classical white Pentecostalism). He states concerning this classification:

> This distinction between Pentecostal and pentecostal is made here to make it clear that these are 2 separate ecclesiastical traditions. Non-White or Black/Third-World pentecostalism has arisen, outside the USA, quite independently of Classical Pentecostalism; and within the USA itself, Black pentecostalism has some claim to have preceded White Pentecostalism in time, to be a phenomenon distinct and separate from it, and to itself be regarded as the classical tradition. (p. 81)

But Barrett's subtypes within each of these main Pentecostal traditions are the same. Barrett's principle of determining distinct classifications within the main traditions is both ecclesiastical and theological. The nature and number of subsequent experiences with the Holy Spirit in post-conversion experience are the main discriminating factor. Barrett's White classical Pentecostal subtypes are:

PeA   Apostolic, or Pentecostal Apostolic (stress on complex hierarchy of living apostles, prophets and other charismatic officials)

Pen   Pentecostal (Protestant; Classical Pentecostal of unspecified type); charismatic, faith-healing (Classical Pentecostal sub-types include PeA, Pe1, Pe2, Pe3, Pe4)

Pe1   Oneness-Pentecostal or Unitarian-Pentecostal: "Jesus only," sometimes unitarian, non/or anti-trinitarian

Pe2   Baptistic-Pentecostal or Keswick-Pentecostal: 2-crisis-experience (conversion, baptism of the Spirit)

Pe3   Holiness-Pentecostal: 3-crisis-experience (conversion, sanctification, baptism of the Spirit)

Pe4   Perfectionist-Pentecostal, Free Pentecostal, Deliverance-Pentecostal, Radical- or Revivalist-Pentecostal: 4-crisis-experience (conversion, sanctification, baptism of the Spirit, deliverance/ecstatic [*sic*] confession/prophecy/perfectionism, also authority/discipling/shepherding) (p. 127)

Barrett's *Non-White* indigenous Pentecostal subtypes are:

peA   indigenous charismatic Pentecostal apostolic (hierarchy of living apostles)

pen   indigenous charismatic (Pentecostal, spirit-dominated): Black/Third-World indigenous body of Pentecostal type (charismatic, enthusiastic, faith-healing); in Africa, spiritual or Zionist or spirit or aladura (praying) churches *pe1* indigenous charismatic oneness-pentecostal, unitarian-pentecostal

pe2 indigenous charismatic baptistic-pentecostal (2-crisis-experience)

pe3 indigenous charismatic holiness-pentecostal (3-crisis-experience)

pe4 indigenous charismatic perfectionist, free, radical- or revivalist-pentecostal or deliverance Pentecostal (4-crisis-experience). (p. 127)

The significance of Barrett's classification is that it recognizes non-Western Pentecostal expressions of the Christian faith. His classification tends to present the worldwide movement as a unity, although the separate traditions are affirmed. This is so, because the focus is on the common Pentecostal experience of the Spirit; it is this that is set forth as the Pentecostal distinctive. Barrett's use of the same subtypes in the indigenous Pentecostal movements shows that he considers them to be parallel Pentecostal expressions of the Christian faith, only in diverse cultural contexts. Also, with regard to the origins of the worldwide movement, the common experience of the Spirit in the diversity of cultural contexts suggests a unity in the movement and the probability of a spontaneous worldwide outpouring of the Spirit. There is evidence of historical-causal linkage between some of the various ecclesiastical traditions, but with others there is *no such historical-causal connection*. This phenomenon is discussed in detail in chapter 2, "A Renewal Movement."

Barrett gives the figure of 21,909,778 in 1980 for the white classical Pentecostals worldwide and 29,257,409 for the non-white indigenous Pentecostals (p. 14). If we add to these 29,257,409 indigenous Pentecostals Barrett's combined figure for all classical Pentecostals and all charismatics—49,235,400—a total of Pentecostal-charismatics worldwide of 78,492,800 emerges for 1980. Barrett appears to know that his estimates are low. In the "Dictionary" section under the heading "Pentecostal-Charismatic" in Barrett's *World Christian Encyclopedia* he states:

A blanket term [is Pentecostal-charismatic] for all Pentecostals, pentecostals, neo-Pentecostals, and charismatics (qv). Global totals (1980) [include]: (a) active regularly-involved persons, 62,200,000; (b) all persons professing or claiming to be Pentecostal-charismatics, over 100 million worldwide. (p. 838)

There is every reason to believe that Barrett's figure of "over 100 million worldwide" for Pentecostal-charismatics was a "reliable estimate."

There is even reason to believe that the actual number of Pentecostal-charismatics worldwide in the 1980s *exceeded* the 100 million figure. The phenomenal growth rate of charismatics and neo-Pentecostals on all continents makes one expect a greater global figure for this category. But in view of the "identity problem" mentioned previously, it is not surprising that the statistics are as low as they are. A statistical picture emerges, however, which is smaller than it should be. The large adherent-unaffiliated communities, or "other believers," that are not always reported in Pentecostal membership statistics tend also to make those figures low and not represent the true scope of this segment of the worldwide movement (see Barrett's discussion on "Belief" in his *World Christian Encyclopedia*, p. 53). The problem of the identification and acceptance of the largest and most rapidly growing Pentecostal group, the non-Western indigenous Pentecostals, is a reason for the probable underestimation of that group. The problem of obtaining *current* statistics is also another factor that tends to make the 100 million figure too conservative.

The conservative nature of the 100 million figure may be illustrated by comparing some statistics gathered in connection with the writing of the first edition of this book apart from Barrett's source. Between 1979 and 1980, the number of classical Pentecostals in the United States and Canada was approximately 4,000,000. Barrett's survey indicates 3,225,701 (pp. 215–16, 720–25). The Assemblies of God alone make up one-third of Barrett's figure. Pentecostal statistics gathered for several other countries also differ. Brazil, a country where 70 percent of the Protestant community is Pentecostal (Miklaus, 1982, p. 117), shows a significantly different statistic. Estimates of the number of Pentecostals in Brazil have been as high as 10 million (Harrison, 1981). Robert Niklaus reports 8,500,000 (1982, p. 117). Barrett's survey, however, shows 3,915,210 (1982, pp. 191–93). In

1980, the Assemblies of God alone reported 3,350,000 *plus 2,750,000 "other believers"* (Division of Foreign Missions, 1981, p. 7). Barry Chant reports an estimated 60,000 classical Pentecostals in Australia (1981, p. 1), while Barrett's survey is nearly half of that figure: 36,000 (1982, pp. 155–56). The reason for the discrepancy may be the rapid rate of growth—156 percent during the period of 1970 to 1980 (Chant, 1981, p. 1). Steve Durasoff estimates the Russian Pentecostal community to be from 500,000 to 600,000 (1982, p. 1)—a very conservative figure—while Barrett's survey indicates a community figure of 120,000 (1982, p. 696). One of the largest Pentecostal churches in the world is in Seoul, Korea; the Assemblies of God membership in Korea is 82,200 baptized members *with 120,000 adherents* (Division of Foreign Missions, 1981, p. 5). But Barrett's survey lists only 82,191 for the whole country (1982, p. 444). His survey lists 296,624 for the classical Pentecostals in all of the Philippine Islands, but the Manila area alone has over 120,000 classical Pentecostals (Seleky, 1982, p. 1). Therefore, there are indications that the 100 million figure for the worldwide Pentecostal movement was too low.

The purpose of the discussion here has been to bring into focus a reliable estimate of the worldwide Pentecostal movement so that its scope and, therefore, its significance and contribution could be considered. Both its scope and rate of growth are phenomenal; the designation "third force" in Christianity is appropriate. In fact, it may approach a literal truth. In Barrett's "Definitions of Types of Christians" graph, he shows three categories of Christians from the standpoint of "belief": (1) 350 million uncommitted Christians, (2) 303 million partially committed Christians, and (3) 780 million committed Christians. The last category is broken down further into 420 million Christians who attend church weekly and confess to be "born again" (Barrett, 1982, p. 49). Of course, Barrett's definitions and qualifications must be read in order to appreciate his categories. However, when the estimates of Pentecostal-charismatics worldwide are placed against this figure of "committed-born again" Christians (420 million), Pentecostalism may not only represent a significant group of Christians and may therefore be called a "third force," but may in reality come close to representing nearly a third of this group of committed Christians.

A Reliable Estimate of
Pentecostalism (2015)

One of the primary reasons for this second edition of *The Third Force in Missions* is to update the statistics on the worldwide Pentecostal-charismatic movement and give a reliable estimate. As previously mentioned, I do not take on the task for the purpose of Pentecostal triumphalism, but rather to draw attention to and corroborate the Pentecostal contribution to Christian missions. The "mission field" of Western Christian missions has become the place where most of the world's Christians live and, for the most part, are Pentecostal in experience. We use the popular term "renewal" for the Pentecostal-charismatic movements in order to emphasize that the movements are renewals of *the gospel of the kingdom of God* and, therefore, renewals of the normative gospel of the New Testament (providing an answer to the question: "What is a Pentecostal?"). We see this focus as crucial for contextualizing this gospel in the many cultures of the Southern Hemisphere. The focus also helps in counteracting the negative influence of a system of theology among evangelicals and Pentecostals: dispensational theology. Dispensationalism denies the movements outright, as well as denying the "presence" of the powerful kingdom of God in the church today (which provides an answer to the question: "What is the gospel?"), thereby denying Jesus' gospel of the kingdom of God.

There are obvious reasons why characterizing the movements as *renewals* of Jesus' good news of the kingdom of God would resonate with the peoples of the Southern Hemisphere, where a majority of the world's Pentecostal-charismatic Christians reside (we return to these reasons in chapter 7, "The Pentecostal and the Kingdom of God"). A prime example illustrating these obvious reasons is Yonggi Cho's contextualization of the gospel of the kingdom of God in Korean culture. The theological core of his "contextualized theology" is the kingdom of God. He primarily focuses on the present kingdom of God and power of the Holy Spirit for Christians in this life, in healings, in overcoming demonic power, and in showing that God is a good God who provides for the needs of his people; Cho does all of this with a focus on the New Testament in which the kingdom of

God is related in a special way to the poor (Synan & Yong, 2013). It is often said that Pentecostalism appears to resonate among the poor, and most of the world's poor live in the Southern Hemisphere. We know, however, that in Jesus' ministry in the New Testament his gospel of the kingdom of God also had a great response from the poor; their hearts were open and they readily responded to his message (James 2:5; Matt. 4:23–25; 5:3; Luke 4:18–19). The great response of the poor in the Pentecostal-charismatic movements in the Southern Hemisphere, therefore, is an example of the poor's response of faith to the normative gospel of the kingdom of God.

In keeping with our purpose in *The Third Force in Missions* of providing the Pentecostal contribution to the Christian mission, we focus on giving a reliable estimate of the movements in the Southern Hemisphere in order to corroborate that contribution. In this regard, we again attempt—as in 1985—to uncover "hidden Pentecostals." Theory concerning the great response of the people of the Southern Hemisphere to the gospel aside, in 2015 the "nuts and bolts" of extracting statistical totals for this group from evangelical institutions reporting on "global Christianity" are still disappointing. Our focus is on this segment of Pentecostalism today, because the same factors causing the information gap in 1985 are still present today, although not to the same degree (ethnocentrism, dispensational theology, and the influence of scholastic theology—the lack of a dynamic view of Scripture, hermeneutics, and theology for contextualizing the gospel in non-Western cultures). The result of the existence of these factors today is the same: an information gap. That the persistent factors are present today is shown in the statistical picture for worldwide Pentecostal-charismatic Christians; this is especially the case in the Southern Hemisphere. They are still understated and, for statistical purposes, there are still "hidden Pentecostals" in that part of the world.

The goal of attaining an *exact number* of Pentecostal-charismatic Christians worldwide is not possible due to the rapid growth of the movements, their ecclesial spread among the churches, and the fragmented reports on global statistics; even surveys from the Pew Forum's research center do not help in filling in the fragmented picture. This is why my goal here is to present an "estimate" based on the many sources available in 2015. Under these circumstances, a reasonable estimate of the movement is hard to come by today. My investigation of the statistics reported indicates that there is a lack of interest and due diligence in reporting on the incredible growth of Pentecostalism in the Southern Hemisphere.

In 1985, we relied heavily on D. B. Barrett's *World Christian Encyclopedia: A comparative study of churches and religions in the modern world AD 1900–2000* (1982). At the time, it was the only work of its kind, and Barrett was a sympathetic source for reporting Pentecostal and charismatic Christians in the developing world. Today, however, there are several such dictionaries or encyclopedias like Barrett's, as well as monographs providing statistics on Christianity worldwide. There are also institutions dedicated to providing statistics on global Christianity, and there is an abundance of works on worldwide Pentecostalism from missionaries and Western theologians, as well as theologians from the Southern Hemisphere. This does not make the task any easier today, and actually makes it more difficult. In spite of the many resources, the resulting statistics on worldwide Pentecostals-charismatics are still incomplete and fragmented; they lack totals for the Southern Hemisphere, are difficult to navigate, and are sometimes contradictory and confusing. This is the case in spite of the notion today that we have reliable statistics on the worldwide movement.

Some of this difficulty is due to use of different methodologies (and definitions) and varying sources of data and reports on worldwide Christianity, but the fact is telling that they often do not even attempt to give clear totals for the worldwide Pentecostal-charismatic movement, or the movement in the Southern Hemisphere. This is an incredible failure on the part of those attempting to survey global Christianity; the growth of Pentecostal-charismatics in the Southern Hemisphere is the *Christian* phenomenon of the twenty-first century. Therefore, I suspect that the factors causing the information gap mentioned previously (ethnocentrism, dispensational theology, and the influence of scholastic theology) are part of the reason for this incomplete picture today. An exception to this failure in reporting on global Pentecostalism is *The New International Dictionary of Pentecostal*

Charismatic Movements (Burgess & van der Maas, 2003), although it does not provide statistics for 2015.

For this update, I first looked at the worldwide statistics at the turn of the twenty-first century—*before* the third wave of Pentecostal-charismatic renewal—and then I reviewed the fragmented data on Pentecostalism in the Southern Hemisphere in order to provide, if not a reliable estimate, a reasonable estimate of the global movement today. However, I first present three statistical factors that have a bearing on both the data at the turn of the twenty-first century and a contemporary estimate of the worldwide Pentecostal-charismatic movement:

1. Gordon-Conwell's Center for the Study of Global Christianity produced "Christianity in its Global Context, 1970–2020"; in the graphic: "Renewalists by type and tradition 1970 & 2020," the Center reported 62,700,000 Pentecostal-charismatics worldwide in 1970 and *projected 709,800,000 for the year 2020.* (2013, p. 2; emphasis mine)

2. Philip Jenkins states in *The Next Christendom: The Coming of Global Christianity* (2002): "Since there were only a handful of Pentecostals in 1900, and several hundred million today, is it not reasonable to identify this as the most successful social movement of the past century? According to the current projections, the number of Pentecostal believers should *surpass the one billion mark before 2050*" (Jenkins, 2002, p. 8; emphasis mine). This is not a casual prediction from Jenkins or Pentecostal triumphalism (Jenkins is not a Pentecostal or a charismatic). In his endnote to this quote above, he cites ten authoritative sources on the growth of the Pentecostal movement. (p. 234, n. 17)

3. *Christianity Today* reported about Pentecostals in "World Growth at 19 Million a Year": "Missions expert David Barrett [reported] to *Christianity Today* that the Pentecostal and charismatic churches are growing by 19 million a year." (Christianity Today, 1998, 16 November)

These three predictions of Pentecostal-charismatic growth point to the movements reaching the one billion mark prior to the years 2020 and 2050. The prior date, 2020, is less than five years away.

A look at the statistics of the worldwide movement in the *first decade* of the second millennium is helpful, because many of the works monitoring the worldwide Pentecostal movement began to report on them at this time. We also present statistics for the second decade; this data is helpful, because it is *before* the third wave of renewal in the Southern Hemisphere, or at least it is at the time when the third wave was "cresting," a time when phenomenal growth begins to take place. That phenomenal growth is shown in the data of our report on the Pentecostal-charismatic Christians worldwide and in the Southern Hemisphere below.

In "AD 2001 Reality Check: 50 new facts and figures about trends and issues concerning empirical global Christianity Today" (Table 1–1) in *World Christian Trends*, D. B. Barrett and Todd Johnson report the worldwide total in 2001 of Pentecostal-charismatic Christians at 524 million affiliated and 602 million unaffiliated. The *New International Dictionary of Pentecostal and Charismatic Movements* (2002), by Stanley M. Burgess and Eduard M. van der Maas (a source we heavily rely on), gives the "global affiliated Pentecostals, charismatics and Neocharismatics [*sic*] at 523,767,390 affiliated and 602,094,900 unaffiliated in 2000. In the second decade of the twenty-first century, however, these two sources have begun to give *significantly differing totals*.

These later statistics, all reported by the Center for the Study of Global Christianity at Gordon-Conwell Theological Seminary (see References for the reports), are shown below in *italics*:

1985	100 million (Barrett, 1982; and my revised estimate)
1995	477,378,000 (Burgess & van der Maas, 2002)
2001	*524,000,000*
2004	*589,000,000*
2007 (mid)	*602,792,000*
2010	*583,208,000*
2014	*631,230,000*
2015 (mid)	*643,661,000*

The above 2007–2015 statistics from the Center for Global Christianity do not show a logical progression of growth in the year totals for the Pentecostal-charismatic movement, nor are the totals clearly portrayed in the reports. The center's total for mid-2015 is frequently reported in contemporary Pentecostal and evangelical literature. Keep in mind that these worldwide totals supposedly include the problematic Pentecostal-charismatic totals in the Southern Hemisphere (Asia/Africa/Latin America/Oceania). However, this growth in the Southern Hemisphere is increasingly hard to find in the center's reports, especially after David Barrett's death in 2011.

Since the 1985–2001 period was *before* the rapid growth of the *third wave* in the decades after the turn of this century, one would assume that the gains in growth would be larger in the 2001–2015 period. This is the period in which Barrett projected the growth of Pentecostalism at 19 million people each year. However, using the center's statistic from 2001 to start with, the years of growth indicate the following: Pentecostalism grew from 100 million in 1985 to 524,000,000 million in 2001, which is a gain of 424,000,000 million in sixteen years. But the center's statistics indicate that Pentecostals grew from 524,000,000 in 2001 to 643,661,000 in mid-2015, which is a gain of *only 119,661,000 in fourteen years*, during a time of explosive growth in the Southern Hemisphere. At Barrett's projection of a growth rate of 19 million per year, using the center's statistics 2001–2015 for the fourteen-year interim, the gain would be *266,000,000*, making the 2015 total 798,000,000.

If indeed Barrett's predictions of growth were correct (Burgess & van der Maas's *Dictionary* confirms they were correct), and we use the 19 million per year growth rate uniformly throughout the years 2001 to 2015 with the center's totals in that period, they then show the totals in the left column below:

Center for the Study of Global Christianity's totals plus Barrett's 19 million per year		Burgess & van der Maas's *Dictionary* totals plus Barrett's 19 million per year	
1995	477,378,000	1995	529,378,000 (unaffiliated)
2000	[no report]	2000	523,767,390 (affiliated)
2001	524,000,000	2001	542,767,390 (?)
2004	581,000,000	2004	599,767,390 (?)
2007	646,000,000	2007	656,767,390 (?)
2010	703,000,000	2010	713,767,390 (?)
2014	779,000,000	2014	789,767,390 (?)
2015	798,000,000	2015	808,767,390 (?)

Using Barrett's growth rate, the annual figure for 2015 according to the center's calculations, their 643,661,000 for 2015, becomes 798,000,000. However, *the center has not given final totals for 2015*; the 798 million (an estimate) is created by using Barrett's growth rate. But, as previously mentioned, the center's totals were uneven and did not show a logical growth progression that the statistical years in the left column now show. Furthermore, in all probability the actual growth rates exceed Barrett's 1998 prediction of 19 million per year; contemporary reports on growth rate shown below exceed his prediction, as they should, in the rapid growth of Pentecostal-charismatic movements of the third wave in the Southern Hemisphere.

The statistics in italics above are only for the purpose of comparison; they show the range of years 2001–2015 based on statistics from *The New International Dictionary of Pentecostal Charismatic Movement* (Burgess & van der Maas, 2002, p. 287), adding Barrett's growth rate and applying it to the *Dictionary's* figure of 523,767,390 for the year 2000 to start the calculation (523,767,390 + 19,000,000 = *542,767,390* for 2001). Therefore, just for the purpose of comparison, the *Dictionary* statistics would show the worldwide total in 2015 for Pentecostal-charismatic Christians at *808,767,390*. The current and often quoted total—600 million—for the global Pentecostal-charismatic movement in the literature in 2015, which is frequently based on the center's statistics, is obviously too low.

The underreported and fragmented statistics on the Pentecostal-charismatic movement in the Southern Hemisphere (shown below) are part of the reason for the uneven growth and low totals for the center's worldwide statistics given previously (see chart on the "Hidden Pentecostals in the Southern Hemisphere" below). I suspect the irregularity of the center's statistics may be due to the same factors in gathering and reporting statistics on Pentecostals and charismatics in the developing world in 1985—bias against Pentecostalism in general, along with the influence of dispensational theology and ethnocentrism. Whether bias is involved or not, there is a statistical information gap in 2015 for the Southern Hemisphere.

In the light of the evidence of declining mention in the center's reports on neo-Pentecostals, not mentioning them at all, or not reporting statistics for the movement in the Southern Hemisphere, it appears that reporting the growth of the Pentecostal-charismatic movement is no longer a priority of the Center for the Study of Global Christianity (see the chart below). Of course, whether this is due to bias, the influence of dispensational theology and ethnocentrism (not seeing the Southern Hemisphere neo-Pentecostals as valid Pentecostal phenomenon), or just a lack of interest, I cannot determine. Whatever the reason, the picture of global Christianity is distorted and the incredible growth of Pentecostals in the Southern Hemisphere is missing.

In the first column below I list the fragmented totals of Pentecostal-charismatic Christians in the Southern Hemisphere (neo-Pentecostals/Renewalists), which also show the lack of statistics for them in the center's reports. We put the reports of the "Center's Statistics" opposite in column two, "Other Statistical Sources," which is footnoted. These two columns represent my search for statistics online, in dictionaries and works providing global statistics, and in monographs. In a third column, I put the above *Dictionary*'s worldwide totals for 2000, 2015, and 2020 in bold type, adding Barrett's growth rate of 19 million a year. With regard to the third column, I am aware that this is an artificial calculation for these years and it is used only for comparison purposes.

"Hidden Pentecostals" in the Southern Hemisphere

The Center's Reports	Other Reported Sources	Barrett's +19 million per year rate
	1985 29,257,409[1]	
	1995 367,177,590[2]	
	2000 406,589,000[3]	**406,589,000**
	2000 200,000,000 (Africa alone)[4]	
2001 295,405,000		
2004 No neo-Pentecostals*		
2005 No report	2005 401,900,000[5]	

---

1. Pomerville, 1985, p. 38.
2. *Dictionary,* Burgess & van der Maas, p. 286.
3. Ibid.
4. Meyer, 2002, p. 451.
5. Pew Research Center, 2006, October 5.

2006		2006	49,700,000 (Han Chinese house churches alone)[6]	
2007	257,161,000			
2010	546,015,000**	2010	400,000,000[7]	
		2010	184,000,000 (Asia alone)[8]	
2013		2013		
2014	No report			
2015	No report	2015		**691,589,000**
		2015	110,000,000 (Africa alone)[9]	
2020	709,800,000	2020		
		2025	*654,167,500*[10]	**881,589,000**

*"No neo-Pentecostals" refers to no neo-Pentecostals being *reported* in the center's reports or a report not having a breakdown of statistical totals for the Southern Hemisphere, or the statistics of the South being mixed together with those of other non-Southern Hemisphere countries, masking the totals for the Southern Hemisphere.

**The 2010 figure supplied is not given in the center's "Christianity in Its Global Context, 1970–2020," but derived from the "Renewalists" discussion in the center's report ("Renewalists in 2010 have grown to 25.8% of all Christians," pp. 7, 14). "All Christians" in 2010 were 2,184,060,000 (Pew Research Center, 2011, December 16, p. 19), 25.8% of which is 546,015,000. The center's report gives no "Renewalists" totals on the Southern Hemisphere, other than the understated 2007 statistic of 67.2 million for Latin America; but that total is masked, because it is reported together with North America. Statements about "Renewalists" indicate that the center has data on them that is not reported (p. 19). Also, there is an elaborate China report (the center's April 2013 report), but no mention of Pentecostal Han house churches. Suico states, "The house church movement in China is persecuted, Pentecostal, and powerful . . . one possible reason for the strength of the Chinese house church movement in the face of persecution and opposition [is] its Pentecostal nature" (Suico, 2005, p. 210). The Han Chinese house churches have 49.7 million members (p. 211).

Several observations may be made about the above comparison of statistics on the "Hidden Pentecostals," especially concerning the center's statistics and those statistics from other sources in columns two and three:

- In the 2001 center figure of 295,405,000, the African Independent Churches *alone* make up two-thirds: 200,000,000. The center uses a lower figure still for *2007* (257,161,000).

---

6. Suico, 2005, p. 211.
7. Stetzer, 2011, December 22.
8. Synan & Yong, 2010, location 282.
9. Patheos Library, online, accessed 2015, July 13.
10. *Dictionary*, Burgess & van der Maas, pp. 287, 301.

- The center's total for 2007 is only 257,161,000, whereas the *Dictionary* gives 401,900,000 for *2005.*

- The center's total for 2010 in the Southern Hemisphere inexplicably approaches parity with statistics from other sources (Pew Forum); this coincides with the passing of David B. Barrett and his participation in the center's work on global Christianity.

- The center has a projected total for 2020 of Renewalists in the Southern Hemisphere, but there are *no center reports on the totals in the Southern Hemisphere from 2010 to 2015.*

- There is reason to believe that the total given for 2015, enhanced by Barrett's growth rate of 19 million a year, of 691,589,000, *is too low*; as is the case with the *Dictionary's* projected figure for 2025 of *654,167,500.* Barrett's growth-rate prediction used for these figures is from the early period, the second wave of renewal. The totals do not indicate the high percentage of Southern Hemisphere Pentecostal-charismatic Christians in relation to overall Pentecostal-charismatics, or their percentage in relation to the Christian faith worldwide.

In *The Next Christendom: The Coming of Global Christianity* (2002), Philip Jenkins stated that "one way or another, inside the Catholic Church or outside it, Third World Christianity is becoming steadily more Pentecostal" (p. 67). The largest number of Pentecostal-charismatics (neo-Pentecostals) in the world, which is two-thirds of all Pentecostal-charismatics, live below the equator, (Hughes, 1998, p. 1). Both statements were made over a decade ago. In 2015 in "World Christianity by the Numbers," George Weigel states: "In raw numbers, then, charismatic and Pentecostal Christianity is the fastest growing phenomenon in world religious history" (2015, February 25).

The center's "Status of Global Christianity, 1970–2020" report, in which the conflicting totals for neo-Pentecostals in the South appear (2007: 257,161,000; 2010: 546,015,000), gives growth rates for neo-Pentecostals in glowing terms:

Over the period 1970–2010 Renewalists movements [neo-Pentecostals] grow at nearly four times the growth rates of both Christianity and the world's population. Looking forward to 2020, they are expected to grow almost twice as fast as both. In 2010, Renewalists made up over one quarter of all Christians worldwide; this percentage will continue to increase in the future. Renewalists are growing the fastest in Asia and Latin America over the 40-year period [1970–2020], and in Asia and Africa over the 10-year period [2010–2020] Latin America will have the highest percentage of Renewalists, followed by North America and Africa. (2013, p. 19)

These rapid growth rates indicate that the center had statistics on neo-Pentecostal/Renewalists in the period from 2010 to 2015, but I could not find them in any of the center's published reports.

The center's mention in the report on Latin America that this region had the highest percentage of "Renewalists" *is not shown in their reports in terms of total numbers*; this would have aided in providing a statistical picture of Renewalists in the Southern Hemisphere. In 2014, however, the Pew Research Center reported that "across all 18 countries and Puerto Rico a median of nearly ⅔ of Protestants (65%) identify as Pentecostal Christians" (Pew Research Center, 2014, November 13, p. 18). The Pew Research Center further stated about Latin America that in the Dominican Republic, Brazil, and Panama, eight in ten Protestants either belong to a church that is part of a Pentecostal denomination or personally identify as Pentecostal Christians. In Puerto Rico, Nicaragua, Guatemala, Argentina, Honduras, Ecuador, and Chile, roughly ⅔ or more Protestants are Pentecostal by denomination or personal identity or both (Pew Research Center, 2014, November 13). In Panama, Brazil, Honduras, Dominican Republic, and El Salvador, at least half of Catholics say they are charismatic (Pew Research Center, "Charismatic Identification among Catholics," 2014, November 13, p. 64). With regard to Pentecostal-charismatic Christians in Asia, Amos Yong states: "There are more Pentecostals in Asia than in any other continent in the world" (Synan & Yong, 2015, e-book location 282).

It is clear from our investigation of Pentecostal-charismatic Christians in the Southern Hemisphere that the totals are incomplete.

Under these circumstances, as in 1985, I am hard-pressed even to arrive at a reasonable estimate; an educated guess is closer to the truth. The literature on Pentecostal-charismatic Christianity shows an interest in what is happening in the Global South; that interest is acute and will intensify in the years to come. It is hoped that a scholarly organization will emerge that is sympathetic, perhaps even Pentecostal in orientation, like the E21 Congresses, to take on the task of reporting on the growth of Pentecostal-charismatic Christianity in the world. Nevertheless, my educated guess is supported by the worldwide totals of Pentecostal-charismatic Christians and neo-Pentecostals/Renewalists in the Southern Hemisphere in the *New International Dictionary of Pentecostal and Charismatic Movements*, statistics from other sources such as the Pew Forum and monographs, as well as the problematic statistics in various reports from the Center for the Study of Global Christianity and others using the center's reports.

Whether or not Pentecostal-charismatic movements are a "third force" in Christianity today is no longer in question. I estimate that out of the 2.1 billion Christians in the world today, Pentecostal-charismatic Christians worldwide make up 40 percent of all Christians. At 850 million strong, they are not just a "third force" in Christianity, but will in a decade or so constitute half of the world's Christians. I estimate that nearly 75 percent of the world's Pentecostal-charismatic Christians, or neo-Pentecostal/Renewalists, live in the Southern Hemisphere and that that total of 637 million Christians will fast become the "first force" in Christian missions in the twenty-first century. Pentecostal-charismatic movements, as renewals of the gospel of the kingdom, show the Christian faith's powerful movement in the world today. The progress of the gospel of the kingdom, however, is under the looming shadow of Islam that is also increasing in the world. As we consider what is happening in the Global South today from the perspective of Jesus' gospel of the kingdom of God that was proclaimed to "the poor" in New Testament times, this should fill us with hope and faith for that powerful gospel to expand among the poor of the Southern Hemisphere and significantly impact and penetrate the world of Islam.

2 A Renewal Movement

A discussion of the origins of the Pentecostal movement is crucial and instructive in discovering its true nature. The matter of origins concerns more than an interest in the historical roots of the movement simply for the purposes of nostalgia or identifying founders and the various streams of Pentecostalism today. It sheds light on the very nature of the Pentecostal movement itself. In the last analysis, the matter of origins concerns a theological issue—salvation history. Therefore, the methodology one uses in attempting to understand a movement whose origins are universal and spontaneous, a renewal of the Spirit in salvation history, must be appropriate to the phenomenon under investigation.

THE TRUE DISTINCTIVE OF PENTECOSTAL-CHARISMATIC MOVEMENTS

Even though the first edition of *The Third Force in Missions* was written before the explosive growth of Pentecostal-charismatic Christianity in the Southern Hemisphere in the twenty-first century, it laid the groundwork for explaining the origins and nature of all three waves of the Pentecostal-charismatic movement. The primary enduring quality of the Pentecostal-charismatic movements (all three waves) is that they represent "renewals" of Jesus' good news of the kingdom of God that he declared had arrived in the first century (Matt. 4:47; 12:28; Mark 1:14–15; Luke 4:43; 11:20; John 3:3–15). The movements are a "renewal" of the *gospel* that Jesus' apostles and followers proclaimed in the early church, including a renewal of the same *normative experience with the Spirit* that they enjoyed. Therefore, the term "renewal" is crucial in evaluating the origins and nature of Pentecostal-charismatic movements. Although it is understandable, it is a disservice to the gospel to focus only on the charismatic phenomena of "Pentecostal-like" renewals we have seen in church history and in the more recent twentieth- and twenty-first-century "waves" of Pentecostal-charismatic renewals. Renewals of the good news of the kingdom of God continue today.

Because the Pentecostal-charismatic movements are renewals of the normative gospel of the kingdom of God, attempts to describe the movements from the viewpoint of "religious phenomenology" alone do not do justice to the biblical-theological core of the movements in salvation history. This is a fundamental error in the analysis of religious movements of any type, and especially of Christian movements. Also, any evaluation of the Pentecostal-charismatic phenomenon in the "mission churches" and the "independent churches" in the Southern Hemisphere (such as the African Independent Churches) requires a cross-cultural understanding of the gospel in its contact with these non-Western cultures and churches in the history of the Christian mission. Some of these independent churches have had little or no contact with Western Christianity and have the character of spontaneous sovereign renewals of the Spirit: God responding to people reaching out in faith in a variety of cultures. Therefore, the missiological viewpoint of *The Third Force in Missions* is of special importance in taking a holistic approach and perspective for understanding the movements with a focus on their theological core, because they amount to divine revelation in human cultural contexts.

It is understandable that there was a focus on charismatic phenomena in the first two "waves" of the Pentecostal-charismatic movements. In the first wave, Pentecostals had to defend the biblical validity of the Pentecostal experience, showing that it was the norm in the early church and that it could be experienced today. In the process, the outward charismatic phenomena of the Spirit became the default distinctive of the Pentecostal movement and, of course, the charismatic phenomena were what attracted attention to the movements. Charismatic Christians in mainline Protestant churches and Roman Catholic charismatic Christians in the "second wave," however, looked at the extraordinary movement of the Spirit as the natural outflow of the gospel. Joseph Grassi, a Roman

Catholic charismatic theologian, recognized two dimensions of the powerful work of the Spirit: the *inner* creative work of the Spirit in spiritual birth, and the Spirit's continuing *outward* charismatic ministry in the life of Christians—a life-source dimension and an outward charismatic dimension. "Full Gospel Businessmen" had the same message during the second wave, bringing attention to what was happening as a renewal of the normative "full gospel" of the New Testament.

Therefore, the renewals are *more than* an a renewal of a Pentecostal experience like the apostles experienced on the day of Pentecost, or a renewal of charismatic phenomena that occurred in the first-century church. Pentecostal-charismatic movements are divine reminders to the church of the normative nature of Christianity in the first century; they remind the church today of the twofold nature of the gospel of the kingdom of God.

Jesus specifically described the good news he brought as the "good news of *the kingdom of God.*" His core teachings focused on his redemptive death and the evident, present powerful kingdom of God in his ministry (Matt. 12:28; Luke 11:20). He taught his disciples that this kingdom was a "kingdom of the heart" and that they would experience it with "power" at Pentecost; Jesus' kingdom, therefore, involved his unprecedented gift of the indwelling Holy Spirit at the midpoint of salvation history (Acts 1:3–8; Luke 24:49; John 14:12–17). His redemptive death on the cross would provide forgiveness of sin and prepare his disciples for the gift of the indwelling Spirit at Pentecost (Acts 2:38–39). Therefore, the good news that Jesus declared present in the first century, and that he said would come upon his disciples with undeniable power at Pentecost, is twofold: (1) his redemptive death on the cross for sin, and (2) his gift of the indwelling Holy Spirit. *This* is the gospel. In contemporary Pentecostal-charismatic "renewals," this first-century gospel's normative claim is refreshed in our minds, and our response to that claim is examined afresh (John 14:26). To say the gospel of the kingdom is twofold, therefore, is not just a handy way to include the Pentecostal experience; it is a way to describe its fundamental character and focus on why it is good news in the course of salvation history.

The Necessity of a Holistic Approach

A holistic approach is necessary for an examination of the Pentecostal movement. We must approach the task recognizing the movement as not only a phenomenon taking place in a human, sociocultural milieu, but one taking place as a divinely initiated phenomenon. The importance of a balanced approach, giving each dimension (divine and human) its appropriate emphasis, is illustrated here by two contemporary European accounts of the American Pentecostal movement. The accounts of both W. J. Hollenweger and Nils Bloch-Hoell represent imbalanced treatments with regard to the divine and human dimensions of causation and, therefore, distortions of the true nature of the movement. Below, theories about the origins of the Pentecostal movement are examined, comparing historical-causal theories with a theory emphasizing the universal and spontaneous origins of the worldwide movement. Giving priority to the divine dimension of the movement is also necessary in formulating a theory of origins.

What is the nature of this movement that in less than a century has become a "third force" in Christianity? Should the various worldwide Pentecostal "outpourings" be perceived as one movement, because they began with a particular Christian group in a particular geographical location? Did the movement then spread outward from its site of origin to other groups in other parts of the world? Can such historical-causal linkage between the various Pentecostal revivals in the world be established? Or is the movement "one" because its origins, for the most part, were universal and spontaneous? A more fundamental question in this regard is, "What is a movement?" Or more specifically, "When does the Pentecostal phenomenon become a movement?"

Some historians focus their treatment on the sociocultural contexts in which the movements emerged, citing various socioeconomic theories of causation. Others emphasize the divine element in the movements, pointing to the factor of the sovereign act of God in connection with their origins. Others, emphasizing the divine element, view the movements as renewals or restorations of certain neglected characteristics or potentials of the Christian faith in contemporary times. Earlier critics of the Pentecostal movement in America, and more recent critics in Europe, emphasized the influence of demonic activity with regard to the question of origins (Hollenweger, 1972, pp. 226, 228). However, most of the recent critics of the movement emphasize its human dimensions by citing psychological, social, and cultural theories of causation.

Due to the incarnational nature of divine revelation, *Christian* movements involve both a divine and a human dimension. The following statement from C. Brumback puts the two major dimensions of the movements in perspective:

> Church historians are prone to interpret revivals solely on the basis of the earthly, rather than the heavenly. So often they emphasize the human element—the social, economic, political, or merely religious problems of the hour, while almost totally ignoring the divine element—the coming again spiritually, of the Lord to His people. The origin and growth of the present-day Pentecostal Revival has been attributed by many authors to mundane causes. It would be folly, of course, to deny the influence of these conditions upon this revival . . . the conditions which all agree provide a background for the rise of the Pentecostal movement. Nevertheless, any investigation, factual though it may be, which fails to yield the First Cause of this phenomenal revival has not "come to the knowledge of the truth." (1961, pp. 1–2)

The divine word is enlivened by the Holy Spirit *in* human sociocultural contexts. Men and women respond in faith in a variety of human circumstances, and some of those circumstances are highly productive in heightening "expectant" faith. Fidelity must be shown toward both the divine and human dimensions in the effort to understand the movements. A holistic, multidisciplinary approach to the subject of origins is needed, with an emphasis on the theological dimension.

An example of this shortcoming can be found in evangelical historian Kenneth Scott Latourette's *A History of the Expansion of Christianity*, an otherwise excellent resource for the influence of culture in the historical expansion of the Christian faith (Pomerville, 2009, pp. 319–27). When the subject "Why the Christian Faith

Triumphed in History" emerges, however, Latourette explains that its growth is due to the moral impact of the "impulse of Jesus," but with a curious "silence on the Holy Spirit." His "impulse of Jesus" criterion is an "energy" of Jesus' spirit (small "s"); he states that the moral example of Jesus, along with the assurance of his resurrection, inspired his disciples to carry out his mission. It is clear that Latourette confines himself to the "impulse of Jesus" criterion not only because a rational post-Reformation evangelical theology would accept this view, but because the scientific methodology of the historical discipline would also accept it. He is in a difficult place in maintaining his scientific discipline in writing the history and explaining why the supernatural, powerful gospel of the kingdom of God has triumphed in history (Latourette, 1969, pp. 167–68, 240; Pomerville, 2009, pp. 319–27).

Another prime example of the failure to hold in tension the two major dimensions of a Christian movement is the case of the scholarly response to the African Independent Church Movement (AICM). The AICM is commonly viewed as a "reaction movement." Observers usually focus on the socioeconomic and cultural dimensions of the movement, the human context. The theological dimension of causation—the deficiency of Western theology in meeting the needs of African society—has had a very low profile in discussions of causation. Focus on the theological dimension reveals a positive response of African Christianity to biblical revelation, appropriating a Pentecostal expression of Christianity. Such an expression of the Christian faith addresses the problems, questions, and needs of African society. The nature of the movement as an indication of God pouring out his Spirit on African Christians who respond to the New Testament is overlooked. This is due to the overemphasis on the human dimensions of the movement's origins, to the point of excluding the divine.

All possible approaches to origins are important in comprehending the complexities of the Pentecostal phenomenon, especially in its non-Western context. In discussing the various contributions of the social sciences and religious phenomenology to such study, Oosterwal qualifies in the following way the meaning of a holistic approach to messianic movements:

> A *holistic understanding* is more than the sum of these different con-
> tributions. It is an insight gained only by an approach that considers
> the social *and* the cultural-historical *and* the psychological *and* the
> religious aspects as parts of one total whole of which the *theological*
> (ideology) is the creative center, and the cement that binds them to-
> gether in one integrated whole. (1973, p. 30)

Emphasis on any one of these approaches to the exclusion of the
others can distort one's perception of the nature of religious movements. Often, one's worldview or presuppositions tend to make one
emphasize only one dimension of the movements. This is especially
the case in Western culture with the scientific approach. Often an
overemphasis is given to the human dimensions of Pentecostal
movements. It should be noted, however, that Oosterwal gives a
special integrative role to the religious or theological dimension.
The reason for this is that divine revelation is involved.

One of the major factors that militates against a holistic approach to religious movements, especially Pentecostal movements,
is the prominence of the anthropological concept of "nativistic
movements" and its corresponding theory of causation: "deprivation." Linton states that a nativistic movement is "any conscious
organized attempt on the part of society's members to revive or
perpetuate selected aspects of its culture" (1979, p. 415). This definition focuses on the *human* dynamics and context of the movement.
A. F. C. Wallace views the nativistic movement as a subclass of a
larger class of phenomena called "revitalization movements." Wallace's processional structure of religious movements (Steady State,
Period of Increased Individual Stress, Period of Cultural Distortion,
Period of Revitalization, and New Steady State) is a helpful framework for comprehending both the human and divine dimensions
of a Christian movement. In discussing the variations within his
basic structure of "revitalization movements," Wallace identifies the
secular and religious dimensions. He notes that both secular and
religious action take place in differing degrees at different stages. He
emphasizes the importance of the religious or charismatic action in
the early stages of revitalization, and the tendency for movements
to become more secular in emphasis in the later organizational
stage (1979, pp. 424, 428). He describes revitalization movements

as "the deliberate, conscious, organized efforts of the members of society to create a more satisfying culture" (p. 429). High stress on the members of society often results in a distortion of their cultural *Gestalt* (Wallace, 1979, p. 429). Wallace, however, does not confine "deprivation" to the human-empirical dimension, as does Linton.

Linton notes that inherent in "deprivation theory" is the assumption that religious change, or a movement's origination, is the result of psychological, social, economic, or political deprivation. He agrees that investigation of nativistic movements must go beyond the secular dimension of society: "An adequate explanation of such movements must go beyond an analysis of the kind of deprivation involved to elucidate the social and cultural context out of which they grow" (1979, p. 414). While Linton advocates a more holistic approach to the movements, he shows a presuppositional bias against the inclusion of the supernatural with regard to origins (pp. 416–17).

Deprivation theory focuses clearly on the human dimension and context of religious movements. While it is useful for the insights it brings concerning the human-cultural context and background of religious movements, it must be used with care. One must disassociate its reductionistic tendencies about the supernatural from its otherwise valid insights. Both of the concepts discussed above view religious movements as reactionary movements. The members of a society attempt to reduce stress on their culture. That stress is usually due to a society's contact with another culture (Wallace, 1979, pp. 422–23). Although the idea of reaction is important for the origins of religious movements, it should not be limited to phenomena originating in the human context (socioeconomic, political, cultural, and so on). This, however, is often the case. Deprivation can also refer to "spiritual deprivation," or deprivation of the supernatural. This appears to be the case with the origins of both the classical Pentecostal movement and the African Independent Church Movement.

To a non-Christian anthropologist, "religious" movements may not include special revelation or the supernatural intervention of God. A "Christian" movement, however, would necessarily involve the dimension of special revelation. A definition of "movement" would necessarily include both the human-cultural dimension and the supernatural-revelational dimension. Both dimensions would be considered in the question of a movement's origins. But even the inclusion of both dimensions in one's approach to the origins of the Pentecostal movement, for instance, is no guarantee of a balanced approach. If one's presuppositions do not allow for supernatural "breakthroughs" in contemporary times, then one's view of the origins of the movement will reflect this bias. The tendency would be to emphasize the human factors of causation. The case of the AICMs, many of which are clearly Pentecostal expressions of the Christian faith in African society, is an illustration of this tendency or bias. Often socioeconomic, sociocultural, and "religious" (pagan) factors are predominantly used to explain causation. The factor of an eschatological Pentecostal outpouring of the Spirit is seldom considered.

The whole discussion of origins, therefore, calls attention to the nature of Pentecostalism. W. J. Hollenweger's description of the American classical Pentecostal movement's origins illustrates the reductionistic tendency mentioned above. He emphasizes the human dimensions of the movement to the extent that its divine nature is called into question. His analysis of the precipitating factors of the movement eclipses the fact of divine visitation. Speaking of the origins of the American movement, Hollenweger states, "The origins of the Pentecostal movement go back to a revival amongst the negroes of North America at the beginning of the present century" (1972, p. xvii). He states further concerning the Azusa Street revival (1906–1915):

> The "Pentecostal experience of Los Angeles" was neither the leading astray of the church by demons (as the German Evangelical movement claimed), *nor the eschatological pouring out of the Holy Spirit* (as the Pentecostal movement itself claims) but an outburst of enthusiastic religion of a kind well-known and frequent in the history of Negro churches in America which derived its specifically Pentecostal features from Parham's theory that speaking with tongues is a necessary concomitant of the baptism of the Spirit. (1972, pp. 23–24; emphasis mine)

This "origins" statement, linking causation with the American "Negro enthusiasm" is followed by the lame qualifier: "I do not wish to assert here that the Holy Spirit was not at work in the Los Angeles revival" (p. 24)! Apparently, Hollenweger sees the operation of the

Holy Spirit limited to an ecumenical effort in bringing together American white and black Christians in the Azusa revival.

Hollenweger's denial of the eschatological outpouring of the Spirit in Pentecostal fashion (the theological issue) is crucial. The central role of African-American "Holiness" Christians in the early American Pentecostal movement cannot be disputed, nor can we doubt that their worldview and West African cultural heritage were reasons for their being open to the Pentecostal expression of Christianity. Hollenweger, however, misuses this information about the context of the revival. He appears to want to give the impression that the Pentecostal movement in the United States was a "Negro enthusiast" expression of Christianity rather than a renewal of New Testament Christianity. A precipitating factor of readiness, or the African-American orientation to the spirit world, is used to explain away the eschatological phenomenon of glossolalia. Of course, Hollenweger denies that speaking in tongues is the initial evidence of the Pentecostal experience. This is in spite of the fact that speaking in tongues is widely held to be the identifying mark of the movement (Atter, 1962, p. 7). This bias leads Hollenweger to attribute the religious phenomena of Azusa Street to African-American enthusiast religion. Furthermore, the growth of the movement is explained in terms of a discovery and exploitation of a "new means of communication" by white Christians, which was "indigenous to North American Negroes." In other words, the phenomenal growth of the movement, according to Hollenweger, was due to the white adoption of the new means of communications which black culture provided: enthusiastic religion. This, of course, would require a major paradigm shift in Western culture—a shift from a written-abstract orientation to the oral-dynamic orientation of the African American (Hollenweger, 1972, p. xvii)! The divine-vertical dimension of God's eschatological act in pouring out the Holy Spirit upon his people is lost in the human-horizontal analysis. Such reductionistic, imbalanced explanations that ignore the creative center of the movement—the renewal of the Spirit in salvation history—seriously distorts its true nature. This "Hollenweger tradition" of overemphasizing social and phenomenological factors in the evaluation of Pentecostal-charismatic movements is still prominent in 2015.

Nils Bloch-Hoell's view of the Pentecostal movement is similarly imbalanced with regard to the divine dimension. While he notes that the Pentecostal movement is regarded as a revival movement even by non-Pentecostal observers, he chooses to disregard the spiritual dynamics of the movement: "The dynamic character of the movement, then, is connected with a primitive emotionalism" (1964, p. 49) and "is ecstatic in nature" (p. 173). His description of those participants in the Pentecostal movement in North America strongly reflects his biases about the nature of the Pentecostal phenomena. He states that Charles Parham was mentally unstable, a homosexual, and "probably was a neurotic" (pp. 19–21, p. 193). Miss Ozman, the first to speak in tongues in Topeka, "must have been of a nervous constitution" (Bloch-Hoell, 1964, p. 23). He notes concerning Frank Bartleman, chief chronicler of the Azusa revival, that he "had ecstatic experiences and was undoubtedly a neurotic" (1964, p. 32). Bloch-Hoell, therefore, sees the early Pentecostal manifestation of tongues as psychological-pathological in nature (pp. 23–24). That view dominates his treatment of Pentecostal phenomena (pp. 26, 28, 42, 199).

Bloch-Hoell attributes the emotional heights of the Azusa revival to the number of women involved. He states that in 1936 in the United States there were 78.5 men to each 100 women. Therefore, he reports, "It is *reasonable* to suggest the marked preponderance of women is explained by the emotional ecstatic character of the movement" (1964, p. 60; emphasis mine). The chauvinistic stereotype is complete when he states that women feel attracted to such forms of religion (p. 60). While the ratio of men to women that Bloch-Hoell cites is neither significant nor relevant for his "reasonable" suggestion, it is interesting to note that in 1980 among the 29 million Pentecostal-charismatics in the United States only 42 percent of the tongues-speaking Pentecostal-charismatics were women (Kantzer, 1980, p. 28). A bias against the emotional, supernatural, and subjective dimensions of Christian experience is quite obvious in Bloch-Hoell's analysis of the classical Pentecostal movement.

A presupposition of empirical scientism controls Bloch-Hoell's evaluation of the Pentecostal movement. Rather than a presupposition of "faith," in which biblical authority is the basis for evaluation, he uses the science of religion as an authoritative base. The Pentecostal experience is described as "rapturous ecstasy and mysticism" and explained in wholly psychological terms (Bloch-Hoell, 1964, p. 174). If there is no rational-scientific explanation for ecstasy, then no explanation exists for Bloch-Hoell. He represents a rationalistic-scholastic response to supernatural phenomena; faith is totally subordinated to reason in the discussion of the Pentecostal experience. Of course, his treatment of the origins and nature of the Pentecostal movement is greatly distorted.

Both of the above approaches to the Pentecostal movement are reductionistic, and behind Hollenweger's reductionism is a theological presupposition concerning the issue of tongues in the movement. His imbalanced treatment about the origins of the American Pentecostal movement violates the theological center of the Pentecostal phenomenon itself—that it is an eschatological renewal of Pentecostal Christianity. Methodologically, he shifts from that theological center to one emphasizing peripheral, precipitating factors.

Bloch-Hoell's reductionism is more severe due to the limits set by the methodologies and presuppositions of the disciplines he uses exclusively. Oosterwal states in this regard:

> The sciences of anthropology, psychology, and phenomenology, which have contributed so much to our understanding of messianic movements, are not able to cope with this aspect of the issue [the relationship between revelation and the crisis context] since it is beyond the limits set by their own disciplines. (1973, p. 13)

Bloch-Hoell's approach to origins rules out that crucial theological center of the movement *a priori* by his scientific empiricism. Presuppositions contrary to those of New Testament Christianity control his analysis. His approach is like that of a truncated biblical theology: historical-critical methodology is present, but biblical theological presuppositions and interpretation are missing. Such methodology is insufficient for probing the depths of a Christian movement, and it is certainly inappropriate for examining the origins of a *Pentecostal* movement.

THE "JERUSALEM-CENTRIFUGAL" THEORY

Perhaps the extensive documentation of the Pentecostal movement in the United States, with the corresponding paucity of information on the worldwide movement and the catalytic nature
of the Azusa Street revival, contributes to why the United States is
often cited as the origin of the worldwide Pentecostal movement.
Another possible source for this viewpoint is the feelings of those
who participated in the Azusa Street revival. In the eyes of Frank
Bartleman, chronicler of the revival, the Pentecostal outpouring in
Los Angeles was the world's second "Pentecost." He states, "I wrote
further in 'Way of Faith,' August 1, 1906: 'Pentecost' has come to Los
Angeles, the American Jerusalem. Every sect, creed and doctrine
under heaven is found in Los Angeles, as well as every nation represented" (1980, p. 63).

Bartleman's account of the Azusa Street revival clearly shows
that he saw what was happening there to be of eschatological significance for the whole church in the whole world. In another statement reflecting the "Jerusalem-Centrifugal" theory, Bartleman
alludes to other revivals in the light of Azusa Street:

> Los Angeles seems to be the place, and this the time, in the mind of
> God, for the restoration of the church to her former place, favor and
> power. The fullness of times seems to have come for the church's com-
> plete restoration. God has spoken to His servants in all parts of the
> world, and has sent many of them to Los Angeles, representing every
> nation under Heaven once more, as of old, come up for "Pentecost,"
> to go out again into all the world with the glad message of salvation.
> The base of operations has been shifted, from old Jerusalem, for the
> latter "Pentecost," to Los Angeles. And there is a tremendous, God-
> given hunger for this experience everywhere. Wales was but intended
> as the cradle for the worldwide restoration of the power of God. India
> but the Nazareth where He was "brought up." (1980, p. 90)

Bartleman did acknowledge previous Pentecostal outpourings
(Wales and India), but he sees the Azusa Street outpouring as central
to the worldwide movement. Today, classical Pentecostals know that
Azusa Street was a source that led to specific outpourings of the Spirit
in other parts of the world, but that there were other outpourings of

the Spirit in the Southern Hemisphere that were not connected to Azusa Street; rather, they had the character of sovereign outpourings of the Spirit. Bartleman's foresight or "vision" concerning the significance of the revival cannot be denied in terms of the revival's influence and the special role it played in the development of the worldwide Pentecostal movement. The parallel between the Los Angeles "Pentecost" and the first-century Jerusalem Pentecost is accurate in terms of the emphasis on the Pentecostal baptism of the Spirit, evidenced by speaking in other tongues. This experience in itself was catalytic for the identity and spread of the movement. Historical evidence shows that the influence of the Azusa Street revival was central to the formation of the Pentecostal movement in the United States, and there is no question that its influence extended beyond the borders of the nation. The beginnings of the Pentecostal movement in Scandinavia were the direct result of the Azusa revival, and Scandinavia's influence aided in the subsequent spread of the movement through Europe and South America. However, the claim that the worldwide Pentecostal movement started in Los Angeles and from there spread to the rest of the world is problematic. It puts too much weight on the centrifugal activities of those who were present or who visited Azusa Street. The claim also detracts from the actual historical development of the worldwide movement, in terms of its universal and spontaneous origins.

As Hollenweger's approach has already illustrated, those treating the Pentecostal movement's history often leave the erroneous impression that the phenomenon is characteristically American. Bruner states:

> Pentecostalism, which we shall see was born in America and appears to have been exported there from around the world, may now perhaps be listed as the most recent contribution to the world's religious groups. (1970, p. 39)

In the introduction to Frank Bartleman's *Azusa Street*, Vinson Synan leaves the same impression. He states that the Azusa revival "ushered into being the worldwide twentieth-century pentecostal renewal" (1980, p. ix). It is Synan's opinion that Bartleman's journalistic reporting of the revival "informed the world about the

Pentecostal movement but in a large measure also helped to form it" (p. xii). In his own history of the Pentecostal movement, *The Holiness-Pentecostal Movement in the United States,* Synan clearly subscribes to what we have called the "Jerusalem-Centrifugal" theory of the origins of the *worldwide* movement, citing the United States as its "Jerusalem" (1971, pp. 37, 109, 114, 215, 217). He states further: "It is also clear that the Pentecostal movement is one of the few major religious movements to originate in America and subsequently become a major force beyond the borders of the nation" (p. 215). But are the origins of the worldwide Pentecostal movement to be thought of as a centrifugal movement arising from America's "Jerusalem," Azusa Street?

Synan's description of the Azusa Street revival as a catalyst for bringing into being scores of Pentecostal denominations in the United States is true. However, his statement that "directly or indirectly, practically all of the pentecostal groups in existence can trace their lineage to the Azusa Mission" (p. 114) is inaccurate concerning the worldwide movement. Even if confined to classical Pentecostal groups, such statements are problematic. They overlook other significant, previous and simultaneous, Pentecostal outpourings around the world that have no historical-causal linkage to the American revival. They also tend to portray the Pentecostal movement as an American expression of the Christian faith. They detract not only from the universal origins of the movement, but they also provide the opportunity for the *nature* of the movement to be misunderstood. The movement appears to some, therefore, as an American contextualization of the Christian faith (Bruner, 1970, p. 39). Or it appears as a mere psycho-sociological phenomenon due to economic and social deprivation (Bloch-Hoell, 1964, pp. 144, 173–74; Hollenweger, 1972, pp. 23–24), rather than a divine renewal of the church in the context of salvation history. My view that the movements are "renewals" of Jesus' gospel of the kingdom of God recorded in the New Testament helps to avoid these opinions.

Walter Hollenweger appears at first glance to agree with the "Jerusalem-Centrifugal" theory when he states, "The origins of the Pentecostal movement go back to a revival amongst the negroes of North America at the beginning of the present century" (1972,

p. xvii). Also, Hollenweger states that T. B. Barratt, a participant in the Azusa Street revival, brought the Pentecostal movement to Norway and other Scandinavian countries, as well as to Germany, Great Britain, and Switzerland (p. 63). Hollenweger, however, mentions prior Pentecostal outpourings of the Spirit in Germany, Wales, and India, *before* the 1906 Azusa Street revival. The apparent contradiction about historical origins and historical-causal linkage between the various movements is resolved when it is understood that Hollenweger does not see the Pentecostal movement in America and the charismatic movement in the denominational churches in Europe as one movement. This dichotomous view of the worldwide Pentecostal movement is clear from: (1) Hollenweger's typology of Pentecostal organizations (pp. 71–72); (2) his discussion of the differences between the charismatic movement in Germany and the Pentecostal-free churches in Germany (pp. 247–49); and (3) his preference for the Pentecostal movement within the established churches and his corresponding criticism of the "come out" churches of American Pentecostalism (pp. 15, 24, 253).

Further evidence of the dichotomy is Hollenweger's methodology of beginning his history of the worldwide Pentecostal movement with a chapter on the charismatic movement, "Pentecost Outside 'Pentecost:' Speaking with Tongues in the Traditional Churches of America" (p. 1). Therefore, when Hollenweger speaks of the "Pentecostal movement" in the preface to his work *The Pentecostals*, he refers to the origins of the *American* classical Pentecostal movement and does not support a "Jerusalem-Centrifugal" theory with regard to the worldwide movement. Due to his critical, and at times somewhat sarcastic, view of the classical Pentecostal movement in America, Hollenweger would especially avoid such a conclusion.

Evidence of Universal Origins

In a balanced and careful statement concerning the role of the Azusa Street revival in relation to other Pentecostal movements, Assemblies of God historian William Menzies states:

> From 1905 to 1910, Pentecostal revivals erupted in widely scattered parts of the world: the United States and Canada, Great Britain, Holland, Germany, Norway, Sweden, Chile, and India. Some of these occurred without visible links with one another; others were the result of revival reports falling on fertile soil. . . . It would not be accurate to ascribe the entire story of the spread of the Pentecostal message to the Great Revival at Azusa Mission in Los Angeles, but without question it was that center that was the most significant instrument in the proliferation of the Latter Rain. (1971, p. 60)

Similar care is taken in Menzies's article "The Non-Wesley Origins of the Pentecostal movement" (1975). He thinks it is necessary to include a fifteen-year span when speaking of Pentecostal origins and states by way of limitation that only the American Pentecostal movement is in focus (p. 83). It is clear that the origins of the movement are somewhat fluid, pointing to a spontaneous, universal outpouring of the Spirit.

While noting the impact of the Azusa Street revival, its centrifugal activities, and its influence in bringing the revival to other parts of the world, Larry Christenson observes:

> Yet during this same period, charismatic manifestations were a common place occurrence in a body of churches outside Pentecostalism. In congregations scattered around the world, but predominantly in Europe and North America, members of the Catholic Apostolic church recorded their experience of tongues, prophecy, and healings— as they had quietly been doing for more than half a century previous. (1975, p. 17)

Christenson's documentation of a charismatic awakening in Great Britain in the 1830s, and a resulting "come out" Pentecostal church led by Edward Irving, suggests that perhaps a similar, but somewhat longer, timespan is also necessary when speaking of the origins of the worldwide Pentecostal movement. Christenson speaks of Irving as a forerunner of the Catholic Apostolic Church *and* the entire Pentecostal phenomenon of the twentieth century (1975, p. 20). But at the same time, he makes it clear that there is no historical connection between the Catholic Apostolic Church and classical Pentecostalism (pp. 22–23).

Based on Christenson's use of the term "forerunner," it appears that he views the movements somehow as a unity. How is it that Irving and the Catholic Apostolic Church are in some way a "forerunner" of classical Pentecostalism in the twentieth century, if there is no historical relationship between the movements? Christenson explains:

> One is faced, at last, with the mystery of two movements existing side by side in history, sharing in considerable measure a unique religious outlook and experience, yet historically unrelated to one another. . . . No serious study of the beginnings of the Pentecostal movement will want to ignore the Catholic Apostolic church. For the story of the Catholic Apostolic church, *precisely because* of the absence of any historical connection between the two movements, sheds a particular light on the origins of Pentecostalism. (1975, p. 23; emphasis mine)

Christenson sees a difference between a "historical-causal relationship," and an "existential-independent relationship," or an independent encounter with the same essential reality—God the Holy Spirit (pp. 23–25).

In Christenson's view, similarities in the particular expression of Christianity may point to a historical-causal relationship between revivals. But they may also point *beyond* any such influence to a sovereign, divine influence, or independent encounters with God the Holy Spirit which are unrelated historically-causally (p. 25). Christenson, therefore, points out the similarity of the movements and the lack of historical-causal linkage as evidence for the *divine origin* of the movements. The "particular light" that the absence of historical-causal linkage sheds on the origins of the Pentecostal movement is that it represents a renewal of Pentecostal Christianity in salvation history. The similarity of pre-Azusa Street revivals in Europe and Asia and the Los Angeles revival, therefore, does not necessarily mean that a historical-causal relationship between those movements exists, as Synan infers (1971, pp. 114–15). Rather, the similarity may point to independent encounters with the same renewing work of the Holy Spirit.

In terms of centrifugal direction and origins of influence, it is much more probable that the original impetus for the Pentecostal movement came from the European continent to the United States, and not vice versa. The influence of the Welsh revival on the Azusa Street revival is well documented (Synan, 1980, pp. xi, xvi; Synan, 1971, p. 97; Hollenweger, 1972, p. 22; Menzies, 1971, p. 49). Furthermore, Atter states that Russia experienced a Pentecostal revival in approximately 1862, and that the Russians took the Pentecostal message to Armenia around 1880. He states that Pentecostal Armenians migrated to the United States in 1900 and were present when the Pentecostal revival broke out in Los Angeles in 1906 (1962, p. 21). Other early Pentecostal outpourings of the Spirit in Northern Europe and Asia at the turn of the last century are evidence of the universal origins of Pentecostalism.

Attempts to assign a "starting point" for the worldwide Pentecostal movement in terms of a geographical location, founder, or group detracts from its universal and spontaneous origins. In this regard, Donald Gee states, "The Pentecostal movement does not owe its origin to any outstanding personality or religious leader; but was a spontaneous revival, appearing almost simultaneously in various parts of the world" (1949, p. 3). Such a view of the movement's origins is held by other historians of the Pentecostal movement (Menzies, 1971, p. 60; Atter, 1962, p. 43; Frodsham, 1946, pp. 9, 53). Concerning the matter of origins, it must be realized that the centrifugal spread of the Pentecostal movement took place not only "horizontally" in terms of historical-causal expansion, but also "vertically" by means of the sovereign activity of God. In numerous places in the world where Christians were expectantly awaiting a divine renewal, Pentecostal phenomena were expressions of the God-given renewal.

The discussion of the origins of the Pentecostal movement raises the question, "What makes the worldwide Pentecostal phenomenon a movement?" Certainly, a combination of factors makes the phenomenon a movement: the political, organizational, psychological, social, economic, and the historical-causal linkage between revivals. But as previously noted, if the movement is *Christian*, then the factor of the sovereign move of God the Holy Spirit must be added. It has been shown that a focus on the human factors alone contributes some confusion to the issue of the movement's origins. When did the Pentecostal "movement" start? In the 1830s with the Irvingites? In 1862 among the Russians, who in turn brought the revival to the Armenians, who were present at Azusa Street? Or were its origins found in Topeka, where the evidence of speaking in tongues was connected doctrinally with the baptism of the Holy Spirit? Or was the "Jerusalem" of the centrifugal worldwide movement at Los Angeles in 1906? Or was it in one of the previous Holiness revivals?

All of these factors—the historical-causal linkage of the revivals, human efforts at organization, doctrinal formulations, and the catalytic impetus of Azusa Street and its centrifugal influence—shed important light on the matter of the Pentecostal movement's origins and development. In the last analysis, however, the universal and spontaneous origins of the movement point to the divine dimension of the movement as crucial in understanding causation. A statement often heard among Pentecostals is " 'Pentecost' is not a denomination but an experience." Clearly, this statement is intended to put the emphasis on the divine dimension of the movement's origin and nature. The statement refers to the movement as a renewal of the Pentecostal experience in contemporary Christian experience.

A Pentecostal worldview and theological presuppositions allow for a view of origins that emphasizes *God's* action. The Pentecostal's emphasis is on the theological "creative center" of the movement, and the movement is a renewal of the Holy Spirit *first* and *foremost.* Only secondly is it an effort of humans to reinstitute a neglected apostolic orientation in the contemporary church. This effort, however, is preceded and accompanied by the divine dynamic. The movement represents cooperation with the eschatological, renewing Spirit of God in the context of salvation history. Whether or not this emphasis on the divine dimension—the theological creative center—is appropriate in defining the origins and nature of the Pentecostal movement will be discussed below. What are the grounds for this emphasis and presupposition? Is it valid to view the Pentecostal movement as an eschatological renewal of the Spirit in salvation history? These questions lead to a discussion of biblical theology and, in turn, an analysis of the theological creative center of the Pentecostal movement. (Again, a contemporary note on this 1985 discussion of the nature of the Pentecostal movement: This discussion leads to the inevitable identification of the Pentecostal movement as a renewal of Jesus' gospel of the kingdom of God.)

THE SALVATION HISTORY NATURE OF THE MOVEMENT

The discussion of the origins of the Pentecostal movement naturally, and eventually, leads to the question of its nature. In a sense, this book's approach in studying the movement so far has been deductive, moving from a discussion of its historical origins to a consideration of its nature. Now the theological question is in focus, the theological core of the movement. The assumption up to this point has been that the Pentecostal movement is a "Christian" phenomenon. However, before the Christian nature of the movement is addressed, it must be realized that substantiation of the movement's Christian validity is a theological matter. It concerns one's worldview and theological presuppositions. The discussion of origins showed that from one ideological viewpoint the movement may appear to be primarily a psycho-sociological response of people to a crisis situation. From another, the movement may appear as a visitation of God to renew his church in salvation history. Of course, no clean dichotomy (in terms of either/or) is possible in assessing the nature of the movement.

Formerly, we saw that a holistic approach to the complex phenomenon of the Pentecostal movement was necessary for understanding its various dimensions. "Christian" movements necessarily have two major dimensions: the divine and the human. This is due to the incarnational nature of divine revelation. God reveals himself in human cultures and he works through them, as the incarnation and the doctrine of Scripture itself illustrates. In dealing with Christian movements, one must encounter not only the social, psychological, and phenomenological, but also the revelational—the dynamics of the divine word and Spirit. The idea of salvation history (*Heilsgeschichte*) also comes to the fore. The German term *Heilsgeschichte* is not to be understood as referring to a "metahistory," but to a Christian view of history in which process (not progress) and direction toward the *eschaton* is primary. It involves the concept of periodization, recognizing epochs in which significant acts of God took place. It envisages a universal history in which God is working with all of humanity. In that complexity and diversity, however, history has meaning and purpose (McIntire, 1977, pp. 51–59). These matters not only reveal the limitations of the sciences that must be used in order to understand the full dimension of Christian movements, but they also determine the controlling ideological context from which the movements must be examined. The character of the movements determines the appropriate orientation and methodology for their examination.

The modifier "Christian" in regard to a movement determines that one's orientation should be theological, and from the evangelical standpoint that theological orientation must be conditioned and controlled by *biblical authority*. This evangelical orientation does not exclude the various orientations, presuppositions, and insights of the social sciences. But it holds biblical content to be the norm for judging their validity and use. Previous erroneous views concerning the nature of the Pentecostal movement emerged from a perspective of origins in which anti-Christian presuppositions were controlling the evaluation of the movement. Biblical authority determines the attitude and presuppositions with which the movement must be evaluated. It calls "faith" into the arena of study. It also determines that the movement be evaluated in the light of biblical theology.

A prior question when approaching the nature of the Pentecostal movement is, "How does it fare under the scrutiny of biblical theology?" Is the claim that it represents an eschatological renewal of New Testament Pentecostal Christianity in accord with a sound biblical theology? Are there biblical grounds for considering the worldwide Pentecostal movement as "one" movement, an eschatological outpouring of the Holy Spirit in salvation history?

An Eschatological Renewal

In attempting to identify the "creative theological center" of the Pentecostal movement, the various definitions of the movement and its common claims are instructive. Menzies's definition of the

movement is clearly eschatological in the salvation history sense
when he states:

> The Pentecostal movement is that group of sects within the Christian
> church which is characterized by the belief that the occurrence men-
> tioned in Acts 2 on the Day of Pentecost not only signaled a birth of
> the church, but described an experience available to believers in all
> ages. (1971, p. 9)

Numerous other definitions of the movement emphasize the same
central thought: God is visiting his people in contemporary times,
just as he visited them in the first century. Atter defines the Pentecostal movement as "that section of the Christian church which
constantly maintains that the church today *should enjoy the same
blessings, believe the same doctrines, and receive the same power as
did the early church*" (1962, p. 6). Bloch-Hoell notes that "Pentecostal" is an appropriate term for describing the classical Pentecostal
movement, due to its implication that the first Pentecost (Acts 2:4)
was to be repeated in the experience of the Christian (1964, p. l). As
an "outsider" speaking of Pentecostalism in general, Henry P. Van
Dusen emphasizes that it is a restoration of the ministry of the Holy
Spirit: "They [the Pentecostals] share a common spiritual aim: to
return, in deliberate imitation, to the content and practices of the
early Christian church" (1958, p. 113). He also notes, "Many features
of this 'new Christianity' bear striking resemblance to the life of
the earliest Christian churches as revealed in the New Testament"
(p. 112). The Baptist World Alliance statement on the charismatic
movement begrudgingly reflects this position:

> 1. The 'charismatic' movement [*sic*] is to be viewed in its historical
> perspective and in particular to be evaluated in the light of certain
> historical features of our time such as alienation, the reactions against
> scientism and rationalization, and the quest for mystical experience.
> . . . 2. Throughout the centuries the Church has owed much to pe-
> riods of experiential religion which has been of value in correcting
> the imbalances of a too rational creedal, or barren Christianity. The
> modern charismatic movement has met with a mixed reception
> among Baptists. Some have found in it a new experience of spiritual
> renewal. Others dismiss it as untrue to Baptist tradition. (McDonnell,
> 1980, p. 80)

The Pentecostal claims and definitions of the movement characterize it as a *renewal movement*. They believe renewal takes place in an eschatological period described as the "last days," a period in which contemporary Christians are now living. Even those outside the movement agree that it represents a renewal. Clark H. Pinnock, a sympathetic evangelical observer of the movement, states, "The new Pentecostalism seems to this observer to be a genuine movement of the Spirit of God renewing His church" (1976, p. 183). Furthermore, Menzies observes that the Pentecostal movement did not add new doctrines, but was rather a "reactionary" movement, calling the church back to historic truth: "The Pentecostal movement has stood within the framework of Orthodox Christianity" (1971, p. 17). The renewal, therefore, has taken place within traditional Protestantism. It is not only a product of the Protestant tradition, but it has also subsequently adopted the traditional beliefs of Protestantism, such as those affirmed by the Apostles' Creed (Gause, 1976, p. 108).

Some would say that the doctrine of the baptism of the Holy Spirit, connected with the initial evidence of speaking with other tongues, is a "new" doctrine. Generally, Pentecostals hold that the distinctive characteristic of the classical Pentecostal movement is the linking together of speaking with other tongues and the baptism of the Holy Spirit. This, of course, addresses a central issue of classical Pentecostalism. But the issue of "new," in the sense of true orthodoxy, rests upon whether or not there is a basis for the doctrine in the New Testament. It does not rest on the historic formulation of the doctrine by a particular group that has experienced a renewing of the Pentecostal experience and therefore theologizes about that experience. Such fresh theologizing often takes place in the history of the church. Theologizing concerning the doctrine of the Trinity in church history is a case in point. The formulation of the "new" doctrine was not outside of orthodox Christian truth; it was firmly rooted in Scripture.

Frederick Bruner also characterizes the movement in terms of renewal when he states:

> In terms of the church's theology and mission Pentecostalism's significance may be that it incarnates a neglected reality of the New

Testament Church: the Holy Spirit in the experience of believers. What to some may seem an overemphasis of the Spirit and especially of the Spirit's more noticeable operations may, perhaps, be intended to startle the church into an awareness of its little emphasis of the same Spirit. Perhaps in the divine perspective a church that gives too much attention to the Spirit is no more culpable—perhaps less—than a church that gives him too little. Perhaps the Pentecostal movement is a voice—albeit an ecstatic and at times a harsh voice—calling the people to hear what the Spirit is capable of saying to and doing with a church that listens. (1970, p. 33)

A renewal movement emphasizing neglected charismatic ministries of the Holy Spirit may, perhaps, appear overemphasized to those outside of the movement. However, those *within* the Pentecostal movement, in both Protestant and Roman Catholic Christianity, do not view the movement as representing an overemphasis. They view the movement as a renewal of normative Christian experience (McDonnell, 1980, pp. 180–81).

It is important at this point to discriminate between the concepts of "reaction" and "renewal." The Pentecostal movement is not merely a reaction to an overly rationalistic expression of the Christian faith. It involves a neglected dimension of New Testament Christianity that God is renewing. The view of the movement as a "reaction" is helpful in emphasizing the human causative factors in it. In this way it may be viewed in an "historical" perspective, but not in a *salvation history* perspective. As pointed out previously, the Pentecostal movement is more than a contextualization of the Christian faith in reaction to certain circumstances of its particular historical moment. It is not merely a phenomenon in history with no necessary connections with the past. It is a renewal of the Holy Spirit in the context of salvation history, in accord with the particular character of the age of the Holy Spirit. While "reaction" indicates causation, by itself it is an inadequate term for addressing the nature of the movement. "Renewal" points to the movement as a phenomenon of the Holy Spirit in the course of salvation history, a *New Testament* phenomenon.

While theological interpretations of the doctrine of the baptism of the Holy Spirit differ among Pentecostal-charismatics, the belief that God is restoring a charismatic dimension of the Christian experience is commonly held. For Roman Catholics especially, the idea of "renewal" is in accord with their sacramental framework for interpreting the charismatic experience. The baptism of the Holy Spirit is viewed as an actualization of what was already received at baptism and confirmation. Although Catholic theologians say that charismatic manifestations were always present in the history of the church, they also see the charismatic experience today as an historical renewal of the church (McDonnell, 1980, pp. 1–6, 51; Grassi, 1978, pp. 7–8). The Pentecostal movement in general views itself as representing a renewal of the charismatic ministry of the Holy Spirit in salvation history (Sandidge, 1976, p. 11).

A Missionary Renewal

Bruner's characterization of the Pentecostal movement as a missionary phenomenon is also in accord with how classical Pentecostals view the movement. This view of the movement as a missionary phenomenon explains, somewhat, their eschatological orientation. Due to the representative nature of the Assemblies of God in classical Pentecostalism, this group is used here in order to illustrate the eschatologically oriented worldview of classical Pentecostalism.

From the beginnings of the Assemblies of God, the fellowship was considered to be a missionary movement. Unlike the creedal affirmations of many Protestant denominations, the "Fundamental Truths" of the Assemblies of God contain a clear statement on mission:

> Since God's purpose concerning man is to seek and to save that which is lost, to be worshiped by man, and to build a body of believers in the image of His Son, the priority reason-for-being of the Assemblies of God as part of the Church is: a. To be an agency of God for evangelizing the world (Acts 1:8, Matthew 28:19, 20; Mark 16:15, 16). (Menzies, 1971, p. 389)

Menzies states further: "Significant is the fact that out of a concern for effective missionary enterprise a semblance of inter-church structure was created" (1971, p. 86). The fellowship's early intense aversion to "organization" was overcome due to the realization that it was necessary in order to fulfill its "missionary calling" (pp. 106, 131). The view of the Assemblies of God fellowship as a "missionary" movement, however, was connected with the idea that it was a missionary movement in an eschatological period of salvation history—the "last days." The outpouring of the Spirit in the twentieth century was seen as an outpouring for the express purpose of accomplishing the church's mission in the world.

Pentecostals view the context of contemporary mission as an eschatological time, characterized by both supernatural blessing and opposition, by Spirit-outpourings and spiritual decline and opposition. Generally speaking, Pentecostals view these times clearly as days of "power-encounter" where the forces of God clash with the forces of evil in cosmic struggle in the "last days." Therefore, the realities of the spirit world are predominant in Pentecostal thinking concerning the church and its worldwide mission. Emphasis varies among Pentecostals between the poles of pessimism and optimism. The position one occupies on the pessimism-optimism continuum is largely a matter of one's view of eschatology. When speaking of evangelicals in general, David Bosch rightly focuses on dispensational theology as occupying the pessimism end of the continuum:

> In the more pronouncedly adventist and dispensational circles all emphasis lies on the coming Kingdom of God. The believer looks forward with longing to Christ's return. The present is empty. All that really matters is the glorious future. (1980, p. 32)

"The present is empty"? Bosch has not wrongly attributed anything here; this is the result of dispensational theology that is highly influential among Pentecostals. The reader should note here that a theological position that states "the present is empty" is a denial of Jesus' *present* good news of the kingdom of God.

Assemblies of God missiologist Melvin Hodges provides a representative, optimistic Pentecostal view of mission. It is a view in which mission is a task that "fills" the present-eschatological "time between the times." Hodges's optimism in regard to the task of mission is clearly linked with his view of the ministry of the Holy Spirit

in the church today. For Hodges, the present is *not empty*, it is filled
with mission. Supernatural intervention is expected as the church
engages in mission. This expectancy is specifically related to his
view that contemporary mission takes place in an *eschatological
context*. Hodges, like the majority of classical Pentecostals, believes
contemporary times to be the biblical "last days," in which God
abundantly pours out his Spirit. Present-day activity of the Holy
Spirit in the world is seen to be the fulfillment of the biblical promise found in Joel 2:28–32 (Hodges, 1970, p. 3). Hodges specifically
connects twentieth-century movements of the Spirit at the beginning and midway through the century with the movement of the
Spirit on the day of Pentecost. The connection is made because of
his view that the unusual activity of the Spirit marks the church age,
or in the Apostle Peter's words, "the last days" (Acts 2:17). There is
expectancy for the Spirit's ministry in mission today because the
church is perceived to live and minister in the *same salvation history time context* as the New Testament church. On the basis of a
biblical promise, Pentecostals look for a supernatural enablement
and ministry in their own contemporary times, like the apostles
and disciples experienced at the beginning of the missionary task.
This enablement is deemed necessary to finish the same missionary task that was started in the "beginning" of the "last days." The
theological basis for such expectancy is the belief that they occupy
the same time context in their engagement in Christ's mission as
the early church occupied—"the last days."

The Pentecostal Movement: A Renewal
of the Gospel of the Kingdom

What is the theological basis for conceiving of an age as the
"last days," extending from the time of the apostles until now? Of
course, this question has great importance for viewing the Pentecostal movement as an eschatological renewal in contemporary
times. The theological basis for this view is the biblical motif of the
kingdom of God. Both the assumption that mission takes place in
an eschatological context and the emphasis on the extraordinary

working of the Holy Spirit in contemporary mission are fundamental to the New Testament concept of the kingdom of God. The
kingdom motif is understood to be a part of a larger theological
context: salvation history. In that context, the Pentecostal movement may be considered a manifestation of the kingdom of God,
for it witnesses to the dynamic redemptive activity of God—the
gospel—in contemporary times.

The Kingdom: Fulfillment without Consummation

Johannes Blauw notes that the eschatological character of
the parables reveals that the meaning of "eschatological" is not
exhausted in its reference to the future. For in the parables, the
coming of Jesus does not mean "*the absolute end,* but rather that
it ushers in *a new period* in the history of Israel and of the world"
(1962, p. 73). In a discussion concerning the continuity of the testaments, Blauw states emphatically: "*The progression of Heilsgeschichte [salvation history] which is here found continues, in that
the 'last of the days' does not mean the end of the days, but a great
turning of the days toward a new future*" (p. 79). Blauw describes the
last stages of history (Jesus' times and the times following his death
and resurrection) as one last phase of salvation history; the "last of
days" becomes a new beginning. The time of eschatological expectation is past (p. 82). Of course, according to Blauw, the "last of the
days" would have begun with the ministry of Jesus and continued
into contemporary times. Blauw's statement above that "the time of
eschatological expectation is past" must be taken in the light of the
New Testament emphasis that in the incarnation Jesus is the *fulfillment* of the law and the prophets. He clearly proclaims the presence
of the kingdom (the "already present" kingdom)—the emphasis of
the New Testament—which does not preclude the "eschatological"
expectation of the second coming of Christ (the "not yet" kingdom).

John Bright states that the "present" aspect of the kingdom of
God was an integral part of the New Testament *kerygma* (Mark 1:14–
15) and that the proclamation of that message is the binding element
in New Testament theology (1953, p. 190). Bright also believes that
the kingdom of God, the dynamic concept of the rule of God, is the

bond that binds the testaments together. This is one of the main points at which dispensational theology conflicts with Jesus' theology of the good news of the kingdom of God. But in *distinction* from the Old Testament, Bright states concerning the New Testament:

> In the New Testament we encounter a change: the tense is a resounding present indicative—the Kingdom is *here!* And that is a very "new thing" indeed: *it is gospel*—the good news that God has acted! . . . Nowhere is it better put than in the word of Jesus which Mark begins the story of his ministry, and which sum up . . . the very essence of his teaching: "The time has come," he said. "The kingdom of God is near. Repent and believe the good news" (Mark 1:15)! What all the ages have desired to see now is here—in this Jesus (Luke 10:23–24). In him has the old order ended and a new order begun. (p. 197)

For Bright, the kingdom invades the world in the person and work of Jesus. His miracles were understood eschatologically in New Testament times; they illustrated the fact that a new age was intruding upon the present evil age; the cosmic end-struggle had begun (pp. 216–17).

George Eldon Ladd addresses the key issue in relation to the eschatological context of mission when he states:

> One of the most important tasks of modern biblical theology has been the search for the key to this problem of how the kingdom can be both future and present so that both sets of sayings—those of present fulfillment and those of future consummation—can be preserved. We believe the solution to this problem [of hermeneutics] is to be found in the dynamic meaning of the kingdom of God. (1974, pp. 120–21)

Ladd notes that both the above sets of sayings in Scripture—present fulfillment and future eschatological consummation—are two central emphases of Jesus' message (p. 33). He finds that the kingdom of God is the reign of God not merely in the heart of the Christian, but that it is also dynamically active in the person of Jesus and in human history. This view of the kingdom allows for present and future, inward and outward, and spiritual and apocalyptic aspects (p. 42). Ladd's central thesis is: "Before the eschatological appearing of God's kingdom at the end of the age, God's kingdom has become dynamically active among men in Jesus' person and mission"

(p. 139). When the church engages in mission, the kingdom of God is a dynamic power at work among people in this age *before* the appearing of the future, outward, apocalyptic kingdom.

Ladd states that the early church claimed the presence of the eschatological blessings of the age to come. The resurrection of Jesus was the beginning of the final resurrection (1 Cor. 15:23); the coming of the Holy Spirit was the fulfillment of the Old Testament promise for the eschatological kingdom (Joel 2:28–32). Paul speaks of the gift of the Holy Spirit as a "down payment" (2 Cor. 1:22; 5:5; Eph. 1:14) of the eschatological inheritance (p. 271). Furthermore, Ladd states that another way of looking at this experience of the eschatological blessing is that the kingdom of God is *present* (p. 271). When discussing the kingdom parables, Ladd notes, "The mystery of the kingdom is the coming of the kingdom into history in advance of its apocalyptic manifestation" (p. 222). He states that the "mystery" of the kingdom "is in short, 'fulfillment without consummation' " (p. 222). I would add to Ladd's explanation that the kingdom refers to the gift of the indwelling Holy Spirit in the gospel of the kingdom of God.

The view that the contemporary mission is a continuation of the age of the Spirit, which broke through at the day of Pentecost and continues to break through today as people engage in mission, is consistent with the kingdom of God motif. The view of the Pentecostal movement as a missionary phenomenon is, in a sense, a manifestation of the very present and powerful kingdom of God in action. For it is evidence of the dynamic, redemptive activity of God the Holy Spirit in contemporary times. Both Bright and Ladd lay the foundation for the kingdom motif being the controlling center of a biblical theology, noting the *continuity* of the Old and New Testaments, but emphasizing "fulfillment," or *discontinuity*, in the New Covenant: that is, that something absolutely *new*—a *unique event*—has taken place in salvation history. However, there must be further description of what that fulfillment is in Jesus' coming at the midpoint of salvation history. Both men, who are non-Pentecostal, reflect a pneumatological gap in their description of the kingdom of God with regard to the *manner* of the Holy Spirit's working in this age of the Spirit, which is by his indwelling presence and power in Christians.

The Kingdom: The New Age of the Spirit

Missing from Ladd's explanation of the kingdom motif is the specific mention of the *manner* of God's active rule and working in the contemporary world. According to Bright, the kingdom of God is dynamic; it is a power already released in the world (1953, pp. 218–19). He speaks of the kingdom as a present power in this age by means of the ministry of the Holy Spirit. Bright, along with Hodges, refers to the church's Pentecostal experience of the Holy Spirit as a demonstration of the beginning of the "last days," based on Joel's prophecy. Floyd Filson also connects the present age of the kingdom with the coming of the Holy Spirit:

> The new order is at hand, and the reference is not merely to a new civilization or a new period of the same sort of world history, but to God's new order, established by divine power as the climax of God's dealings with this world. . . . Similarly, in Acts 2:16 the gift of the Spirit is connected with the prediction of Joel 2:28–32 that in the last days the Spirit will be given. The fact that in the Greek text of Acts usually followed the reference to "the last days" is not found in Joel shows that to the writer of Acts the phrase is no meaningless item, but is rather inserted precisely because the Apostolic Church regarded the gift of the Spirit as an eschatological event. (1950, pp. 75–76)

Filson states that the promise in the Synoptic Gospels that Christ will give the Spirit must be read in the light of the preaching of John the Baptist and Jesus, who both proclaimed that the kingdom was at the threshold. Bosch further explains:

> The future, including the future *before* the end, is not empty but filled with the Kingdom. Admittedly the Kingdom is still hidden and can be perceived only by the eyes of faith; admittedly the form the Kingdom takes is still inchoate; yet this does not imply that the presence of the Kingdom is illusory. We live on the basis of the "already" en route to the "not yet," but in such a way that the challenge of the "already" outweighs the vision of the "not yet." . . . Eschatology does not refer only to a future divine answer which we have to accept blindly or on authority; it also refers to anticipations in human experience now. (1980, p. 236)

The term "last days" represents an age that is characteristically an age of the Spirit. Pentecost was the crucial turning point of those "eschatological days." Filson states, "Pentecost therefore has an eschatological quality which modern interpretation of Acts frequently fails to mention" (1950, p. 76).

Blaauw likewise speaks of the presence of the kingdom in terms of the coming of the Holy Spirit: "In the New Testament, 'the last days' can mean the days which have broken forth with Christ (Heb. 1:1) and the Holy Spirit (Acts 2:17), but also the time of the Last Judgment and the Second Coming (e.g., John 11:24, 12:48; 1 Pet. 1:5)" (1962, p. 111). Blaauw shows that the evidence of the presence of the kingdom is the power of the Holy Spirit. The view that mission takes place in an eschatological context is firmly rooted in the New Testament concept of the present kingdom of God. That eschatological context in salvation history represents a new era—an era of the Holy Spirit. The Pentecostal view that the contemporary church engages in mission in the *same period* and the *same power* as the early church finds theological support in the biblical motif of the kingdom of God. Bosch states that mission is an eschatological event, due to the certainty that the kingdom of God is not only a future reality but is present in contemporary times. He states that Israel expected salvation exclusively from the future, but Christ divided that future into two; in him the forces of the coming age have flowed into the present (Bosch, 1980, p. 236).

While Filson speaks of the kingdom as coming at Pentecost, and the others quoted above speak of the Spirit in the new age with the church and the "kingdom" filling the new age, the conversation is not sufficiently specific for a Pentecostal theology. The *manner* of God's rule indicated by "the kingdom" is the indwelling Spirit in Christians.

The Kingdom: God Working in Salvation History

It is important to recognize the dynamic nature of the kingdom of God, that it represents God's working in salvation history. Often the term is used in the Bible in a way that emphasizes that the kingdom is a realm to be entered, or a sphere in which God rules. But the dynamic nature of the kingdom also needs to be emphasized.

The crucial point is that the manner of God's working in contemporary times is by means of the ministry of the Third Person of the Godhead—the Holy Spirit. It is a *mediated* working of God. Significant mission issues are decided on this pivotal theological point. This specific identification of the manner of God's working in the church age introduces the necessity for a full-blown Trinitarian view of mission. In John 14–17, Jesus emphasizes the indwelling of the Spirit of God in a Trinitarian context, but with emphasis that the Holy Spirit will be the primary actor in an age of the Spirit, which is also an "age of mission."

The kingdom of God is God's dynamic power at work *among men and women* and his power at work in salvation history. The presence of the kingdom is characterized by the activity of God the Holy Spirit. The miracles of Jesus illustrated that the new age had come and the cosmic end-struggle had begun. The kingdom's presence meant that a power was already released in the world (Luke 11:20); the powers of the coming age were visible in the power of the Holy Spirit, in the present working of *God himself* (Ladd, 1974, p. 144).

The nature of the kingdom cannot be determined if it separates God from his kingdom. The kingdom of God is an expression of the ontic presence of God, God's present rule, God's action, God encountering men and women in history. In Jesus, therefore, God has become present among humanity; the kingdom is God himself actively at work among men and women (Ladd, 1974, p. 145). The kingdom of God is not the ideal good to be realized in a spiritual universal kingdom, or inevitable progress or an abstract principle of divine rule, but God's redemptive working in history. Nor can the kingdom be identified merely as God's working in and through historical events in general; it is God's supernatural breaking into history in the person of Jesus (pp. 188–89). "The coming of the kingdom into history . . . is [a] miracle—God's deed" (p. 189). These statements by Ladd, while correctly describing the nature and function of the kingdom today, nevertheless reflect his consistent silence on the Holy Spirit; this is discussed in detail in chapter 7.

While it is important to emphasize the kingdom as God actively working in history, it is clear in Jesus' teaching that the kingdom is a "kingdom of the heart," and his promise was that the kingdom would come in power at Pentecost to work powerfully *in* his disciples (John 14–16); it would be a *mediated* revelation of power. Jesus' declaration of the good news of the kingdom of God involved the gift of the Spirit to men and women (John 3–4). Jesus' theology of the good news of the kingdom of God was not the rule of God through a worldly kingdom or a nebulous sovereign power working in the world, but a kingdom of the heart where God rules *in* Christians *through* the Holy Spirit.

Joseph Grassi, a Roman Catholic theologian, also identifies the Spirit as the "manner" of God's working among men and women:

> The new age would be an age when all of God's power and Spirit would be evident in the world. In the Bible, the Spirit was the name given to God as manifest in the activity and life of people. It was first of all the source of all life, as when God breathed into the first human being to give life (Gen. 2:7). But the Spirit was also the source of all that showed God's presence in people in quite an extraordinary or unusual way. The coming of the new age would be accompanied by the discovery of a *new full dimension and depth of the Spirit of God* that would result in exciting *new manifestations of God's power and presence.* (1978, pp. 7–8; emphasis mine)

Grassi goes on to quote Joel 3:1–2 in connection with the above description of the extraordinary experience that the people of God would have in the new age. Grassi identifies *two dimensions* of the working of the Spirit: a life-source dimension and what could be called an outward, charismatic dimension.

In summarizing his study of the growth of a biblical tradition of the Spirit, George T. Montague likewise views the Spirit as another way of referring to the work of God himself: "This Spirit was not really other than a way of saying that God himself was moving those whom he touched" (1976, p. 366). In the Deuteronomist tradition, Montague identifies the Spirit that at times comes upon the recipient in an ecstatic way (p. 32). The nature of the kingdom, therefore, involves the people of God experiencing the full dimension and depth of the Spirit of God. God is present and actively working by means of the Holy Spirit, both inwardly as the source of spiritual life and outwardly in charismatic power. He also works immediately in the world apart from the church.

In summary, the Pentecostal-charismatic claim is that the Pentecostal movement represents an eschatological renewal of the Holy Spirit in salvation history. The theological creative center of the movement is Jesus' gospel of the kingdom of God, the charismatic working of the Holy Spirit in contemporary times. The experience that the apostles had with the Holy Spirit is also available in this present age. This claim is not founded on a naive biblicism. It is founded on *New Testament* theology. The hermeneutical horizon for Pentecostal theology is the biblical concept of salvation history; its hermeneutical key is the *already-present* kingdom of God. The "new age," according to New Testament theology, is an age of the Spirit, one characterized by his rule and the manifestation of his power in the people of God. The nature of the dynamic, present kingdom of God is such that it provides the people of God with an experience of the full dimension and depth of the Holy Spirit's ministry as they engage in their mission in the world.

3 A Correction of a Western Distortion

How does Pentecostalism represent a potential correction for a distortion in current-day missions? The answer to this question is found in Pentecostalism's focus on the experiential dimension of the Christian faith. In terms of the dynamic and evidential experience of the Holy Spirit, Pentecostalism contrasts with the static intellectually oriented expression of Christianity inherited from the post-Reformation period. The impact of Protestant Scholasticism on Western theology and the imbalanced nature of its theological orientation are well documented in contemporary theology (Berkouwer, 1952, 1975, 1977; Dunn, 1970; Green, 1975; Kraft, 1979; Ramm, 1959, 1977; Rogers, 1966, 1977; Rogers & McKim, 1979; Webber & Bloesch, 1978). Pentecostalism represents a restoration of the experiential dimension of the Christian faith in the wake of its scholastic reduction. In view of the excessive impact of Western culture on the Christian faith as it was contextualized in the West, Pentecostalism may be seen as a renewal movement that restores the significance of its experiential dimension. It brings a needed correction to a Western distortion of the faith.

Therefore, the Pentecostal's orientation corresponds to a theological hiatus in Western theological tradition, specifically a *pneumatological hiatus, "silence on the Holy Spirit."* This chapter identifies that theological hiatus in Western theology and in the Protestant missionary heritage. The demise of pneumatology in Western tradition is outlined, as well as the evidence of that demise in the recent history of the Christian mission. General areas of mission impacted by the "silence on the Holy Spirit" in Western Christianity are mentioned. The full discussion of the results of this silence on contemporary mission issues is the subject of chapters 6 and 7. In this chapter, the orientation of Pentecostalism is shown to address the theological hiatus in a significant way. It restores balance to Western theology and opens up new vistas for solutions to contemporary issues in mission theology.

Evidence of Distortion in Western Theology

The correction that the Pentecostal orientation provides for contemporary missions is clarified when the theological and historical context of its origin is brought into focus. To speak of the Pentecostal movement as restoring a crucial orientation of the Christian faith infers the demise or loss of that orientation in the course of the history of the church. An opposite theological orientation to that of Pentecostalism is when the intellectual dimension of the faith is emphasized to the point where the dynamic and experiential—the very dimensions that Pentecostalism epitomizes—are eclipsed. Historical, theological, and missiological evidence follows that points to a theological hiatus in Western theology—a pneumatological hiatus. This hiatus has impacted Western missions and contemporary mission theology, bringing considerable distortion and confusion.

A Pneumatological Hiatus: Historical Evidence

In an article surveying the development of pneumatology in the history of the Western church, "The Holy Spirit in Christian Theology," William Menzies outlines the areas in which it is underdeveloped. He also suggests reasons why the doctrine was neglected. Menzies shows that until the Reformation the doctrine developed only in terms of the essential being of the Third Person of the Trinity (1979, p. 69). The historic creeds of the church, as well as some Western systematic theologies, testify to this underdevelopment (pp. 71, 74). Little is said about the function or mission of the Holy Spirit in theology during this period. Menzies suggests two possible reasons for the lack of development: (1) a practical or ontological subordinationism of the Third Person of the Trinity, and (2) the contextualization of theology in the period; the fact that theology focuses on the issues and questions of the historical moment, and therefore theological development reflects this narrow focus (p. 71).

A possible third reason is implicit in the second reason cited above. Not only does theology naturally narrow its response to certain issues, due to the questions that need theological attention, but there is also often a reaction against certain questions and issues. "Selectivity" is an active principle in theological development, both positively as response to issues and *negatively as avoidance* of other issues. The subjective dimension of the Spirit in Christian experience was one issue that was avoided. Such avoidance was due to excesses that occurred regarding the experiential-subjective dimension of the faith, both at the beginning of the period (due to Montanism) and at its end (the *Schwarmerei*) (Menzies, 1979, p. 73).

Also, due to the contextual focus of Reformation theology, the theology of the Spirit was mostly developed along the lines of the Spirit's relationship and function with the Scriptures (Menzies, 1979, p. 74). What was not developed in the period was the mission of the Spirit and his outward expressive ministry. There was an almost immediate move into a scholastic period following the Reformation. Because of the effort to systematize the "theological deposit" of the Reformers, this contributed to the underdevelopment of pneumatology and the eclipse of the Spirit in his missionary role. Menzies notes that this neglected dimension began to receive attention in the theological traditions that represent the roots of modern Pentecostalism: Wesleyan-Holiness and Keswickian theology of the eighteenth and nineteenth centuries (pp. 74–75).

Under the title "The Reticent Spirit," Harry Boer discusses the question as to why the church is so unaware of the Spirit's ministry as the source of its witness. He notes that this question could be asked concerning *all* of the Spirit's work. He suggests reasons why the doctrine of the Spirit tends to be neglected, especially in an age strongly influenced by empiricism and rationalism.

First, Boer states that, in relation to the other persons of the Trinity, the Spirit has remained in the background and has been overshadowed by the more concrete figures of the Father and Son in theological reflection. The very name "Holy Spirit" contributes to the obscurity of the Third Person of the Trinity in our thinking. Boer suggests, "Perhaps it is because of the hidden role which the Spirit plays in redemption that he has been given a name which, as contrasted with that of the Father and the Son, allows of no concrete representation or association in our minds"—*Holy Spirit* (1961, p. 134). Such a factor would be influential in a scholastic-apologetic period in which the objective dimension of Christianity received primary attention. While the church has produced developed theologies and Christologies, there has been no unified and clearly circumscribed pneumatology developed (Boer, 1961, pp. 130–31). Perhaps the very systematic and controversial theological context in which pneumatology developed has contributed to the "silence on the Holy Spirit." In that context, the Holy Spirit has been chiefly viewed in terms of his subordination and representation with respect to the other persons of the Trinity.

Second, as the "Spirit of *God*," the qualitative or representative aspects of the Holy Spirit stand in the foreground, rather than his own personality and personhood (Boer, 1961, p. 131). Furthermore, he is the "Spirit of *Christ*"; his ministry of bearing witness to Jesus is emphasized in the New Testament (John 15:26; 16:13–15). In the Synoptic Gospels, Christ is prominent in that this Spirit anoints and empowers Christ for his mission (Luke 4:1, 14, 18–19). Since the Spirit's "anointing" also serves a similar function in his relationship with the church, the Holy Spirit recedes into the background. For he is the power of witness; the church is the organ of the Spirit's expression (Boer, 1961, p. 133).

Boer observes that the Holy Spirit is the *loving* Spirit, *life-giving* Spirit, and *witnessing* Spirit; in each case, he directs attention away from himself to the object of his ministry—the object of love, the expressions of life, and the content of the witness: Christ. The Spirit does not press himself on the attention of the church; he is a *reticent Spirit*, remaining in the background (Boer, 1961, p. 133). For several reasons, therefore, it is not surprising that pneumatology was neglected, especially in an age of controversy and rationalism: (1) the historical circumstances in which theological reflection took place, as well as the scholastic methodology of theologians; (2) the

difficulties the subject matter itself presented in an age of reason
and controversy; and (3) the representative and reticent nature of
the Spirit. Scholastic theologians were also reticent in dealing with
the "subjective" dimension of the Christian faith.

The Scholastic Roots: Theological Evidence

Historical and theological perspectives that find their source in
Western culture contribute toward this "silence on the Holy Spirit."
They have fostered the development of negative attitudes toward the
Holy Spirit that range from a passive neglect to studied repression
of his outward charismatic ministry. Considerable theologizing has
taken place to justify the absence of the Spirit's charismatic activity
in segments of the church. Scholasticism and dispensationalism
have been frequent sources for this. This theologizing has eroded
"expectancy" and has contributed to the inability of many to enter
into the full potential of the present gospel of the kingdom of God.
Without question, this constricting of the activity of the Spirit in
mission theology has weakened the missionary thrust of the Western church in the developing world.

In discussing the question "Should we expect to see the charismatic gifts in the church today?" Michael Green suggests a Western
cultural reason for the frequent negative response: "Both Catholic
and Protestant camps have been heavily infected by the rationalism of the Enlightenment, and our Christianity has been unduly
cerebral" (1975, p. 197). This statement refers to the word-oriented
nature of the faith we have inherited from the post-Reformation
period. Green's statement about the impact of scholastic thought
on Western Christianity equally applies to the Western missionary heritage. The historic moment in which William Carey made
his appearance to appeal for foreign missions was during the Enlightenment. Protestant missions had their beginning in the post-
Reformation period—a truly scholastic, Cartesian age.

In an age of rationalism and empiricism, and scientific and
philosophical breakthroughs, as well as under the pressure of the
Roman Catholic Counter-Reformation, the Protestant church

began defending the Reformation's "theological deposit." Attention moved away from the functional nature of Scripture and the experiential dimension of the faith to the form of Scripture—the text—and rationalistic apologetics.

In the immediate post-Reformation period, therefore, theologians began systematizing the writings of the Reformers. McClintock and Strong state concerning this phenomenon:

> Whenever the Church begins to let the writings of any of its eminent ministers stand between it and a free and direct interpretation of the Scriptures in the light of intuition and experience, that moment it enters into its scholastic stage. (1970, p. 422)

Under the impact of the Enlightenment, the post-Reformation period produced a scholastic theology. Theology was a theoretical discipline, an abstract-technical science, a logical system of belief cast in an Aristotelian mold. It was static in nature, with an emphasis on a rational defense of a settled deposit of doctrine (Pomerville, 1980, p. 94). The view of scholastic theologians was that they were working with a "finished" theological deposit. In its systematic form, theology consisted of propositional statements rather than an ongoing, dynamic process of theology in which biblical revelation was constantly interacting with historical and cultural contexts. Rationality and system were characteristic of the methodology of scholastic theologians. Theology, therefore, was viewed as a scholastic science rather than a practical discipline.

The primary role of reason in eighteenth-century theological work was the result of a philosophical shift. Anselm's "I believe that I may understand," which emphasized reason's subordination to faith, shifted under the impact of the Enlightenment to Protestant Scholasticism's "I know that I may believe." Such a confidence in reason led to a naive realism, which in turn led these theologians to believe that there was a direct correspondence between their Western perception and reality. Human reason was elevated to such a point in Reformed Scholasticism under the influence of Scottish Common Sense philosophy that theologians assumed they were thinking the thoughts of God after him. That is, they assumed they saw things objectively as God saw things (Pomerville, 1980, pp. 79–81). This perception of theology tended toward a view that theological speculation was *absolute*.

In this age of controversy, the noetic principle of theology (reflection, reason, epistemology, propositional statements on the confrontation of being) eclipsed the ontic principle (immediacy, presence, "there-ness" of God, confrontation with reality). The apologetic tools of the Age of Reason did not involve the subjective dimension of the Holy Spirit. Rather, the church's apologetic stance manifested itself in Reformed Scholasticism. The church implemented a medieval scholastic methodology. However, the Reformation principle *sola scriptura* (scripture alone) now eliminated church tradition as an apologetic means *and as an arbiter* functioning to withstand the impact of the Enlightenment on theology. Also, the church made an effort to objectify religious authority by limiting the concept of revelation to Scripture alone (Pomerville, 1980, pp. 66, 73–75).

This effort to objectify revelation in order to defend it against Roman Catholic claims and the claims of science resulted in a reduction of Reformation theology. As Reformed Scholasticism developed, the reduction chiefly took the form of *limiting the activity of the Holy Spirit at the contemporary end of biblical revelation*. Rogers and McKim state: "By the nineteenth century, the Princeton theologians would allow the work of the Holy Spirit only in inspiring the original authors of Scripture, and not at all in enabling modern readers to understand their Bibles" (1979, p. 176). Therefore, due to the apologetic nature of theology in the period, and the value placed on empirical and "objective" truth, theology was inflexible and static in nature. A correlative of this was a de-emphasis on the subjective dimension of theology, and a reductionism with regard to the Holy Spirit's ministry at "this end" of biblical revelation.

These scholastic historical roots greatly influenced the continuing tendency in Western missions to neglect the subjective dimension of the Holy Spirit in both theory and practice. The limiting of the activity of the Spirit to the author-end of Scripture and the prominence of the noetic principle of theology both tend to militate against and, in their extreme application, deny the Pentecostal's fundamental belief that God is dynamically present today in Christian experience and ministry in the person of the Holy Spirit.

In *I Believe in the Holy Spirit*, Michael Green speaks of the contemporary neglect of the Third Person of the Trinity under the provocative title, "The Spirit: Unknown—or Domesticated?" He speaks of one group of Christians to whom the Holy Spirit is virtually unknown, due to their lack of expectancy with regard to his intervention in their everyday lives. Green suggests that the neglect of the Spirit among other groups may be characterized by efforts to circumscribe his activities and hem him in with respect to his charismatic workings. These groups attempted to "domesticate" the Spirit, believing him to be a disturbing influence. Green represents these Christians as saying:

> Let him [the Holy Spirit] therefore be paid lip service, but for all practical purposes be shut up in the Bible where he can do no harm. Let his presence attend the confessional statement of our particular brand of Protestantism. Let the bizarre and miraculous elements which the New Testament documents narrate about his activity be relegated to those far-off apostolic days: it would be very embarrassing and doctrinally untidy if the Holy Spirit were to speak to men today, or to enable miracles to be performed and men to speak in tongues not their own. The Bible, accordingly, is the safest place for the Spirit. That is where he belongs; not in the hurly-burly of real life. (1975, p. 12)

Although a caricature, Green's description of the modern response to the Holy Spirit captures the influence of the Enlightenment's prejudice against the supernatural. It also expresses the truth that some Christians are *affectively closed* to the notion of the outward charismatic working of the Holy Spirit today. That "closed" attitude of some results in a studied repression of the Holy Spirit and represents the antithesis of the Pentecostal's theological and practical orientation to the Spirit.

Green also rejects the theological position that restricts the work of the Spirit to his inward work, claiming that the ebb of the charismatic dimension of the Spirit's ministry is based on dispensationalism: "It is simply not the case that healing, prophecy, exorcism and speaking in tongues died out with the last apostle" (1975, p. 198). Green states concerning 1 Corinthians 13:8, a passage often used as support for the position that the charismatic gifts disappeared with the apostolic age, "Still less can a passage like 1 Corinthians

13:8 ('as for prophecies, they will pass away; as for tongues, they
will cease . . . ') be adduced to attest the supposed demise of these
gifts. They will pass away only when 'the perfect comes,' i.e. at the
Parousia—not at the end of the apostolic age or the formation of
the New Testament Canon" (1975, p. 198)! Green goes on to state
that there is plenty of evidence that in sub-apostolic days, and pe-
riodically throughout church history, this charismatic ministry of
the Spirit did not die out. He also elaborates on the place of such
ministry in the church today (pp. 198–204).

While evangelical missiologists readily confess the neglect of
the Holy Spirit in mission theology and practice, they may not express that neglect in terms of the charismatic dimension of the
Spirit's ministry. However, Geradus van der Leeuw suggests that
any neglect of the Spirit's ministry should be avoided:

> Mission is a vital expression of the Holy Spirit whom we may never
> hem in. For this very reason every constricting of the activities of
> the Holy Spirit to the individual or the Church or orthodox doctrine
> drains the vital force of missions. (Bosch, 1980, p. 199)

Protestant Scholasticism represents the theological roots of the silence on the Spirit in Western missions. The neglect and hemming
in of the Spirit is part and parcel of that theological tradition. This
weakness is due to the influence of Western worldview in the period
and the apologetic methodology used. Central in the tradition is
the prominence of abstract reason with its precedence over faith
and the experiential dimension of Christianity. The residual effect
of that imbalance is evident in evangelical theology today.

NEGLECT OF THE SPIRIT'S ROLE IN MISSION THEORY AND PRACTICE

Neglect in Mission Theory: The Western World

There is evidence in Protestant mission history and theology
that the neglect of pneumatology has adversely impacted the Western missionary heritage. It is not surprising that Lindsell (1949),

Allen (1960), Boer (1961), Kane (1974), and Hodges (1977) all see the role of the Holy Spirit in modern missions to be greatly neglected. Allen emphasizes that the revelation of the Holy Spirit as a missionary Spirit in the Acts of the Apostles causes that portion of the New Testament to stand alone. He states that the missionary role of the Holy Spirit is crucial for any true understanding of the Holy Spirit and his work:

> This revelation embraces one whole hemisphere of the Spirit. If we ignore it, or treat it less seriously than the revelation of truth or righteousness, we lose sight of the perfection of the Spirit. Our view is necessarily one-sided, our understanding of the past is robbed of its true foundation, our conception of our present duty is incomplete, and our hope for the future is rendered doubtful and indistinct. (1960, p. 21)

Allen discusses the neglect of the Spirit in terms of limiting his ministry to only certain areas: the revelation of truth, of holiness, and of church government and order (1960, p. 21). He thinks the missionary role of the Spirit, found in Acts, is largely neglected. This "whole hemisphere of the Spirit" in Acts involves largely the outward-expressive dimension of the Spirit's ministry. Allen says the neglect of this dimension destroys the "perfection" or completeness of the Holy Spirit, rendering a "one-sided" view of the Spirit. The development of pneumatology in the area that Allen spoke of still remains largely undeveloped. Such neglect could only adversely affect one's concept of mission theory and practice.

In *Pentecost and Missions* (1961), Harry Boer shows how the eclipse of the missionary role of the Spirit was partly due to the emergence of the Protestant missionary movement in the post-Reformation period. Boer concentrates on explaining why the Protestant missionary movement emphasized the Great Commission as its motivation for missions, the *written* command, over the New Testament's emphasis on the inner motivation of the Holy Spirit. The influence of scholastic thought in the post-Reformation period is illustrated by the role the Great Commission played as the motivation for missions in the history of Protestant missions. Boer notes a striking contrast between the different foundations that have undergirded the missionary witness of the church in the early period and the recent period of the church. The first contrast he notes is that since the post-Reformation period there has been a heavy emphasis on the Great Commission as motivation for missions, but in the early church there is a complete absence of this motivation as a conscious factor. The second contrast Boer notes is the lack of attention paid to Pentecost in relation to missions through the history of Protestantism, and the major emphasis Acts gives to Pentecost in terms of initiating and "wholly conditioning the missionary witness and expansion of the early church" (1961, p. 15). This apparent misunderstanding of the role of the Great Commission has contributed to the eclipse of the Holy Spirit's missionary role.

The Great Commission played such a major role because it was connected with a theological misconception of the Reformation period and the circumstances of the post-Reformation period. The Reformers and the majority of seventeenth-century theologians believed the Great Commission was binding only on the apostles. They believed that when the apostles died Christ's command died with them. They held that since the apostles were extraordinary officers with no successors, that which was binding on them was no longer binding on the church (Boer, 1961, pp. 17, 20). The Reformers (Calvin, Luther, Melanchthon, and Zwingli) saw the expansion of the church in terms of witness in the immediate community, or an extended witness as a result of scattering due to persecution. The Reformers believed another occasion for an extended witness was the non-Christian areas of the colonies. They believed that it was the duty of Christian governments to bring the gospel to them. The church, however, was believed to have had no mandate to preach the gospel and plant churches in distant lands by means of a program of missions. They believed the gospel was *in principle* declared to the whole world by the apostles (Boer, 1961, pp. 18–20).

Latourette confirms that this theological misconception concerning the Great Commission existed in the Reformation period. He adds that Luther and Melanchthon both believed that the end of the world was so imminent that no time remained to spread the gospel throughout the world (1967, p. 25). Stephen Neill suggests that the stance of the Reformers on the binding nature of the Great Commission may have been defensive in nature. Roman Catholic controversialists charged that "the Lutherans compare themselves to the apostles and the evangelists; yet though they have among them a very large number of Jews, and in Poland and Hungary have the Turks as their near neighbors, they have hardly converted even so much as a handful" (1964, p. 221). Rather than admit they should have missions, they tended to say missions were not obligatory (p. 222).

Even though some voices were raised in opposition to this misconception about the Great Commission, the view held until it was assailed by the Pietists in the post-Reformation period. William Carey's *An Enquiry into the Obligations of Christians to Use Means for the Conversion of the Heathen* argued that the Great Commission given by the Lord was still binding on the church (Boer, 1961, p. 16). Due to the success of Carey's argument in proving the continuing missionary obligation of the church on the basis of the Great Commission, it became the basis on which the missionary witness of the church was built (pp. 24–25). The emphasis on the command of Christ for mission's motivation has prevailed until today. But the theological context and historical circumstances out of which this emphasis came have been largely forgotten. It is clear that the appeal to the Great Commission, among other factors, was powerful during an age when emphasis was placed on the written word of God and obedience. The appeal to the command continued to revive missions for about one hundred fifty years.

Boer questions "whether an emphasis whose origins lie embedded so strongly in reaction to a long held theological misconception is also a *scriptural* emphasis" (1961, p. 27). The fact that Jesus actually gave the command is not in doubt. Neither is there any doubt that the Scriptures are authoritative. An examination of the role of the Great Commission in initiating mission in Protestant history shows it to function in the biblical sense. It acts as a corrective, a reminder, and an objective command to return the church to a task that is in accord with its purpose and its very nature—mission. However, the historical circumstances of the mobilization of the Protestant church in centrifugal mission do not reflect the original biblical basis for

mission. Nor do those circumstances reflect the church's true motivation for mission. Rather, the emphasis on the Great Commission
represents the historical mobilization of the Protestant church, its
return to an activity that was in accord with its purpose for being
and its inner nature. Furthermore, as Boer shows, an examination
of Acts reveals a complete absence of the Great Commission as the
motivating impetus for mission. Instead, *the Holy Spirit predomi-
nates the scene of mission.*

Allen captures the significance of the absence of command for
mission in Acts and the emphasis of the Spirit as an inward dynamic for witness. He believes that Acts stands alone in the New
Testament in its revelation of the Holy Spirit as a *missionary Spirit*
(1960, p. 21). In the new age, the new people of God are by *nature*
a witnessing community, because they have received a witnessing
Spirit (John 15:26). Allens states concerning this inner motivation:

> St. Luke fixes our attention, not upon an external voice, but upon an
> internal Spirit. This manner of command is peculiar to the Gospel.
> Others direct from without, Christ directs within; others order, Christ
> inspires; others speak external words, Christ gives the Spirit which
> desires and strives for that which he commands; others administer a
> dead letter, Christ imparts life. This is the manner of the command in
> St. Luke's writings. He speaks not of men who, being what they were,
> strove to obey the last orders of a beloved Master, but of men who,
> receiving a Spirit, were driven by that Spirit to act in accordance with
> the nature of that Spirit. (1960, p. 5)

The primary motivation, therefore, is not an outward command,
but an inward Spirit. Acts is governed by one dominant, overrid-
ing and all-controlling theme: the expansion of the church through
missionary witness in the power of the Holy Spirit (Acts 1:8).

It is interesting to note that in his book *I Believe in the Great
Commission,* Max Warren personifies the Great Commission as the
Spirit of Christ within the believer. He states that Jesus himself is the
Great Commission (1976, p. 13). In the new covenant we are not confronted by an ethical demand; we are confronted with a person. The
claim of the New Testament is that the message is Jesus and Jesus is
the Great Commission—the revealer of God. "To have received that
revelation is to have entered into a particular relationship with the

Great Commission. It is to know oneself commissioned" (pp. 23–24). Warren is consistent in his personification of the Great Commission throughout the book (pp. 26, 29, 45, 67, 136, 172). This emphasis on the inward motivation and dynamic of mission agrees with Allen's statement, and is in accord with the theology of the Holy Spirit and mission of the church in the Acts of the Apostles.

Warren is correct when he speaks of the Great Commission as personified, Christ dwelling within the believer by the Holy Spirit. However, this is only evident when the Holy Spirit's relation to Christ is clarified, when Christology is properly related to pneumatology. St. Luke begins volume two of his work (the book of Acts) by referring to volume one (his Gospel) in which he says he wrote about all that Jesus *began* to do and teach (Acts 1:1). Then he immediately speaks of the promised Holy Spirit. The implication is that now, through the inward presence of the Spirit in his people, Jesus would *continue* his mission (Mark 16:20; John 14:18; 17:26). For Luke, it is the Holy Spirit who provides continuity between the period of the church and the period of Jesus—the same Spirit is operative in both. This is shown by the many parallels of the early community with the experience of Jesus (Montague, 1976, p. 268).

Both Warren and Allen capture Luke's thrust in Acts: the impetus for mission is internal—the word of command is internalized. The commission is no longer merely an outward command, an ethical demand. It is now personified by the missionary Spirit's indwelling presence. Therefore, the Great Commission derives its meaning from this internalizing event. The Pentecostal event, then, is decisive for an understanding of the Spirit's role in initiating and universalizing mission. Of course, this does not take away from the function of the objective command in Scripture. It is a constant reminder of the missionary nature and purpose of the people of God. Nor does it take away from its value in providing the church with a strategy for mission.

Warren's work appears to be an effort to correct the misconception inherent in the Western missionary heritage concerning the church's motivation for mission. In this way, he addresses the demise of the experiential dimension of the faith. The Great Commission is honored in its function as a reminder of the church's missionary purpose in the world. But for Warren, the emphasis is on the experiential dimension, the inward impetus of the Spirit of Christ in initiating and universalizing mission.

A result of the emergence of the Protestant missionary movement during the Enlightenment, therefore, was that the Holy Spirit's missionary role was neglected. The beginnings of the movement were characterized by an emphasis on the written command to the point where the outward-expressive dimension of the Spirit's missionary ministry was severely limited. This neglect by Western theologians compelled Roland Allen to stress this problem (Branner, 1975, p. 18). Boer's study on the role of the Pentecost event and the Holy Spirit's role in the missionary expansion of the church illustrates the extent of the scholastic distortion in the post-Reformation period. It shows the impact of that theological tradition on the Western missionary heritage, with the written command of the Great Commission becoming the motivation for mission rather than the inward imperative of the Holy Spirit. Part of the great potential for missions in the Southern Hemisphere in the twenty-first century is that the "neo-Pentecostal's" sense of "missions" came in the midst of a Pentecostal-charismatic movement in which the full dimension of the Spirit's ministry was considered the norm. It was not in Western culture, with its rationalistic, scholastic theology and cerebral gospel. The "reminder" that the Pentecostal-charismatic movement gives to Western Christians is the gospel of the kingdom in the New Testament and the notion that what they are experiencing in the Holy Spirit is the same experience of the apostles in Acts. There is not much of a chance that the written command would eclipse the inward missionary impulse of the Holy Spirit for them as a motivation for missions.

Neglect in Mission Practice: Pentecostal Independency Movements

Further evidence of the pneumatological hiatus in the Western Protestant missionary heritage, perhaps the greatest evidence of all, concerns the impact of the Western expression of Christianity and its theology on non-Western cultures. The phenomenon of "independency" movements in the wake of the impact of Western missions in the developing world is important contemporary evidence of the neglect of the Spirit. These movements have already been noted in chapters 1 and 2. How are these movements in the non-Western world *evidence* of the "silence on the Holy Spirit" in Western Christianity? How has Western Christianity helped to provoke, or inspire, such movements? There is no doubt that Western Christianity has been chiefly instrumental in causing independency movements. Peel is representative of the consensus in his somewhat general statement with regard to Christianity's role:

> Christianity has been both cause and catalyst of social change in Africa; and one of the most prominent features of modern Africa has been the emergence of independent churches, founded by Africans in protest at some feature of the Christianity of the missionary societies. (1968, p. 1)

Previously, we have noted that Ngoni Sengwe clarified the issue of causation when he stated that the movements were the result of the clash of Western culture and African culture, not the clash of the gospel and African culture (1981, p. 94). Contrary to popular belief, in terms of cultural clash, the roots of causation lie not in African culture but in *Western* culture. The loss of value for, and perception of, the supernatural in Western culture is an all-important antecedent factor in the study of independency movements. Horton notes regarding the disparate nature of the two worldviews, "So far as a confrontation of modern Christianity with traditional African religion is concerned, then, it looks as though the essential aspiration of the one is often the marginal aspiration of the other" (1979, p. 250). Western Christianity's "practical anti-supernaturalism" (i.e., neglect of the Spirit) in supernatural-oriented societies forms the conceptual framework for the study of independency movements.

The excessive impact of Western culture on the theology brought by the missionary to non-Western cultures resulted in an extremely naturalistic, rational, and abstract-oriented theological product being introduced into supernaturalistic, intuitive, and concrete-oriented societies. The contextualization of the Christian faith in such cultural situations should have involved both a fidelity to cultural context and a fidelity to biblical revelation. Where independency movements occurred, there appears to have been a failure on the part of Western missionaries at *both* points of fidelity.

The more obvious failure, often noted, is the failure to consider the non-Western cultural context with sufficient sensitivity. The less frequently observed failure concerns *the lack of articulation and application of the very supernaturalistic-oriented New Testament view of life* by the Western missionary in African society. The lack of fidelity to the African cultural milieu was directly related to the lack of fidelity to divine revelation in the missionary's own culture first. The area of non-Western culture that was consistently neglected by the Western missionary in African society was the transempirical "middle world" of spirits. This area permeated every aspect of native culture. The neglect of this area represented a neglect of the life-supporting matrix of those cultures and, therefore, was the increasing point of stress in them.

The failure to provide a biblical worldview regarding the spirit world and the role of the Holy Spirit in the church is a Western lack of fidelity to biblical revelation. "Neglect," therefore, is to be perceived not only in a passive-avoidance of, or aggressive reaction against, the needs of African society, but it also should be perceived *a failure to respond positively and biblically to those needs.* The failure concerns not only the cultural insensitivity of Western missionaries, but also involves their failure to respond biblically to needs for which *the New Testament amply provided.*

In a real sense, explaining the origin of the African Independent Churches as a reactionary movement in the African cultural milieu alone is inconclusive. The reaction in African society is the "fruit," not the "root" of causation. The "root" concerns the missionary neglect in articulating the biblical view of the supernatural in connection with the African view of reality (Sengwe, 1981, p. 95). The failure to be faithful to biblical revelation, because of the obscure nature of the supernatural-experiential dimension of Christianity for the Westerner, directs the discussion of causation away from the reactions of African society to the "root-cause": *a Western worldview.*

Further evidence of the obscurity of the spirit world for Western missionaries is found in their denial of that dimension in traditional societies and in their studied attack on traditional institutions that dealt with that dimension in non-Western cultures. Oosterwal addresses this "blind spot" of Western missionaries and its effects in the developing world in the following manner:

> For, it is precisely the absence or the lack of the power of God as a reality people can live by that has been a precipitating factor to these movements. In the African, Asian or Melanesian traditional religious setting, power was at the center of their thinking, life and experience. And the spirit—of God, the gods or the ancestor—was a tangible reality. How remote, how intellectual, how powerless seems to be the God and the Spirit missionaries preach about or we [Western] Christians show in our lives. As one leader once expressed it in a conversation with a missionary: "you have held back the Spirit." The movements challenge our understanding of God, and our pneumatology. (1973, p. 36)

Oosterwal also observes that Western dichotomizing tendencies have cut Westerners off from a dimension of the Christian faith that is readily accepted by non-Western societies:

> In the West . . . the biblical message becomes demythologized . . . but it has become fatal in the African and Asian setting, where the whole of life is (still) sacred and the world view is essentially a religious one. The Kingdom of God is a reality; its signs of healing, hearing the Spirit's voice, speaking in tongues, dreams and miracles of all sorts are tangible experiences of its presence. (p. 41)

In his thesis on "African Independency," Avery states that in evaluating independency movements, some Western missionaries demanded that a "clean break" with paganism be a qualification before the movements could be considered Christian. However, the "clean break" was defined as the total repudiation of other supernatural forces, all forms of magic, benevolent or malevolent, and traditional medicine (1969, p. 31). It appears that often missionaries took a God-against-culture position in African societies. Avery himself may betray a Western bias against the supernatural when he says, "Evil spirits and curses of sorcerers are daily problems and *try & feel what the people feel.*

"Put yourself in someone else's shoes. Don't just 'feel bad', actually clues:

fears; the wrath and blessings of the 'living dead' [ancestors] are present experiences. To preach that these forces do not exist is only displaying one's ignorance of the reality *from the African's viewpoint*" (1969, p. 3; emphasis mine).

That missionaries preached that the spirit world did not exist, as well as Avery's mention that one must know reality "from the African's viewpoint," both reveal the anti-supernatural bias. It is not just a matter of understanding the African's viewpoint, if I have interpreted Avery's statement accurately, but about affirming that the African's viewpoint about the existence of evil spirits is *biblically correct*. Whatever the case, the provision of the Christian answer for that African viewpoint is the crucial issue. However, Avery does mention the tremendous stress produced by Western Christianity when he quotes Mitchell:

> In short, Christianity was too Western on the whole, too rationalistic and other-worldly to gain the confidence of its adherents at their deepest levels of experience. This showed up most plainly in those times of personal crisis, such as barrenness and sickness, when many baptized believers, thinking that Jesus Christ did not have any interest or worse, the power, to improve their state of affairs, felt they had to visit the traditional healer. (1969, p. 64)

Mitchell goes on to contrast this Western expression of Christianity with that of the African Independent Churches: "It is precisely to this spiritual malaise that the independent churches preached their naïve, yet deeply biblical, theology of power. They proclaimed a God who acts, a Saviour who saves *in* the world" (Avery, 1969, p. 64).

In his article "Missions Churches, Independent Churches, and Felt Needs in Africa," Jacob Loewen gives several case studies where mission churches were found to have no way of dealing with phenomena of the transempirical dimension of spirit. He states that the mission churches had no way of dealing effectively with de-witching processes and with witchcraft itself. But he points out that both traditional African society and the Independent African Churches did (1976, pp. 406–7). Loewen outlines the felt needs of African Christians that were met by the shaman in traditional societies: protection against witchcraft, the need for physical and psychic health, the need for supernatural sanction for confession, and the need for protection against evil spirits (pp. 409–10). Concerning the avoidance of these areas by Western mission churches Loewen states:

> Verbally missionaries tend to confess a belief in spirits, especially the Spirit of God. But it seems to be more lip service than anything else, because most of them have never seen or experienced an evil spirit. Their knowledge is entirely conceptual, rather than experiential. In fact, their whole educational system in the Western scientific world has taught them that there is a deep cleavage between the material and the spiritual, and whether they want to or not, they tend to accept the material as much more real than the spiritual. (pp. 414–15)

Loewen's mention of the "deep cleavage between the material and the spiritual" is another way of saying that the "middle" transempirical dimension of spirit is obscure in Western culture.

The missionary assault on African traditional society was comprehensive. Barrett lists the following ten major areas that were attacked from tribe to tribe in varying degrees: community structure, land and property, laws and taboos, religious concepts, religious leadership, religious symbolism, magical concepts, rituals, worship, and the vernacular languages (1968, pp. 266–67). Barrett describes the resulting period of stress and cultural distortion:

> Africans now realized with some *bitterness* that the hopes aroused by the early days of Christian preaching would not materialize. They had not anticipated the consequences in the severe strain being put on their traditional institutions. They had failed to obtain the *force vitale*, the mysterious power of the whites—either material, financial, cultural, religious, spiritual or ecclesiastical. Their societies were not being fulfilled by the new religion, but were being demolished. In the place of the secure religion they thought they had of old, there was now a religious void. (p. 267)

An emasculated Western gospel could not possibly have filled that social and spiritual void. The neglect of the dynamic dimension of the Christian faith and the failure to articulate the biblical view about the spirit world in African society was disastrous.

On the other hand, the discovery of a dynamic, power-oriented expression of the Christian faith was like a *resurrection* for African

Christians. This took place increasingly when the Scriptures were translated into the vernacular. The discovery of a Pentecostal expression of the faith did not result in a resurrection of traditional religion or in a bridge to paganism. But the discovery of an expression of Christianity in the New Testament, which spoke to the needs of the Africans in their cultural context and provided Christian means for dealing with the spirit world, became the impetus for the African independency movements.

Barrett's investigation into the causation of independency movements in Africa emphasizes the sociological and ecclesiastical dimensions in the clash between the Western mission and the African traditional societies. His thesis concerning the root cause of the movements reflects the social level of his investigation:

> The root cause common to the entire movement of independency, therefore, may be seen in this one aspect of culture clash: *a failure in sensitivity, the failure of missions at one small point to demonstrate consistently the fullness of the biblical concept of love as sensitive understanding towards others as equals, the failure to study or understand African society, religion and psychology in any depth, together with a dawning African perception from the vernacular scriptures of the catastrophic nature of this failure and of the urgent necessity to remedy it in order that Christianity might survive on African soil.* (1968, p. 156)

The inadequacy of Barrett's "love theory," as well as theories focusing on social, political, and economic deprivation as the cause of the movements, is evidenced in the continuation of the movements and in the circumstances in which they continue to emerge. H. W. Turner states that polygamy and economic deprivation are contributory rather than basic causes of the movements, and that there are many instances where they cannot be applied. Ghana has the highest standards of living among African peoples, yet movements have proliferated during the very period of prosperity there (Turner, 1963, p. 114). Also, the wealthy are involved in the movements, and the economic principle is applied to explain the prophet movements in political terms. There is some truth to this, especially in certain areas of Africa. But it does not account for the wide-ranging phenomenon in Africa (p. 114).

The inadequacy of the economic-political grounds for causation is seen in the continuing growth of the movements after the colonial period. Turner states that a deeper probe into causation shows that the movements represent a creative response to the breakdown of old forms of African society. The new movements represent groups that provide fellowship, security, and some sanctions and guidance for living—a life in which the Africans work out the expression of Christianity according to their own way of life (Turner, 1963, p. 115). Of course, this is especially true when that expression of Christianity is Pentecostal.

Barrett's thesis (he is not Pentecostal or charismatic) concerns the "fruit" of causation, not the "root." He emphasizes the African response to the neglect of their culture and the resulting ecclesiastical problems. The attack on traditional institutions *in toto*, not differentiating the good elements from the bad, is only the surface manifestation of the inadequacy. The comprehensive attack of the Western missionary on society is evidence of a deeper level of causation, at a *worldview level.*

Barrett's "lack of love" theory appears to be imposed on the evidence of his investigation. Perhaps this is due to the centrality of "love" in the Christian gospel and its application on the level of Barrett's investigation—church/missions tensions. Certainly, more than a "lack of love" was behind the ethnocentrism that kept missionaries from learning African culture. Often the missionary failure is excessively characterized as "intentional." This intentional charge is especially prominent in the African viewpoint—that Western missionaries deliberately withheld "the fullness of the biblical welcome" (Barrett, 1968, p. 154). But the failure to teach the full benefits of the Holy Spirit was due more to the *deficiency of that dimension in Western Christianity* than to deliberate withholding of the truth. Rather than a discovery of divine love when the Scriptures were translated, it was the discovery of *New Testament pneumatology* that was so revolutionary for the African. The catastrophic nature of the missionary failure concerned the power of the Holy Spirit in the Christian life. This failure arose from an ethnocentrism rooted in a worldview that caused Western missionaries to neglect the same dimension of the Spirit in their own culture. The investigation of causation must probe deeper than the socio-ecclesiastical level. It must focus on the deficiency of a Western worldview with its aversion toward the spirit world. Such a deficiency in the Christian message in African society provided the catalyst for the independency movements. Therefore, the deprivation in African society goes beyond the social and economic. It primarily concerns a "spiritual" deprivation.

The Western doubt as to the authenticity of these movements as to their "Christian-ness" appears to be rooted in Western Christianity's awkwardness with the subjective and experiential dimensions of the Spirit, and in a latent ethnocentrism. What appears to be problematic to Western missionaries is the movements' indigenous expression and their orientation to the dynamic-experiential dimension of Christianity. Establishing the validity of independency movements, therefore, must be done against the backdrop of Western ethnocentrism, its inadequate grasp of the experiential dimension of the faith, and a deficient pneumatology. The ease with which Westerners reject New Testament models for evaluating Pentecostal phenomena in the movements speaks to the inadequacy of the Western theological apparatus. The rejection takes place in spite of the lack of any biblical or Reformation principle that would preclude the manifestation of contemporary Pentecostal phenomena. The same pneumatological deficiency that precipitated independency movements, therefore, is also a liability in their contemporary evaluation.

4 An Experience with the Spirit

The purpose of this chapter is to outline the distinctiveness of Pentecostalism. Central to this whole study is the question, "Who are the Pentecostals?" A concise definition is elusive when we view the worldwide phenomenon. In a sense, the answer to this question is found only in the context of the whole study. This chapter examines the common denominator of the Pentecostal movement, the Pentecostal experience of the Spirit. The issues of a "subsequent" and "evidential" experience with the Spirit are analyzed, which are the issues most frequently questioned by non-Pentecostals. The primary motive for this focus is not to present an apologetic for Pentecostal doctrine. Rather, it is to promote an understanding of the movement, and thereby allow Pentecostalism to make its maximum contribution to contemporary missions.

The notion that Pentecostalism provides direction for contemporary missions is based on its emphasis on the experiential dimension of the Christian faith, the dynamic experience of the Spirit. As a renewal movement, emphasizing a neglected dimension of the Holy Spirit's ministry, Pentecostalism sets the subtle influence of post-Reformation Protestant Scholasticism in bold relief. It is at this point that Pentecostalism functions as a "corrective" in contemporary missions. Criticisms of Pentecostalism often emerge from the above theological context, showing the influence of scholastic tradition in modern evangelicalism. It is at this point that Pentecostalism's "God with us" experience makes its major contribution to contemporary missions. Paradoxically, the chief criticism of the movement—the distinct, dynamic experience of the Spirit—reveals its chief contribution for contemporary missions.

WHO ARE THE PENTECOSTALS?
A COMMON DENOMINATOR

The historical study of the phenomenon of the Pentecostal movement has pointed to a common Pentecostal distinctive within a movement with diverse denominational and cultural traditions. The possibility of a common denominator in Pentecostalism is indicated by the spontaneous origins of the movement and its distinct nature as a divine eschatological renewal. A common denominator is suggested by the belief among the three streams of Pentecostalism that God is renewing the church by restoring the full spectrum of the Holy Spirit's ministry today. Any common denominator having to do with the Pentecostal distinctive, therefore, will concern the outward charismatic work of the Holy Spirit among classical Pentecostals, neo-Pentecostals, and Catholic charismatics. The initial stage of this ministry of the Spirit after conversion is commonly called the "baptism of the Holy Spirit."

There are several evangelical criticisms that arise when one speaks of the "Pentecostal experience." Perhaps the chief objection is that charismatic manifestations of the Spirit belong to a past period of the church, the apostolic period. However, this objection to Pentecostalism has been largely abandoned since the charismatic movement began midway through the twentieth century. Those evangelicals holding to dispensational theology still object to believing that charismatic phenomena are normative today. It appears, however, that this objection is influenced by Western culture under the impact of the Enlightenment as much as it is by dispensational theology. In chapter 2, New Testament theology focusing on the kingdom of God motif was seen to support the present-day occurrence of charismatic phenomena. The biblical evidence and theological underpinnings for contemporary charismatic phenomena rest in the New Testament concept of the dynamic, present kingdom of God. Pentecostalism was viewed as an *eschatological* phenomenon, a movement consistent with the biblical meaning of the term. The dispensational objection to Pentecostalism is therefore the weakest criticism in terms of biblical theology.

Another criticism concerns the Pentecostal belief that the Pentecostal experience is normative for contemporary Christian experience. While some non-Pentecostal traditions hold to an experience with the Spirit subsequent to conversion, they object to the Pentecostal's emphasis on speaking in tongues in connection with the experience.

The Pentecostal's answer to these criticisms of this doctrine and experience can be formulated by the question, "Is not Scripture normative?" Of course, this is not a simple question, for it involves the matter of hermeneutics. While that question is discussed here, especially in connection with the Acts of the Apostles, chapters 5 and 6 also discuss Pentecostal hermeneutics. There the question arises, "What is the Pentecostal view of biblical revelation, and how does it use Scripture to support the Pentecostal experience?" In this chapter, the focus is on the dynamic nature of Christianity itself. In addition to the question on the normative nature of Scripture, the Pentecostal would ask, "Is not Christianity the demonstration of God's power?" This last question brings into focus a chief contribution of Pentecostalism for contemporary missions—the very nature of the Christian faith.

A Renewal Experience

In order to understand and evaluate Pentecostal pneumatology fairly, it must be viewed within the context of renewal. It concerns a neglected dimension of the Holy Spirit's ministry, and it is a response to, and restoration of, New Testament Christian experience. "Renewal," therefore, explains the Pentecostal's emphasis on the outward-charismatic dimension of the Spirit's ministry. Pentecostalism's emphasis on the baptism of the Spirit and his charismatic gifts does not indicate a truncated, narrow pneumatology. Rather, in dealing with a *restoration* of the Holy Spirit's outward charismatic ministry of power, it represents a return to a New Testament pneumatology. Pentecostal pneumatology is no different from that of Protestantism in general, except for this emphasis on the Holy Spirit's subsequent baptizing and charismatic work. It also includes the inward work of the Spirit in Christian initiation (initiation and growth in Christ, and in the fruit of the Spirit). As a *renewal* movement, however, it emphasizes the charismatic-power dimension of the Spirit's ministry. While the Pentecostal distinctive *does* concern this dimension of pneumatology, it does not indicate the full spectrum of even classical Pentecostal pneumatology, contrary to Bruner's assertion (1970, pp. 57–59). The evangelical criticism that Pentecostals overemphasize the Holy Spirit in the Godhead must also be seen in this context. Michael Green observes that the charge of overemphasizing a particular person of the Godhead could also be leveled against Roman Catholicism and evangelicalism, and that only a fully Trinitarian Christianity can stand the test of orthodoxy (1975, p. 53).

A common denominator among all of the streams of Pentecostalism is the belief in a further experience with the Holy Spirit in addition to that of conversion. This experience is believed to be related to the experience of the early Christian community in the New Testament—their experience with the gospel. All view their Pentecostal-charismatic experience as *normative*, in the sense that it follows the pattern or experience of the early church in the New Testament. "Renewal" indicates that Pentecostals believe a *neglected dimension* of the Holy Spirit's ministry is restored in contemporary times. In addition to the Holy Spirit's ministry as the principle of life in regeneration and sanctification, the outward-charismatic ministry of the Spirit is the dimension that is being renewed.

The discussion of the contemporary Pentecostal-charismatic experience as "subsequent" is especially fitting under the title of this section, "A Renewal Experience." When seen in an historical renewal framework, some difficulties with the acceptance of a "subsequent" experience with the Holy Spirit are dispelled. Difficulties in accepting this "other" experience with the Holy Spirit are due to the long periods of church history where the full experience of the Spirit was lost. This "ebb and flow" phenomenon with regard to the charismatic experience in church history is addressed in greater detail in chapter 7.

The recognition of two dimensions of the Holy Spirit's work, even in terms of his initial and subsequent work in Christian experience, is found in Wesleyan-Holiness theology, Keswickian-Reformed theology (Menzies, 1975, p. 86), and Roman Catholic theology (Grassi, 1978, pp. 7–8; Montague, 1976, p. 32). The Wesleyan stream of Pentecostalism made a distinction between subsequent experience and conversion in connection with the Holiness view of sanctification and perfectionism. That tradition in Pentecostalism holds to a three stage view of the Christian's experience with the Holy Spirit. However, the Keswickian tradition views a subsequent experience as an enduement of power for service (Menzies, 1975, pp. 86–88; Dunn, 1970, pp. 2, 32). These two theological traditions in Pentecostalism represent the subsequent experience as necessary or normative, and may be classified as *subsequence theologies*. Subsequence theologies hold to two or three crisis experiences with the Holy Spirit in Christian experience. Other Protestant neo-Pentecostal groups also fit within this theological classification, in terms of their view of a subsequent experience with the Holy Spirit (Menzies, 1978, p. 1). We should note here that those receiving a "Pentecostal" or "charismatic" experience with the Spirit, for the most part, are unaware of the above theological distinctions.

When Bruner treats this subsequent experience in Pentecostalism entirely in terms of Wesleyan eradication theology (1970, pp. 94, 117), he is mistaken. He emphasizes a "doctrine of conditions" as though this was an accepted norm in the movement instead of a matter where there is a wide diversity, even a plethora of opinions in classical Pentecostalism alone. Actually, Bruner only speaks of one theological tradition when he says:

> The doctrine of conditions, then, is actually a corollary of the doctrine of subsequence and a premise for the doctrine of evidence and as such occupies a cornerstone position in the edifice of the distinctive Pentecostal doctrine. (p. 88)

The Keswickian wing of Pentecostalism, however, does not view the Spirit's work in the subsequent stage as eradication of sin with the above-mentioned corresponding "condition." Rather it is viewed as an enduement of power received by *faith* for witness.

Bruner's fixation on a "doctrine of conditions" (1970, pp. 87–116) appears to be due to his distaste for the Arminian theology of the Wesleyan-Holiness doctrine, which emphasizes the will of man in connection with faith. However, Roman Catholic theology stresses, and rightly so, the importance of "subjective dispositions": awareness, expectancy, and openness with regard to the faith-appropriation of the charismatic experience (McDonnell, 1980, pp. 27–29). This point is dealt with in detail in chapter 7 from the standpoint of Scripture. Bruner appears to be strongly influenced by Protestant Scholasticism in his denial of the dynamic, continuing nature of faith. This is evident in his extremely static-punctiliar view of faith. This contrasts to that view which sees faith as a principle by which the believer is justified in the forensic sense and as a continuing principle by which he or she lives (Rom. 1:17).

The Roman Catholic theological tradition also includes two distinct experiences with the Holy Spirit in the Christian life, but the emphasis is on the *growth process* in the Christian experience (McDonnell, 1980, pp. 38–39). The subsequent experience of the Spirit is viewed more in terms of the Spirit, who was given at water baptism, coming to the believer's conscious experience at a particular point in the Christian life. They consider this experience as a "new relationship to the Holy Spirit." However, it is sometimes seen as a new imparting of the Spirit in connection with a particular ministry in the Christian community (pp. 38–39). The Protestant neo-Pentecostal traditions that view the subsequent experience with the Holy Spirit in the sacramental sense as described here, as well as Roman Catholic tradition, may be classified as *actualization theologies*. Menzies states concerning these theologies, "The normal expectation of the believer is to bring to conscious experience what is incipient from baptism or new birth" (1978, p. 1).

There is no doubt that the impact of the Enlightenment on Western Christianity in the post-Reformation period has much to do with the difficulty of accepting the restoration of the Pentecostal-charismatic experience in contemporary Western Christianity. A Western difficulty in evaluating subsequent Pentecostal experiences is the theological paradigm inherited from the scholastic theology of the post-Reformation period. In this paradigm, the role of the Spirit is reduced to his work in connection with Scripture (almost exclusively with his work at the author-end). This in turn has eliminated the "witness of the Spirit" in verifying Christian experience, which was not only an emphasis in Reformation theology but also in the Acts of the Apostles. Biblical authority was, therefore, reduced to the "objective" written word. Its locus was wrongly conceived as the text of Scripture rather than the *witness of the Spirit* in conjunction with that written word *in the heart of the Christian*—the Reformation view. This deficiency in pneumatology leaves the impression that biblical authority is primarily *noetic* in nature (having to do with reflection, thinking, and propositional statements on the confrontation of being—inerrancy), rather than *ontic* (having to do with immediacy, presence, "there-ness," confrontation with reality—the witness of the Spirit). Biblical authority is ontic in nature in that it deals primarily with the witness of the Spirit to the word in the heart of the believer. Therefore, the tendency is to limit the Spirit's work to New Testament times, or at least to his inward work of regeneration and sanctification in the believer today.

In the conclusion to James Dunn's study, *Baptism in the Holy Spirit*, Dunn sees the Pentecostal emphasis on "experience" as a correction of the above Western distortion of pneumatology:

> Against the mechanical sacramentalism of extreme Catholicism and the dead biblicist orthodoxy of extreme Protestantism they [the Pentecostals] have shifted the focus of attention to the *experience* of the Spirit. Our examination of the NT evidence has shown that they were wholly justified in this. (1970, p. 225)

The counterpart of the Pentecostal experience of the Spirit is the scholastic theological articulation of the Spirit, which Dunn calls the "biblicist orthodoxy of extreme Protestantism." Dunn addresses the Westerner's difficulty with (or aversion to) the experiential and subjective:

> It is a sad commentary on the poverty of our own immediate experience of the Spirit that when we come across language in which the NT writers refer directly to the gift of the Spirit and to their experience of it, either we automatically refer it to the sacraments and can only give it meaning when we do so . . . or else we discount the experience described as too subjective and mystical in favor of a faith which is essentially an affirmation of biblical propositions, or else we in effect psychologize the Spirit out of existence. (pp. 225–26)

The notion of a subsequent experience with the Spirit collides with the Protestant orthodoxy represented by the post-Reformation period. The relatively new and sustained restoration of the full experience of the Holy Spirit in the history of the church via Pentecostalism is both a reaction to scholastic orthodoxy and a challenge to it. The above Western aversion to the subjective dimension of the Spirit in Protestantism (and evangelicalism) has a direct bearing on the evangelical criticisms of the Pentecostal claim to a subsequent experience with the Holy Spirit. Discussion of a "subsequent" charismatic experience of the Spirit uncovers a *Western disposition* that militates against renewal of this neglected dimension of the Spirit.

As mentioned previously, "renewal" reveals that "subsequence" is in one sense necessary, due to the *historical* restoration of the charismatic dimension of the Spirit's ministry in the contemporary church. A. J. Gordon also referred to this historical restoration of the Pentecostal experience. He stated that God has offered a higher position in this matter of the experience of the Spirit than the church has been able to occupy. He believed that the full experience of the Spirit was, and is, offered to each person at conversion, and that it is only from want of faith that a subsequent experience of the Holy Spirit becomes needful (Gordon, 1964, p. 86). Normally, the Pentecostal experience is received when one is convinced it is a valid dimension of the full experience of the Spirit and there is "expectancy," an important dimension of faith. In terms of a renewal in the history of the church, therefore, the Pentecostal experience *is* an experience "historically subsequent" to conversion for Christianity in general.

The above Protestant explanation of "subsequence" is nearly identical to that of Roman Catholic theologians on the subject. They stress the charismatic experience of the Spirit in terms of renewal, both historical and personal. Speaking for an international group of Roman Catholic theologians, Kilian McDonnell states that the differences between the early Christian community and the community of Christians in the contemporary church is to be found in a "difference of awareness, expectation and openness" (1980, p. 28). Roman Catholics strongly emphasize that the charismatic renewal does not mean the church or Christians receive something they do not already possess, but rather "the renewal points to an expanded awareness, and this awareness and expectancy affect experience and the total life of the church" (p. 36). While it is recognized that the Spirit is sovereign and free, it is pointed out that he ordinarily deals with individuals "at the point of where they are, and that subjective dispositions in some sense affect experience" (p. 30). Where communities do not expect the Holy Spirit's outward-charismatic ministry, that ministry is not usually operative.

In terms of awareness and expectancy, faith is especially crucial for those holding to "actualization theologies." The "subsequence theologies" of classical Pentecostalism also stress faith and the already-present, indwelling Holy Spirit in the Christian life. This is contrary to the supposition of many non-Pentecostals. But "subsequence" is interpreted not only as a *historical necessity* for the contemporary church in general, but also as *personal necessity* for every Christian. Pentecostals believe that the experience of the full spectrum of the Holy Spirit's ministry is the *normative* Christian experience, for both the early and contemporary church.

[handwritten annotation: I feel like miracles will happen in front of a believer for God to build a type of repoir with the person (His child).]

A Normative Experience

Classical Pentecostals would say the Pentecostal distinctive is a conscious-crisis experience with the Holy Spirit called the baptism in the Holy Spirit. It will be clear in the description of that experience by classical Pentecostals that "subsequence" is conceived in a different sense than the mere historical renewal of the Pentecostal experience to the contemporary church in general. They believe that this subsequent experience is normative for contemporary Christian experience. The theological underpinnings of this view were discussed in chapter 2 and the new preface to this edition: Pentecostal-charismatic movements are renewals of the gospel of the kingdom of God.

The Assemblies of God statement on the Pentecostal experience is discussed here in order to bring into focus a classical description:

2. (7) THE BAPTISM IN THE HOLY GHOST

All believers are entitled to and should ardently expect and earnestly seek the promise of the Father, the baptism in the Holy Ghost and fire, according to the command of our Lord Jesus Christ. This was the normal experience of all in the early Christian Church. With it comes the enduement of power for life and service, the bestowment of the gifts and their uses in the work of the ministry (Luke 24:49; Acts 1:4–8; 1 Cor. 12:1–31). This experience is distinct from and subsequent to the experience of the new birth (Acts 8:12–17; 10:44–46; 11:14–16; 15:7–9). With the baptism in the Holy Ghost come such experience as an over-flowing fullness of the Spirit (John 7:37–39; Acts 4:8), an intensified consecration to God and dedication to His work (Acts 2:42), and a more active love for Christ, for His word, and for the lost (Mark 16:20).

(8) THE EVIDENCE OF THE BAPTISM OF THE HOLY GHOST

The baptism of believers in the Holy Ghost is witnessed by the initial physical sign of speaking with other tongues as the Spirit of God gives them utterance (Acts 2:4). The speaking in tongues in this instance is the same in essence as the gift of tongues (1 Cor. 12:4–10, 28) but different in purpose and use. (Menzies, 1971, p. 388)

Before addressing the issue of "subsequence" in Pentecostalism, a comment on the nature and purpose of creedal or confessional statements, such as this Assemblies of God statement, is useful. The Assemblies of God statement, "The Baptism in the Holy Ghost," like all creedal statements, focuses on particular problems, issues, or needs in the context of contemporary Christian thought and life. As such, creeds can never be viewed apart from the context of their authors or their existential historical moment. Nor should they be viewed as statements of "pure" theological truth or content. They are "contextualizations" of Christian truth, serving the church in its contemporary effort to understand the faith, to articulate it in accordance with that understanding, and to obey it in practice. Such statements *do* focus on biblical content, but they also have a particular focus on the context of contemporary belief and practice in a particular historical moment. They are *selective* in nature and purpose as opposed to being *comprehensive* in nature and purpose.

Creedal statements, then, are the result of the church's response to Scripture in the light of particular issues and problems. In other words, they are the result of fresh theologizing on the basis of

Scripture about issues arising out of a particular historical context. Regardless of the particular ecclesiastical confession involved, such statements are never absolute or complete statements, nor are they perennial in nature. This is true, not only because of their contextual focus but also due to the imperfect (though not necessarily incorrect) nature of all human articulations of divine truth (1 Cor. 12:8). From time to time, therefore, they must be updated and sharpened through fresh theologizing on the basis of Scripture and the changing contextual problems facing the church. Chapter 5 discusses this "reinterpretation of dogma" phenomenon in detail.

With this introductory statement concerning the nature and purpose of confessional statements in general, the Assemblies of God statement can be analyzed in terms of its nature and purpose. The Pentecostal distinctive that the statement articulates are those scriptural points about the Pentecostal experience that tend to preserve its uniqueness in a period of controversy. The *normative* nature of the experience ("all believers . . . normal experience of all in the early Christian Church . . . power for life and service") and the *distinct* nature of the experience (subsequence and evidence) are emphasized. The statement's purpose in preserving the distinctive nature of the Pentecostal experience is evident, as well as its reactionary-apologetic nature, in that a separate article exists for the evidence of the Pentecostal experience.

The distinct way the Pentecostal experience is described in the Assemblies of God statement is due to the historical controversy surrounding the experience and its distinctive—tongues. Such controversy within the movement was settled in the General Council of 1918 (Menzies, 1971, p. 129). Menzies states concerning this distinctive, "Many evangelicals have accepted the concept of a filling with the Holy Spirit as an experience subsequent to conversion, but the Pentecostal touchstone has always been on the definition of the evidence" (p. 125). Controversy was not so much over the fruit of the Spirit, which is also evidence of a genuine baptism of the Spirit, but on the "initial outward evidence" of the experience. Menzies states that the point of clarity on the evidence of the baptism in the Holy Spirit was not "merely sectarian narrowness"; rather, the motive was the preservation of a doctrine believed to be "basic to a full-orbed New Testament Church" (p. 125). The statement, then, should be understood in the context of its purpose—to preserve the distinctiveness of the Pentecostal experience—which in terms of the New Testament witness involved the outward charismatic ministry of the Spirit as well as his inward life-giving work.

Bruner's analysis of an earlier Assemblies of God statement focuses on the points above (subsequence and evidence) and a third point ("conditions") in receiving the experience (Bruner, 1970, pp. 61, 87–88, 111). However, the third point ("conditions") appears to be arbitrarily extracted from the statement. We might ask, "Why does Bruner arbitrarily separate "earnestly seek" from "entitled to" and "ardently expect" in the same sentence from the Assemblies of God statement on the baptism of the Holy Ghost? Bruner reads into the Keswickian-oriented statement the alleged "conditions" in order to carry out his polemic against the explicit Arminianism in the Wesleyan-Holiness tradition in Pentecostalism (p. 61). Furthermore, "conditions" are not indicated in the earlier Assemblies of God statement. Rather, the normativity of the Pentecostal experience, in terms of its availability and value for all Christians, is expressed. Bruner makes the statement carry more theological weight than its authors intended it to carry.

The relatively concise statement on the baptism of the Holy Spirit and its evidence is not intended to be a full statement on pneumatology. The doctrinal statement centers on the task of preserving the Pentecostal experience as a distinct conscious-crisis experience, in which the full spectrum of the Holy Spirit's ministry is kept in focus. This "preservation purpose" is evident in the Assemblies of God statement. One could say, then, that the matter of "subsequence" focuses not so much on the *time-sequence* as on the *full experience of the Holy Spirit* (of course, a logical subsequence is not in question here, that the Spirit's regenerating work logically precedes his charismatic work). The statement emphasizes the Pentecostal experience as "distinct" from conversion; it is on the neglected dimension of the Spirit's work in salvation history.

In referring to Dunn's study on the baptism in the Holy Spirit, Gordon Fee speaks somewhat indirectly to this idea of the full experience of the Spirit:

In a carefully argued exegetical study of all the relevant passages in Acts, Dunn (*Baptism in the Holy Spirit*) concluded that for Luke the real evidence (and chief element) of Christian experience was the presence of the Spirit. What seems to be important for Luke in this narrative is that the validation (and completion) of Christian experience in the initial spread beyond Jerusalem is tied to the Jerusalem church and signified by a dynamic quality similar to theirs. If Dunn is correct, and it surely is defensible exegesis, then the concept of subsequence is irrelevant. What is of consequence is the experiential, dynamic quality of the gift of the Spirit. (1976, p. 130)

The problem with subsequence appears to be asking questions of a text that is speaking of something else. The element of "time sequence" with regard to subsequence is not the important issue, or Luke's intention. Rather, the validation and completion of Christian experience is.

Fee then observes that if "subsequence" as "distinct from and subsequent to" cannot be established as being "taught" in the New Testament as the pattern for Christian experience, then "there is a pattern is Acts which *may* be derived not only from historical precedent but also from the intent of Luke and Paul" (1976, p. 130). Following Dunn's lead, Fee describes that pattern as focusing on the experience of the Spirit as a chief element in the process of Christian conversion, as well as its *validating element*. He states that in Acts the presence or coming of the Spirit had a dynamic, charismatic nature (p. 131). He adds to this observation that Pentecostals see speaking in tongues as a repeated pattern in the New Testament (p. 131).

About the Pentecostal attempt to preserve the dynamic dimension of the Spirit's ministry, Fee states:

> If in his attempt to recapture this New Testament pattern, the Pentecostal saw the dynamic element as "distinct from and subsequent to," he should not thereby be faulted. The fault perhaps lay with the church which no longer normally expected or experienced life in the Spirit in a dynamic way. (p. 131)

The New Testament witness emphasizes a pattern of dynamic, Spirit-oriented Christian initiation that, in the eyes of the Pentecostal, is being restored in the contemporary Pentecostal movement. The presence of examples of a subsequent charismatic experience in Acts, whether exegetically sound or not, corresponds with contemporary experience. Christians *are* experiencing a subsequent, dynamic experience with the Spirit, which *is* identical to that of the first-century church!

The parallel between the contemporary charismatic experience of the Spirit and that of the first-century church, however, may be more than coincidental. Luke's reason for recording those examples of a subsequent charismatic experience of the Spirit, where Christians did not experience the full dimension of the Spirit immediately upon conversion, could be that he intended to emphasize that the full reception or experience of the Spirit was *normative.* The same reason why contemporary Christians do not experience the full dimension of the Spirit—a matter of faith-awareness, faith-expectancy, or faith-openness—could be the key to the interpretation of the often quoted "subsequence experiences" in Acts (8:12–17; 9:1–19; 19:1–7). Luke intends by these incidents to emphasize the necessity of experiencing the full dimension of the Spirit's ministry—the dynamic charismatic dimension included—even if it is hindered for some reason. Imperfect knowledge and dispositions, such as those mentioned above, would prevent the normal experience of the Spirit (Montague, 1976, pp. 293–94).

The outward dynamic dimension of the experience of the Spirit, in terms of the Spirit's witness, appears to have played an important role in validating Christian experience, especially as the gospel moved across cultural and prejudicial frontiers (Acts 3, 9, 10, 19). Green sees Luke's purpose in the problematic account of the Samaritans (Acts 8) as an effort to stress the links between the church at Jerusalem and the expanding circles of Christian outreach. The distance in miles was not as dangerous to the potential loss of unity in the early church as the "cultural distance" the gospel traversed. Green suggests that God did not give the supernatural manifestations of the Spirit—tongues and prophecy—to the Samaritans at once upon their conversion, so that Jerusalem representatives could come down and express solidarity with them. He explains:

> It was not so much an authorisation from Jerusalem or an extension of the Jerusalem church, as a divine veto on schism in the infant

church, a schism which could have slipped almost unnoticed into the Christian fellowship, as converts from the two sides of the "Samaritan curtain" found Christ without finding each other. (1975, pp. 138–39)

Green, therefore, states that the account is recorded for the purpose that it is not typical for Christian initiation (p. 137). The outward evidence of the Spirit's coming was that which validated Christian experience in such cases and was the means for preventing schism that might arise on the basis of the gospel's diverse cultural expressions as it took root in the cultures of Gentile peoples.

One may well ask why the Pentecost event itself (and the disciples' experience of the fullness of the Spirit) is not used here for the discussion of "subsequence." The Pentecost event marked the ushering in of the era of the Spirit in salvation history in which the full experience of the Spirit is made possible for all Christians. The disciples' example, while clearly illustrating the full experience of the Spirit, does not provide a normative "subsequence" pattern for Christian initiation now. Their unique position in bridging two eras of salvation history prevents this; they were with Jesus and saw the power of the kingdom in his ministry, as well as experienced it themselves pre-Pentecost. Their example *does,* however, support a distinctive, conscious-crisis Pentecostal experience for the church today. The example of the disciples is valid according to the hermeneutical principle for the *type* of experience but not the *time* of the experience. Dunn is correct when he states concerning their example:

> The epochal significance of Pentecost raises the whole course of salvation-history to a new plane. As the beginning of the new age of the Spirit, the new covenant, the Church, it is what happened at Pentecost and not before which is normative for those who would enter that age, covenant and Church. The (pre-Christian) experience of the 120 prior to Pentecost can *never* provide a pattern for the experience of new Christians now. (1970, p. 53)

Dunn does not deny that what happened in the lives of the disciples prior to Pentecost is not applicable today, following an extreme dispensationalism. He merely points out that the disciples occupied a unique position in the transition of dispensations (old and new), and that the era ushered in by Pentecost is the normative context for viewing Christian initiation in the age of the Spirit. He adds this qualifying statement to his previous statement,

> In one sense, therefore, Pentecost can never be repeated—for the new age is here and cannot be ushered in again. But in another sense Pentecost, or rather the *experience of Pentecost*, can and must be repeated in the experience of all who would become Christians. As the day of Pentecost was once the doorway into the new age, so entry into the new age can only be made through that doorway, that is through receiving the same Spirit and the same baptism in the Spirit as did the 120. (pp. 53–54; emphasis mine)

Although Dunn means by this statement that each Christian today does experience "Pentecost" at conversion, in that he or she is initiated into the same Spirit, the Pentecostal would find no fault with the above statement if it referred to the distinct, charismatic, dynamic, repeatable Pentecostal experience of Acts 2:4 today.

Dunn's view of the Pentecost event in the course of salvation history emphasizes the matter of subsequence in terms of a distinct, dynamic experience of the Spirit that is repeatable. But the event is not viewed as a pattern of Christian experience where "subsequence" is viewed as a *normative time sequence* for contemporary Christian initiation. In their unique salvation history position, bridging the old and the new eras, the disciples' Pentecostal experience is clearly subsequent to their conversion. However, the "Gentile Pentecost" (Acts 10) does not involve disciples in a period of salvation history transition (of the same sort) like the one hundred twenty. Therefore, their baptism in the Holy Spirit (for example, Cornelius's household) is not a "necessary" subsequent experience. The Holy Spirit came on Cornelius and his household *while they were listening to Peter's sermon* (Acts 10:44); there is no reference to them having believed, that belief and reception of the Spirit with the outward evidence of speaking in other tongues (Acts 10:47) was simultaneous. It appears that Dunn argues for the Cornelius-type, simultaneous, and dynamic experience of the Spirit, but without the outward charismatic evidence. Though the Pentecostal experience of Caesarea was simultaneous with conversion, and in spite of it taking place in the unlikely Gentile context of God-fearers, its validity is unquestioned when related to the Jewish Christians in Jerusalem. This is a significant point to recognize. The witness of the Spirit in the *evidential manner of his coming* at Caesarea was identical to that of his coming at Jerusalem. The Jewish Pentecost, therefore, represents that "normative pattern" in terms of the distinct, charismatic type of experience with the Spirit; it has validation-value for Christian initiation. The Gentile Pentecost, on the other hand, could represent the normative pattern in terms of time-sequence for Christian initiation today, post-Pentecost. Affective dispositions and deficient knowledge, the same factors that prevented the full experience of the Spirit in the occurrences in Acts, could be a major reason why the Gentile Pentecost is not the normative pattern for common Christian experience today. People just do not *expect* a Cornelius-type baptism of the Holy Spirit at the point of conversion today. What if they did?

Dunn also views the baptism of Jesus at Jordan in a salvation history context, and is especially supportive of the Pentecostal's view of a distinct experience of the Spirit apart from conversion. But for Dunn it is supportive in the Keswickian sense, as an enduement of power for service. However, Dunn argues that "subsequence" with respect to Jesus' experience of the Spirit at Jordan, while hermeneutically possible in terms of the personal experience of Jesus, is a secondary matter (1970, p. 24). The primary matter is the event as a pivotal point in salvation history. Dunn states:

> In other words, we are dealing not so much with stages in the life of Jesus, which belong to the same dispensation of salvation-history and so can be appealed to as the pattern for all who belong to the same dispensation; we are dealing rather with stages in salvation-history itself. The experience of Jesus at Jordan is far more than something merely personal—*it is a unique moment in history: the beginning of a new epoch in salvation-history*—the beginning, albeit in a restricted sense, of the End-time, the messianic age, the new covenant. (p. 24; emphasis mine)

Commenting on how the first baptism of the Spirit (Jesus') could be taken as typical for all later Spirit-baptisms, Dunn states:

> Pentecostals are right to recognize that Jesus' anointing with the Spirit was what equipped him for his messianic ministry of healing and

teaching (Acts 10:38). This empowering for service should not however be taken as the primary purpose of the anointing—it is only a corollary to it. The baptism in the Spirit, in other words, is not primarily to equip the (already) Christian for service; rather its function is to initiate the individual into the new age and covenant, to "Christ" (= anoint) him, and in so doing to equip him for life and service in that new age and covenant. (p. 32)

In view of the sometimes crude and theologically inaccurate "subsequent" experience (as though prior to that time Jesus did not experience the fullness of the Spirit!), Dunn's emphasis is helpful. He states:

The descent of the Spirit on Jesus effects not so much a change in Jesus, his person or his status, as the beginning of a new stage in salvation-history. The thought is not so much of Jesus becoming what he was not before, but of Jesus entering where he was not before—a new epoch in God's plan of redemption. It is not so much that Jesus became what he was not before, but that history became what it was not before. (pp. 28–29)

The baptism of the Spirit still can be conceived as an *initiation* (belated, of course) to the new age. The Christian is ushered into the *charismatic dimension* of the Spirit's ministry. Initiation into that dimension is also an anointing and empowering for service. The Pentecostal, therefore, sees in Dunn's statement above a certain redundancy, both actual and conceptual. For the person baptized in the Spirit, the experience is *both* an initiation to the potential of the age of the Spirit *and* an anointing or empowering for service in that age. Of course, the Pentecostal experience thus conceived does not involve a "quantitative" reception of "more" of the Spirit. This is only possible figuratively speaking, not theologically speaking. Rather, it represents a qualitatively different relationship with the Spirit and should be viewed as the Spirit getting more of the Christian (in terms of responding to the Spirit, being led by him, "walking in the Spirit," and so on), not vice versa. The emphasis is on the Spirit's control of the believer, due to his or her new awareness, openness, and expectancy.

The Pentecostal's claim that the Pentecostal experience is normative finds strong support in the New Testament. It emphasizes the "full" experience of the Spirit, both his inward life-giving ministry and his outward charismatic ministry. The "given" of an historical renewal of a neglected dimension of the Spirit's ministry has forced the issue of "subsequence" to the fore. The Assemblies of God statement on the baptism of the Holy Spirit shows the results of the doctrine being contextualized in a period of controversy. The issue of subsequence is tied to the purpose of preserving the full experience of the Spirit. The dimension that is neglected is in focus in the statement—the outward, charismatic dimension. The distinct, conscious-crisis experience that is believed to usher one into a new dimension of the Spirit's ministry—the baptism of the Holy Spirit—is that which is in focus.

The historical renewal of the Pentecostal experience and the effort to preserve its distinctive nature has caused Pentecostals to emphasize the evidence of "subsequence" in Acts. Bias in Western culture and worldview, which tends toward an emphasis of discrete categories and time sequences, perhaps has much to do with the attention paid to the subsequence issue as well. Westerners tend to "see" more categories and divisions in the holistically oriented biblical material than is warranted. "Subsequence" in the New Testament witness, however, is connected with Luke's purpose in emphasizing the complete experience of the Holy Spirit's ministry. The time element does not appear to be in the category of normativity but rather in that of abnormality, due to various "subjective dispositions" on the part of believers that prevented the full experience of the Spirit. The complete experience of the Spirit in the New Testament is normative, and it is concrete in nature. It is a conscious experience and it is accompanied with charismatic phenomena.

Their Message: "God with Us"

In dealing with the subject of "evidence" for the Pentecostal experience, or just supernatural evidence in contemporary Christian experience in general, the following questions are important. First, "Should there be evidence for this further experience with the Holy Spirit?" Second, and more fundamentally, "Should there be further evidence for the Christian experience *at all* beyond the written word of God?" Finally, "Should the initial evidence for the Pentecostal experience be speaking in tongues?" The first two questions are fundamental in evaluating evangelical criticisms of the Pentecostal movement. The third question is only of secondary theological importance for many evangelicals. The first two questions address a prevalent theological orientation among conservative evangelicals—that of Protestant Scholasticism. This orientation is the antithesis to the theological orientation of Pentecostal theology.

The matter of the initial outward evidence of the baptism of the Holy Spirit has been reserved for discussion under this section dealing with the unique message of Pentecostalism. But it is not here because Pentecostalism's unique message is speaking in tongues. It is appropriate to treat it at this point, because speaking in tongues is the phenomenon that so commonly represents the dynamic experience of the Spirit in Pentecostalism. That the Spirit's coming in the Pentecostal experience is an *evidential* coming points to both a *chief criticism* of the movement and its *chief contribution*.

"Evidence": Bankrupt Faith or New Testament Faith?

The chief criticism mentioned above concerns the Pentecostal claim that the baptism of the Holy Spirit is accompanied by the initial evidence of speaking in other tongues. Often the criticism is part and parcel of dispensational theology that limits outward Pentecostal-charismatic type phenomena and the miraculous to the apostolic period only. To critics holding such theology, the notion of "evidence" reveals a bankrupt faith on the part of the Pentecostal. They say that one should be content with the authority of *the written word* alone. This statement, at first glance, sounds quite Reformation-based. But such a view reveals the influence of *post-Reformation* Protestant Scholasticism. It points to the absence of statements regarding the "witness of the Spirit" and the outward charismatic working of the Spirit in conservative evangelical theology.

The criticism of the "evidential" coming of the Spirit reveals a weakness in evangelical theology, and also brings to the fore the unique Pentecostal contribution (unique in terms of contemporary evangelical theology). The Pentecostal would simply reply to the evangelical charge that the doctrine of evidence suggests a weak faith, "Isn't Christianity the demonstration of God's power?" Or one might ask, "Has not the kingdom of God broken through into this present age?" Or perhaps more specifically, one might ask, "Isn't the Holy Spirit's witness, both inward and outward, to be expected today?" The Pentecostal contribution, therefore, concerns the dynamic experience of the Spirit and his active witness in validating Christian experience today.

In the Introduction, this emphasis on the dynamic dimension of the Christian faith was referred to as the "eighth principle," which Pentecostalism adds to the seven evangelical principles. Pentecostalism believes in the continuing activity of God today by means of the inward and outward ministry of the Holy Spirit. It is concerned with the ontic principle of theology, the immediacy of the presence of God, the "there-ness" of God (God with us) in Christian experience and mission. Pentecostals see the validity of their Pentecostal experience today, its contemporaneity, to be founded on biblical theology and the witness of the Spirit. They are not reluctant to admit the latter, as it is together with the former a renewal of a Reformation principle—the indivisible nature of word and Spirit. The notion of the Spirit validating Christian experience in contemporary times is a New Testament concept, amply illustrated in the Acts of the Apostles.

The Pentecostal's emphasis on the evidential coming of the Spirit presents a bothersome theme for conservative evangelical theology. Pentecostalism's pneumatology brings a pervasive dynamic orientation to its theology as a whole. The evangelical criticism concerning "evidence" points to the uniqueness of the Pentecostal message itself. It points to the dynamic nature of the Christian experience, as opposed to the cerebral "faith-alone" nature of Protestant Scholasticism. The distinctive Pentecostal message, therefore, brings a corrective to the pervasive influence of post-Reformation Scholasticism in evangelical theology. Pentecostalism's message of "God with us," the renewal of the dynamic experiential dimension of the Christian faith, is a corrective to the Western distortion. Under the influence of the Enlightenment, an expression of the faith arose that reduced it to a noetic, rational system of belief, effecting a separation of word and Spirit. At the root of the evangelical criticism of Pentecostalism, therefore, is a theological orientation that rejects the notion of "evidence" as either superfluous or anti-faith. The problem is with evidence *per se*, not merely the evidence of tongues.

Of course, speaking of the "eighth principle"—the dynamic dimension of the Christian faith—is just another way of saying that Pentecostalism brings fresh attention to the activity of the Holy Spirit in Christian experience and mission today. If its formally articulated theology does not do so, the phenomenon of the Pentecostal movement itself brings to light the neglect of pneumatology in Western theology. The doctrines of biblical revelation and biblical authority are in focus when discussing the "evidence" of the Pentecostal experience. But a scholastic view of these doctrines is ill-equipped to evaluate Pentecostal phenomena. I have already illustrated its inadequacy in confronting certain issues in contemporary mission theology (e.g., the African Independent Church Movement).

The impact of Protestant Scholasticism in evangelical theology is clear when Bernard Ramm explains that in his research for the book *The Pattern of Religious Authority*, he found that the doctrine of the internal witness of the Holy Spirit had almost disappeared from evangelical literature and theology (1959, p. 7). The dynamic nature of both biblical revelation and biblical authority are important with regard to the Pentecostal doctrine of evidence. Pentecostals focus on the activity and witness of the Spirit at "this end" of biblical revelation, not only in connection with the authors of Scripture in the apostolic period.

The contrast of the theological orientations given above may be illustrated by comparing the historic Reformed view of biblical revelation with the Reformed scholastic view. (A chart showing this contrast can be found in the Appendix.) The diverse approaches to Scripture illustrate the contrasting theological orientations discussed here. The historic Reformed view emphasized the *function* of Scripture in its saving purpose. Scripture was dynamic in nature; it was enlivened by the Spirit. The Reformed scholastic view was preoccupied with the *form* of Scripture, the written text, and was static in nature. It represented a rationalistic approach to Scripture that resulted in the concept of the dynamic word of God being reduced to its written form only (Pomerville, 1980, p. 95). These contrasts are important to recognize so that the Pentecostal orientation to biblical revelation and authority may be brought into focus. A principle contrast in the chart is the activity of the Holy Spirit in the historic Reformed view and his absence in the Reformed scholastic view, with the exception of his work with the authors of Scripture. In its dynamic view of biblical revelation and authority, then, Pentecostalism follows in the tradition of historic Reformation theology.

In Bruner's *Theology of the Holy Spirit: The Pentecostal Experience and the New Testament Witness,* he argues against the doctrine of the initial evidence of the baptism of the Holy Spirit and the supposed necessity of evidence (the Pentecostal's requirement of evidence). The argument centers on the Wesleyan-Holiness stream of Pentecostalism, which in Bruner's view violates *sola fide* most. The inclusion of "evidence" in the Assemblies of God doctrinal statement on the baptism of the Holy Ghost, in his view, detracts from the Reformation formula of saving faith, or *sola fide* (1970, p. 115). The idea of evidence *per se* receives specific attention in the argument and is always in a pejorative context. The experiential dimension is also invalid with respect to a verification of Christian experience (p. 82). Only propositional statements from the text of Scripture are valid in this regard. Anything outside of "simple faith" in Christ is, in Bruner's view, an occasion for criticism. The scholastic, rationalistic view of *sola fide* in Bruner's argument, however, is not that of the Reformation (see chart in the Appendix).

In Bruner's view, "evidence-less" faith is what *sola fide* and *simplex fide* (apart from the evidence of Scripture, that is) signify. All of this discussion, however, is not about the conversion experience. It is in connection with the Pentecostal's subsequent experience of the baptism of the Holy Spirit and its evidence. The whole discussion against "necessity" of evidence made in connection with saving faith is imposed on the theological issue of evidence in regard to the Pentecostal experience. Not only is faith held to be "evidence-less" in terms of personal conversion, but the activity of God the Holy Spirit in contemporary times is also thought to be "evidence-less." This reveals not only a very static view of faith but also a scholastic, noetic view of revelation and biblical authority. An underlying theological orientation shapes the theological argument—Protestant Scholasticism.

George Peters' evaluation of the twentieth-century revival in Indonesia, *Indonesian Revival: Focus on Timor*, represents an argument against the miraculous and New Testament charismatic phenomena in contemporary times. It reflects Peters' dispensational theology. However, the same underlying theological orientation that was evident in Bruner's criticism of Pentecostalism's "evidence" doctrine is found in Peters' evaluation of the Timor revival. To expect New Testament phenomena, or to show an interest in the supernatural, is interpreted as anti-faith. According to Peters, it is an indication of weak faith! He states:

> No aspect of the Timor revival has received more attention and wider publicity than the miracles that are supposed to have accompanied it. Such interest may be the result of massive publicity, but in general it seems to me that this unusual attention to the miraculous indicates that *American Christians* are so destitute of spiritual reality that they look for the spectacular to substantiate and bolster their own faith in the truth of the Gospel. The faith of the average Christian is evidently so bankrupt, and his life so empty, that he needs this kind of demonstration. (1973, p. 57)

Peters' position on present-day miracles is that they are a *possibility*, but not necessary or probable (pp. 50–60, 62). This position is maintained throughout the debunking of the Timor revival. It is also maintained in spite of his acknowledgement that there is no conclusive New Testament exegetical evidence that would preclude such supernatural manifestations. Nor, he states, would any New Testament truth be violated if all the miracles of the book of Acts were to be repeated today (pp. 58, 60).

The scholastic dichotomy of word and Spirit and Scholasticism's limitation of the Spirit's role in contemporary supernatural manifestations are evident when Peters states:

> If miracles are made *necessary* for our age to verify the power of the Gospel of Jesus Christ, we show on the one hand the bankruptcy of our faith in the Word of God written, and on the other hand we reflect negatively upon the sufficiency of God's past revelation and manifestations. (p. 60)

As in Bruner's argument, the issue boils down to the objection of any evidence for Christian experience beyond the written word. The outward ministry of the Holy Spirit is admitted as a "possibility" but not a "necessity," or even a "probability" today. This "domestication of the Spirit" is not absolute, however, as Peters mentions an exception to this dispensational rule. The exception would be when the gospel is introduced to a people for the first time—that is, pioneer situations in missions (Peters, 1973, p. 60). Another exception would be to counteract the "magical miracles" of an animistic people (p. 71). In view of the thousands of unreached people groups among the two and a half billion people who are powerfully and pervasively influenced by animism, these "exceptions" appear to address the task of evangelism among the majority of the non-Christian world! According to Peters' own argument, then, supernatural phenomena would not be the exception but the contemporary *rule*. At the writing of this second edition of *The Third Force in Missions*, historical perspective has allowed us to see that such charismatic phenomena in Pentecostal movements among the animist peoples of the Southern Hemisphere indeed has been the rule.

While the miraculous is never spoken of in normative terms in Peters' argument, but only to meet the needs of animistic peoples, it appears that dispensational theology alone is not the reason for his reluctance to admit to the probability of supernatural New Testament phenomena. In spite of the clear references to such phenomena in the New Testament, and his own admission as to their biblical nature, Peters chooses to explain away the supernatural phenomena of the Timor revival. He attributes them for the most part to the "mentality" of non-Western peoples, or to nativism (1973, pp. 63–71). Having lived in East Timor for two years, it was quite evident to me that the society that experienced revival during the second wave of the charismatic movement had been a strongly influenced *Roman Catholic society* since the early sixteenth century. Peters' prejudice against Pentecostal phenomena echoes Sundkler's "bridge to paganism" view—the somewhat astounding matter of attributing supernatural phenomena in a non-Western expression of Christianity to nativism, rather than to a New Testament expression of the faith. The pervasive and subtle influence of Protestant Scholasticism appears to be part of the reason (along with a latent prejudice against Pentecostalism and a latent ethnocentrism).

A theological orientation that sees revelation as static in nature appears to control Peters' evaluation of the miraculous phenomena of the Timor revival. Anything beyond the rational-propositional proof of the written word of God, in terms of Christian experience, is seen to militate against an alleged Reformation "faith-alone" stance. Such a position, however, is not representative of the Reformation but of post-Reformation Scholasticism. *Sola scriptura* and *sola fide* in the context of the Reformation do not even address the matter of the supernatural evidence of the Holy Spirit in his outward ministry among men and women.

"The Bible-Only Mentality" Whuunt!

Is Scripture the only evidence for validating Christian experience? Does *sola scriptura* mean that the only criterion for validating Christian experience is the biblical text? What of the period prior to the writing of the New Testament? Were not the oral tradition that was taught and the preaching of the kerygma authoritative? Was it not the word of God? What of the whole prophetic tradition of the Old Testament? What of the Reformation doctrine of the *testimonium*, the witness of the Spirit (Ramm, 1959)? Would none of these constitute the "word of God," due to the fact that the revelation was not *written*? Is the concept of biblical authority to be tied only to the text of Scripture? All of the above questions are leveled at a view of revelation that is static and tends to limit divine revelation to its objective dimension—Scripture.

In his article "Is 'Scripture Alone' the Essence of Christianity?" Bernard Ramm outlines a scholastic view of biblical revelation

[handwritten margin note: Scripture is 'God-breathed'. The breath into my life filters through my life experiences.]

prominent in conservative evangelicalism. He calls it "the Bible-only mentality":

> The Bible-only mentality confuses the *sola scriptura* of the Reformation with criteria of theological scholarship. The Bible-only mentality makes the record of revelation more primordial than the original revelation; it makes the history Scripture reports of second order to the scriptural report. The Bible-only mentality in principle reduces theology to the simplicities of proof-texting theological convictions. . . . Finally, a Bible-only mentality virtually equates spiritual reality with the text of Scripture itself, whereas the Scripture is a pointer to or witness to that reality. (1977, p. 116)

Ramm speaks of a reality, a dynamic acting of God beyond his written word. He is not demeaning Scripture. Rather he is putting it into the perspective of God's dynamic activity among humans. A reductionistic view of revelation, "the Bible-only mentality," is evident with Bruner and Peters when they discuss the matter of supernatural evidence in contemporary times. Equating the text of Scripture with spiritual reality eliminates the Reformation *testimonium* and effects a separation of word and Spirit. Ramm states elsewhere concerning the *testimonium* (the ontic witness of the Spirit), "The *testimonium* may occur wherever God's truth exists. It is not bound to truth in written form" (1959, p. 66).

Sola scriptura is a phrase coming out of theological disputations with Roman Catholic theologians on the subject of the ultimate reference of authority. The debate contrasted the authority of the church with the authority of Scripture. It did *not* contrast the authority of Scripture with the authority of the Holy Spirit! *Sola scriptura* was never intended to mean Scripture alone in the sense of alone or apart from the Spirit. The Bible-only mentality eliminates the witness of the Spirit in the doctrine of revelation, replacing it with rational proofs and argumentation about Scripture's authority. The witness of the Spirit and faith are subordinated to human reason in that mentality; the ontic principle is replaced by the noetic.

Reformation theology had no such dichotomy of word and Spirit. Calvin strongly affirmed the priority of the testimony of the Spirit:

> The highest proof of Scripture derives in general from the fact that God in person speaks in it . . . we ought to seek our conviction in a higher place than human reasons, judgements, or conjectures, that is in the secret testimony of the Spirit . . . the testimony of the Spirit is more excellent than all reason. (Institutes I.vii.4)

It is clear from Calvin's doctrine of Scripture's self-authenticating nature that he views the word and the Spirit in an inseparable relationship. He said concerning this doctrine,

> Let this point therefore stand: that those whom the Holy Spirit has inwardly taught truly rest upon Scripture, and that Scripture indeed is self-authenticated; hence, it is not right to subject it to proof and reasoning. And the certainty it deserves with us, it attains by the testimony of the Spirit. For even if it wins reverence for itself by its own majesty, it seriously affects us only when it is sealed upon our hearts through the Spirit. Therefore, illumined by his power, we believe neither by our own nor by anyone else's judgment that Scripture is from God; but above human judgment we affirm with utter certainty . . . that it has flowed to us from the very mouth of God by the ministry of men. (Institutes I.vii.5)

Furthermore, Calvin believed that the preaching of the word of God *was* the word of God in dynamic living form. Preaching was another form of God's accommodation, a way that God condescended to communicate by means of human instruments. Clearly, Calvin viewed the Holy Spirit as active at the preaching-end of Scripture just as he was present at the writing-end of Scripture. God was active at both ends of biblical revelation; word and Spirit are inseparable (Pomerville, 1980, p. 47).

It is that activity of God the Holy Spirit at *this contemporary end of revelation* that points to the distinctive of the Pentecostal movement. This emphasis on the activity of God in turn points to the movement's capacity for giving contemporary mission direction. The two criticisms from Bruner and Peters of the movement's claim to an "evidential" coming of the Spirit revealed the influence of Protestant Scholasticism on their view of Christian experience and mission. It is a view that severely distorts the nature of the Christian faith itself and impairs its impact among non-Western peoples. The essence of Christianity is not merely intellectual commitment to a written revelation. It concerns a dynamic encounter with God the Holy Spirit in connection with that written revelation. Revelation concerns not merely knowledge and information; it refers to the *activity* of God the Holy Spirit (Kraft, 1979, pp. 179–80).

The Pentecostal's emphasis on evidence, therefore, is not due to bankrupt faith. It is due to the Pentecostal's emphasis on the dynamic experience of the Spirit. The evidential coming of the Spirit, the gospel with signs following (Mark 16:20), is not only a valid means for authenticating Christian experience, but it is also an effective means for evangelism and mission among animistic peoples. The issue of the "necessity" of supernatural signs is not within the purview of humans but of God. He alone knows what is "necessary" in bringing men and women to a saving knowledge and experience of Jesus Christ. A faith that looks to both the inward and outward evidence of the Holy Spirit in Christian experience today is in accord with the New Testament witness. It is New Testament faith. There is no Reformation principle against the notion of "evidence" for the baptism of the Holy Spirit; in fact, Reformation tradition supports the notion. The question remains, however, whether the witness of the Spirit in that experience involves speaking with tongues.

The Evidence Points to "The Evidence"

In his article "The Evidence Points to the Evidence," D. V. Hurst surveys the experiential and biblical evidence for tongues as the initial, outward evidence of the baptism of the Holy Spirit. He asks several prior questions before addressing the question of the initial evidence of the baptism of the Spirit. One of them is, "Is it [speaking in tongues] evidence of the baptism of the Spirit *at all?*" (1968, p. 22). Then he points to the millions of contemporary "Bible-believing" Christians who confess they have had an experience after the New Testament pattern. Then he points to the clear references concerning the experience of the Spirit in Acts and the Epistles. Therefore, he speaks of two categories of evidence: *biblical* and *experiential.*

In this chapter, a survey of the biblical evidence has shown the baptism of the Holy Spirit to be a "distinct" experience, a conscious-crisis one, dynamic and evidential in nature. That it was evidential in the New Testament is shown by the fact that it was a means for validating Christian experience (Dunn, 1970, p. 66). This is especially the case in prejudicial and cross-cultural contexts, as the gospel spread beyond its Jewish confines. As Green states, the experience of the Spirit in New Testament times was of a "concrete nature" (1975, p. 146). According to the New Testament witness, there should be nothing opposed to an evidential coming of the Spirit, nor are there any grounds in Reformation theology that would preclude an evidential coming of the Spirit. In answer to Hurst's first question above, "Is it [speaking in tongues] evidence of the baptism of the Holy Spirit *at all?*" both the New Testament witness and contemporary experience produce an unquestioned affirmative answer. Hurst's last question, "Is speaking in tongues *the* initial outward evidence?" brings to the fore the issue of tongues as the unique evidence of the Pentecostal experience.

The biblical evidence for the Pentecostal baptism of the Spirit has been discussed thoroughly by Pentecostals and their critics. The New Testament support for the Pentecostal position derives from the historical precedent of the occasions of the Spirit's coming in the Acts of the Apostles account. The New Testament witness's contribution to this question thus concerns the hermeneutical use of historical precedent (Fee, 1976, pp. 131–32). According to the New Testament witness, the historical precedent may be summarized as follows: (1) the presence of the Spirit was the main characteristic of Christian conversion and practice; (2) in Acts and in the Pauline churches, the charismatic dimension normally accompanied the reception of the Spirit; (3) speaking in tongues was a repeated expression of that charismatic dimension; and (4) on the basis of the New Testament pattern, Christians today may expect that dimension as an integral part of their conversion (pp. 131–32). Fee concludes about the use of historical precedent:

> If the Pentecostal may not say one *must* speak in tongues, he may surely say, why *not* speak in tongues? It does have repeated biblical precedent, it did have evidential value at Cornelius' household . . .

and—in spite of much that has been written to the contrary—it does have value both for the edification of the individual believer (1 Cor. 14:2–5) and, with interpretation, for the edification of the church (1 Cor. 14:5, 26–28). (pp. 131–32)

Furthermore, the initial evidence of tongues took place at crucial points in Luke's history. It occurred at the Jerusalem Pentecost, the central event for the rest of Luke's history of the church (Allen, 1960, p. 17; Montague, 1976, pp. 271–72). And it occurred at the "Caesarean Pentecost," which marked the transition of the gospel from the Jewish cultural context ("Jerusalem, and in all Judea and Samaria") to the Gentile world ("and to the ends of the earth"; Acts 1:8). The crucial nature of the Caesarean outpouring of the Spirit is seen in Peter's recounting the incident when he is questioned by Jewish believers about the validity of the Gentile Christian experience (Acts 10:45–47; 11:15–17; 15:8–9). The evidential manner of the Spirit's coming is the crucial argument for the Jewish believers. Donald Gee states that Luke's explanation following the outpouring at Cornelius' house ("For they heard them speaking in tongues and praising God"; Acts 10:46) "is so emphatic that it approaches a definite statement of the doctrine" concerning tongues (Gee, 1949, p. 3). Hurst also states about this evidence at Cornelius' house, "The root evidence supporting all action and conclusions was 'tongues.' The Holy Spirit was poured out, water could not be forbidden, and repentance was available to the Gentiles—all based on *the* evidence" (1968, p. 27; emphasis mine). The evidential, outward witness of tongues is connected with the idea of authority, the authority of the Spirit. Its use in validating Christian experience points to the importance of the prophetic tradition in the experience of the early Jewish Christians.

MacDonald notes that the former crucial outpouring at the Feast of Pentecost is significant because "this [speaking in tongues] was the first perceptible expression *from within* the disciples that they had been filled with the Spirit" (1964, p. 4). The "initial" evidence from the disciples themselves at Pentecost, therefore, was speaking in tongues as the Spirit enabled them (Acts 2:4). However, Pentecost's significance and the evidence of speaking in tongues among the proselytes of the Diaspora go beyond the personal experience of the disciples with the Holy Spirit.

The Pentecost event has primary theological significance for salvation history itself. It is the third great work of God in salvation history. It follows creation and the incarnation, and marks the beginning of a new phase in salvation history, the "last days." In the "last days," the Holy Spirit is powerful and active in the church until the Parousia (Cullmann, 1964, p. 73). A chief characteristic of this age of the Spirit is the universal witness of the gospel. The tongues are significant in that they symbolize this universal witness at Pentecost (Acts 2:4–11), and the ever-expanding movement of salvation history that encompasses the whole Gentile world. The appearance of tongues at both Jerusalem and Caesarea, which are *transitional outpourings of the Spirit*, points to the phenomenon as significant and unique New Testament evidence.

In addition to the biblical evidence of tongues, which involves biblical precedent-pattern and prominence in the context of salvation history, the experiential evidence for tongues is significant. The belief that the Pentecostal experience, the baptism of the Holy Spirit, is accompanied by the initial, outward evidence of speaking with other tongues is held by the majority of classical Pentecostal denominations (Sandidge, 1976, p. 138). They do not hold that speaking in tongues is the only evidence, but that it is the only *initial* evidence. Some classical Pentecostal groups, neo-Pentecostal groups, and the Catholic charismatic renewal in general deny that tongues is *the* sign for the Spirit's baptism. Catholic writers, however, point to glossolalia as the *first* spiritual gift to be operative upon the "release of the Spirit." Ranaghan states, "The gift of tongues is not the baptism of the Holy Spirit. Rather it is a consequence, normally the first consequence, of receiving the baptism of the Holy Spirit" (1969, p. 220).

While speaking in tongues is not uniformly held to be the initial evidence of the baptism of the Holy Spirit by the Pentecostal movement in general, glossolalia is a common practice. Other gifts of the Spirit are also believed to be the initial evidence of the baptism of the Spirit. One could say about the Pentecostal movement in general that it is characterized by a belief that the Spirit's coming is accompanied by perceptible outward evidence.

Dynamic, Continuing Revelation?

The question surfaces in connection with the "experiential" evidence of tongues in the lives of millions of contemporary Christians: "Why should this New Testament witness of the Spirit be disparaged in theological argument today?" "Why does not the witness of the Spirit have the credibility today that it had at Cornelius' house, or with the first-century church in general?" The reason why such questions must be posed is due to the estrangement of Western Christianity and the Spirit. The experiential dimension of the faith had evidential value for the early church because of its nearness to the prophetic tradition, the renewal of that tradition in Jesus, and its renewal in their own experience. Their view of divine revelation was far from being static; it was dynamic, and at the advent of Jesus, it was seen to be renewed and continuing.

According to Yehezkel Kauffmann, the fall of Jerusalem was the great watershed of the history of Israelite religion. The life of the people of Israel ended and the history of Judaism began. The exile brought a central focus on the written word of God, and the age of compilation and canonization began. Israel's questioning as to whether God's presence was with them, in view of the fall of Jerusalem and the exile, caused the spirit of prophecy to die. Emphasis was on the objectified word (written word) rather than on the dynamic word of prophecy (1972, pp. 447–51). This was the stance of many in the first-century Jewish community.

Judaism's concentration on the written word, and their identity as a people being tied to the fact of Jewish ancestry and their custodianship of the Scriptures, may have been the focus of Jesus' allusion in John 5:39–40, "You diligently study the Scriptures because you think that by them you possess eternal life. These are the Scriptures that testify about me, yet you refuse to come to me to have life." Jesus' statement is filled with irony; as the Living Word stands before the custodians of the written word, they do not recognize him! Their static, "high view" of Scripture was devoid of the living dynamic of the prophetic spirit (2 Cor. 3). Bromiley states that this "high view" of Scripture in Judaism carried with it a threefold danger:

In the first place it tended to abstract the divine nature and authority of the Bible from the human authors and situations, i.e., from the whole movement of God's saving work in and through the history of Israel and the persons concerned. Second, it clearly abstracted the Bible from the objects of its witness, thus being left with a mere textbook of doctrine, ethics and ceremonial. Third, in rejecting Jesus Christ it refused the witness of the Holy Spirit, so that in its reading the Old Testament was deprived of its living power. (1958, p. 206)

For the early Christian (Jewish) church, however, the authority of the Old Testament Scriptures was seen in the context of faith and the witness of the Holy Spirit. They had experienced a renewal of the prophetic tradition in Jesus and in their own experience (Acts 2:17–21). For them, the Scriptures were linked with the Holy Spirit's work in witnessing to Jesus Christ (Rogers, 1977, p. 17).

A parallel to Israel's earlier view of dynamic revelation (prophecy), and first-century Judaism's somewhat static view of revelation, are those views of Pentecostalism and post-Reformation Scholasticism, respectively. In the post-Reformation period, under the barrage of questions leveled at the Christian worldview, the dynamic view of revelation shifted to Scholasticism's apologetic, static, and text-centered view. A "high view" of Scripture in evangelical circles today often refers to a view of biblical revelation that parallels the Judaistic view. It emphasizes the written "form" of Scripture at the expense of its dynamic, functional nature. The living prophetic voice of the Spirit is silent under the "captivity of the Enlightenment." The three dangers Bromiley mentioned above tend to be repeated in conservative evangelicalism, with the exception that the second danger (the abstracting of the Bible from the object of its witness) manifests itself as the abstracting of biblical revelation. Its dynamic, functional nature is denied (John 5:20–32, 39). Rather than Scripture's authority resting in the witness of the Spirit, his speaking through the written word as he transforms the lives of believers, its authority is perceived as resting in the "form" of Scripture, in arguments concerning the perfection of the text.

This emphasis on an objectified and static view of revelation has to do with a demise of the role of the Holy Spirit and his activity in contemporary Christianity. Pentecostalism believes that revelation is dynamic, because the Holy Spirit continues to be active at "this end" of biblical revelation. Revelation is a divine activity, not simply the finished product of that activity (Kraft, 1979, p. 184). The discussion of this theological point is continued in detail in chapter 6. Pentecostalism testifies to, and exemplifies, the fact that the continuing activity of the Spirit is not limited to his inward work with the written word. His activity also involves his outward charismatic work in the lives of believers (John 14:12–14; Acts 1:1–5).

The witness of tongues among millions of Pentecostal Christians is valid evidence for the Pentecostal belief that the initial evidence of the baptism of the Holy Spirit is speaking in tongues. To say this is not to say that every manifestation of tongues today is Christian or is of the Holy Spirit. This was not true in the first century and it is not true today. Those biblical guidelines given in the Epistles, as well as the gift of the Spirit—the ability to distinguish between spirits—are to be used by the people of God (1 Cor. 14; 2 Cor. 12:9; 1 John 2:18–23; 4:1–3). However, the witness of the Spirit today is biblical evidence and a valid means for verification of Christian experience within the biblical guidelines.

A point of difficulty in conservative evangelicalism's dealing with tongues as "evidence" is the subjectivism involved. The authority of the Spirit appears strange in a theological tradition so highly impacted by Scholasticism. The Pentecostal movement represents a "corrective" influence for contemporary mission at this point. Also, the possibility of Pentecostalism providing a theological contribution emerges here. As an established Christian tradition that is experiencing renewal of a neglected dimension of the Spirit's ministry, their contribution is obvious. It is a renewal that emphasizes the experiential dimension of the Christian faith. In terms of mission, this emphasis on the experiential dimension is relevant for mission strategy among the non-Christian animistic-oriented peoples of the developing world. It is the dynamic, powerful dimension of the Spirit that is crucial in evangelizing the animist. Rational arguments about biblical doctrine do not meet this challenge, regardless of how "sound" they may be.

PART TWO

PENTECOSTALISM,
A MISSIONS CONTRIBUTION

5 The Pentecostal and Mission Strategy

While the Pentecostal-charismatic movement focuses on the "experiential" dimension of the Christian faith, it may surprise the reader that in the discussion of the Pentecostal contribution to Christian missions a "theological" contribution emerges. In the discussion of Pentecostal "mission strategy" it becomes clear that Pentecostals utilize a dynamic biblical theologizing in mission. It is evident that the loss of this dynamic ongoing theologizing—with Scripture as the "horizon" for "doing theology"—has been eclipsed by the impact of a static Scholastic theology from the post-Reformation period, which has had an inordinate influence on evangelical theology. It also becomes clear in the discussion that a Christ-centered "biblical theology" is needed to replace an "Israel-centered" dispensational theology. Also, when we consider the true distinctive of Pentecostal-charismatic movements—that they are renewals of the gospel of the kingdom—the contention about the failure of dispensational theology becomes clear.

The contribution that Pentecostalism makes to contemporary mission theology concerns the discipline of theology itself. Considering its emphasis on the experiential dimension of the Christian faith, it may seem paradoxical that Pentecostalism has a theological contribution to make. Hollenweger notes that its contribution is not in the area of "dogmatic" theology, but rather in the area of "religious practice" (1972, p. 500). While Hollenweger does not agree with classical Pentecostal theology concerning religious practice (the tongues issue), he does view the experiential dimension of the faith as a theological dimension. Pentecostalism emphasizes the fact that theology is a practical discipline concerned with Christian experience and the activities of men and women engaged in mission. Thinking of mission strategy as mission "theologizing" points to the purpose of Scripture in providing direction for Christian obedience in life and ministry.

However, the idea of "theology" is often confined to theoretical reflection and theological systems that have been worked out in previous periods of the church. Confining theology to a historical *product* has produced a dichotomy between theory and practice in theology. Theology in scholastic tradition tends to leave the impression that mission strategy does not qualify as "theology." This notion has severely impacted mission strategy and its practice.

In contemporary mission literature, the theologizing done in the arena of mission is often viewed as pure pragmatism. This charge of pragmatism intends to focus on the alleged lack of theological/ biblical orientation in mission theologizing, not the philosophy of pragmatism. The critics are not so unkind as to level the charge of William James's philosophical pragmatism (no absolutes, crass relativism). The misconceived criticism is due to missiologists and theologians failing to recognize the dynamic, continuous nature of theology and the validity of using insights of the social sciences in mission theologizing. The roots of this misconception are discussed in this chapter, focusing on the occasion when Pentecostals and the "church growth" school of missiology are accused of pragmatism and a lack of theological orientation. The theological framework from which this criticism emerges is often Protestant Scholasticism, and a static view of theology and revelation are basic to this misconception.

This chapter discusses the nature of Pentecostal theology as a dynamic theologizing. It shows how that theological orientation, in this "doing theology" sense, provides insights and direction for contemporary mission theology. The Pentecostal view of theology is that it is a dynamic, continuing biblical process of applying Scripture to the problems and opportunities of mission. The Pentecostal view of revelation is that it is dynamic in nature.

Mission Strategy: Pragmatism or Theologizing?

A frequent criticism of schools of missiology that are oriented to church growth is that their mission strategy lacks theological sophistication and support. Their focus on evangelistic results, in terms of men and women converted and made responsible members of multiplying churches, has been characterized as "American pragmatism." Their scientific focus on the context of mission and their advocacy for the use of the social sciences in mission strategy has also led to this charge (Wasdel, 1980, p. 1; Padilla, 1977, p. 14). Some of the emphases that have been the occasion for criticism of the church growth school of missiology are: (1) the optimum growth of the church and the multiplication of churches; (2) a priority on evangelism as accomplished communication—men and women reconciled to God; (3) the focus on receptive people; (4) the necessity of research on the church and its mission; (5) the homogeneous unit principle; and (6) people movements. This configuration of emphases has been referred to as church growth strategy, or a "theology of church growth" (Hesselgrave, 1978b, p. 173).

Frequently, the theological and biblical adequacy of this view of mission strategy is questioned because of its nonsectarian nature (i.e., that it is not related to a particular confessional system of theology). Also, the use of research techniques appears to be problematic. In short, its in-mission or praxis origin is the object of criticism (Conn, 1976, p. 12; Padilla, 1977, p. 14). It is important to note that the biblical nature of church growth mission strategy is not in question. Rather, it is the in-mission use of Scripture, the theological methodology that is in question (Conn, 1976, pp. 45–46). The criticism shows the influence of Protestant Scholasticism (theology as a product). It is not even considered that the theologizing taking place in missions might be on the basis of a "biblical theology" found in the Scriptures. In a summary of his book, *How Biblical Is the Church Growth Movement?* J. Robertson McQuilkin writes, "Is Church Growth thinking biblical thinking? Yes, it is. This is not to say that all the people associated with Church Growth think biblically in all applications and interpretations of the principles. But the underlying presuppositions of the Church Growth movement rest on a solid theological foundation grounded in the Word of God" (1973, p. 62). The charge of pragmatism, then, is specifically related to the alleged improper theological base and improper methodology, challenging the validity of the very idea of using a theology (a biblical theology) other than a sectarian systematic theology, as well as the very idea of a dynamic biblical theologizing as a methodology in missions.

While not emphasizing the scientific approach to church growth, Pentecostals also could be characterized as having a mission strategy that is oriented to church growth. In a statement that echoes the church growth strategy of Donald McGavran, the father of the church growth school, Melvin L. Hodges states, "Whatever other good things the church may do, its success in promoting the Kingdom of God must be measured by the number of people it can bring into vital relationship with Christ and the number of local units of the Body of Christ that it can produce" (1977a, p. 144). In addition to some emphases similar to those given for the church growth school at Fuller Theological Seminary's School of World Mission, characteristic emphases of Pentecostal mission strategy are: (1) the planting of indigenous churches; (2) the evangelization of the humble, responsive masses; (3) the mobilization of the laity in witness; (4) spiritual gifts; (5) the spiritual dynamic of supernatural power in the power-encounter of mission; and (6) the development of spiritual leadership.

Pentecostal mission strategy has also been characterized as pragmatic and lacking theological sophistication, but for some different reasons than those mentioned above. Pentecostals would fall under the criticism of having a nonsectarian theology, as well as having a mission strategy of a pragmatic nature, but the charge of pragmatism in their case relates more to their pneumatology. Some of the more prominent reasons that non-Pentecostals give for the pragmatic nature of Pentecostal theology are their experiential orientation, their emphasis on the leading of the Holy Spirit in mission strategy, and the manner in which Scripture is used (Hesselgrave, 1978b, pp. 45, 65).

The charge of pragmatism primarily concerns the Pentecostal's belief concerning the active guidance of the Holy Spirit in mission. A response to the gospel is often considered evidence of the leading of the Holy Spirit. Classical Pentecostal missiologist Melvin Hodges believes mission strategy must be flexible in order for the church to take advantage of each opportunity for evangelism. He states, "The Pentecostal's deep conviction that the guidance of the Holy Spirit must be sought for each situation makes for flexibility and insures variety in method" (1977a, p. 142). However, this flexibility, due to the leading of the sovereign Spirit, the chief Strategist, also means that certain biblical principles are inviolable (p. 146). At the beginning of his article "A Pentecostal's View of Mission Strategy," Hodges states, "Pentecostals have roots imbedded in *The Book*. They strive constantly to follow the New Testament in every aspect of faith and practice. If follows that Pentecostal missiology should be based on biblical doctrine, experience and methodology" (p. 142).

Both of these church-growth-oriented schools of mission strategy are clearly committed to a biblically oriented strategy of mission, but somehow not in the sense that their critics would want them to be. Both are charged with the improper use of Scripture; both are charged with a pragmatic approach to strategy, with a flexibility that appears to be outside of the boundaries of a sectarian system of theology. Critics find their theology originating in the encounter with the missionary task itself. Their theological horizon, however, is *not* the context of mission, like some conciliar theologies of mission. For these schools (church-growth-oriented schools), the world does not set the theological agenda. Rather, the authoritative starting point for mission strategy is clearly Scripture.

Certainly, both church growth missiologists and Pentecostal missiologists are trained in their respective theological traditions. But in the opinion of their critics, their mission theology does not reflect those theological systems. When they engage in mission, do those missiologists holding to church growth principles really discard their theological traditions because of the American value of pragmatism? Should Pentecostals be written off as theologically deficient enthusiasts because they speak of the leading of the Holy Spirit in mission strategy? Or does the problem rest with their critics, who perhaps are unable to see beyond their own sectarian theological tradition and concept of theology?

In contrast to the view of theology as a static theological deposit, a dated theological tradition, all of the above "symptoms" of a supposedly theologically deficient mission strategy indicate a different view of theology than sectarian systematic theologies. They indicate a view in which theology is a dynamic, biblical process of reasoned reflection. They indicate the use of a "biblical theology" methodology in a different phase of theological work from that of dogmatic or systematic theology. This theology represents a dynamic interaction between Scripture and the missiologist who is immersed in a mission context. It represents a search for biblical solutions to contextual problems in the execution of mission. The criticism of this dynamic, biblical theologizing stems from the failure to tell the difference between theology as the cultural-historical *product* and theology as the continuing biblical *process*.

The content of both a sectarian systematic theology and a biblical theology of mission function as presuppositions that guide the missionary engaging in this fresh theologizing. Although this theologizing takes place in the context of the missionary endeavor, focusing on specific problems of mission, these problems are not the hermeneutical horizon. They are not the controlling, authoritative issue that determines the direction of theologizing. Due to the new situations and cultures involved in the Christian mission, there is a return to Scripture for answers to questions not addressed in a systematic theology contextualized in another time and place. The hermeneutical horizon, that authoritative starting point and guide, therefore, is Scripture.

Thinking of mission strategy as *theologizing* helps in bringing biblical solutions to many of the problems involved with the concept of "strategy." For evangelicals, it brings the concept of mission strategy clearly within the confines of biblical authority. Thinking of mission strategy as "biblical" activity in the context of mission brings the concept into focus as a "biblical theologizing." This theologizing involves a twofold task (a descriptive-historical task and an interpretive-theological task). That twofold task in turn involves a twofold fidelity (a fidelity to biblical revelation and a fidelity to the cultural context of mission). The identification of mission strategy as a valid phase of theological activity also closes the gap between mission theory and mission practice. It outlines the relationship between systematic theology and dynamic, biblical theologizing in the total theological enterprise.

The charge of pragmatism, or lack of theological orientation, in mission work is sometimes valid. However, this is not because of a dynamic, biblical theologizing on the part of the missionary. The charge of pragmatism draws attention to the methodological pitfalls involved in this dynamic theologizing. Sometimes the view of mission strategy is taken from the secular definition of "strategy." Many terms and phrases are used as synonyms for "strategy," or at least are used in a definitive way to describe the concept of mission strategy. Some representative terms in missiological literature are: "the missionary approach" (Bavinck, 1960, p. 179); "philosophy," "management theory," "planning," "pragmatism," "discovering God's strategy," and "incarnating the norms of the Bible" (Dayton & Fraser, 1980, pp. 26, 38, 49, 270, 297–98, 365, 443). Other terms are: biblical "paradigms for mission" (Shenk, 1980, p. 160); "practical missiology" (Anderson, 1961, p. 133); "the contextualization of the gospel" (Stott & Coote, 1980, pp. 77–78); "mission theory" (Conn, 1976, p. ii); and "theology of mission" and "practice of mission" (Bosch, 1975, pp. 1, 3). The terms used to define the concept cover both activities prior to and during the engagement in mission. The context in which the various terms are used infers a biblical hermeneutic, but often it is not articulated. Some of the terms connote a biblical hermeneutic; others are purely secular, signifying nothing concerning the role of Scripture in the activity. The problem of pragmatism rests in the latter usage. At times, the indiscriminate use of insights from the various social sciences is the occasion for the charge of pragmatism. The danger is not that insights from the secular sciences are used. Rather, the danger is in removing mission work from its theological-biblical base by failing to recognize mission strategy as preeminently *theological activity*. As theological activity, it requires that mission decisions and strategy be intentionally related to Scripture at all times.

Because of the various usages of the term "strategy," and some of its misleading connotations, it is necessary to let the term be defined by the concept of "theology" for various important reasons. Viewed as theology, or theologizing, the term "strategy" is immediately characterized as "biblical thinking" about mission. It is thinking that is related to Scripture in a special way (the previously mentioned twofold biblical task of hermeneutics). The biblical is a given as indicated in the term "theology," in spite of differences of opinion as to hermeneutics. When we approach the theological enterprise from an evangelical persuasion, the place and role of Scripture is somewhat precise, at least in terms of its authority. We know that to discuss "theology," we must be confronted with the content of Scripture, and that it plays an authoritative role. Any thinking about God's mission in the world must be biblical; that is the "bottom line" of the doctrine of biblical authority (Berkouwer, 1975, p. 105). Viewing mission strategy as "theology," then, focuses on the particular way that the Bible is related to theology. The term "theology" implies a hermeneutic, or biblical methodology (in evangelical theology), which can be used to evaluate the various terms used in missiological literature that *appear* to be synonymous with the term "strategy" when it is coupled with the term "mission."

Viewing mission strategy as biblical theologizing provides a constant reminder that such thinking is to be under Scripture's authority, even though it involves the use of extra-biblical knowledge and insights. Often mission strategy loses its biblical orientation, or it is heavily impacted by the missiologist's worldview or science when it is not recognized and articulated as a theological process.

The term "strategy" as a secular term has connotations that, if emphasized, are misleading when the word is used in a theological or missiological context. The term "strategy" may be defined in such a way as to infer that it only has to do with thinking *prior* to an action or event and excludes any thinking *during* the execution of an action (Dayton & Fraser, 1980, pp. 7, 19). "Strategy" is thereby differentiated from "tactics" in its secular usage, in that it involves planning and broad principles utilized prior to an action. Tactics, on the other hand, deals with carrying out general plans and principles during an encounter with specific situations. On the basis of this definition of strategy, any biblical thinking done while engaged in a missionary task would not be mission "strategy," nor would it be "theology." From a theological viewpoint, however, this is an erroneous conclusion. The conclusion is derived from the secular usage of the term "strategy," not from a theological evaluation of the activity of the missionary. Would not tactical, biblical thinking done by a missionary engaged in mission be "theology"? Actually, according to the secular usage, strategy-as-planning and principles would represent mission theology-theory (a particular systematic theology), and tactics would represent a dynamic phase of theology, mission theology-practice (a biblical theology). Therefore, the "dynamic theologizing" we refer to is the missionary applying Scripture to contemporary issues and problems of mission.

The secular definition and usage of the term "strategy" should not be allowed to determine the guidelines and nature of this crucial missiological issue. The dichotomy between strategy and tactics above contributes to a divorce of Scripture's influence on tactical thinking during the execution of the missionary task, which is actually a biblical theologizing (see Dayton & Fraser, 1980, pp. 7, 263, 266–77, 294–98, 344, 365). This apparent dichotomy has been the occasion for the charge of pragmatism with regard to church growth mission strategy. Whether thinking about mission is *prior* to missionary activity itself, *during* the activity, or *following* it, it is still biblical thinking and therefore is "theology" (Thielicke, 1974, pp. 196–99). The time when the thinking is done in relation to the missionary task does not change its nature.

The dynamic, pragmatic nature of the activities involved in mission strategy is often not recognized as "theology," because of a preconceived idea of theology as a static deposit. Also, missiologists often employ secular concepts or paradigms to describe missionary activity that tends to distance that activity from its theological-biblical base. The charge of pragmatism, therefore, concerns a failure to recognize the true nature of theology. Mission strategy involves a dynamic, biblical theologizing in the context of mission.

THEOLOGY AS THEORY AND PRACTICE

In introducing the topic "The Theology of Mission," David Bosch observes that the theology of mission can never be isolated from the practice of mission. He sees theology of mission as involved with the basic presuppositions and underlying principles that determine the practice of mission. Both theologies of mission and practical mission work are viewed in a relationship of creative tension (Bosch, 1975, pp. 2–3). Bosch brings into focus the danger of crass pragmatism in the practice of mission (the absence of theological orientation). But he also introduces the possibility of a danger in the other direction—in the direction of theology. He states: "There is a risk (and it is more than imaginary) that the practice and the theology of mission can become so estranged from one another that theological reflection can come to reject any practical application almost as a matter of principle" (p. 3). This would mean that any fresh theologizing done in the context of mission would be suspect, because of its dynamic and practical nature. The danger in the other direction is that theology can be separated from the practice of the church until it becomes a closed world of abstract reflection, which is sometimes the case in systematic theology (Thielicke, 1974, p. 23). This danger denies the mutual influence that exists between "theology" and "practice." Also, it often results in the irrelevancy of that theology in terms of the issues immediately concerning the church in mission. It just does not address them directly (e.g., teaching theological students in an animistic society the ten Western arguments for the existence of God, instead of giving biblical answers relating to the spirit world).

Hendrik Kraemer dramatically illustrated the danger of a dichotomy developing between mission theory and mission practice when he refused to write a theoretical essay on "Syncretism as a Theological Problem for Missions" for Gerald H. Anderson's *The Theology of the Christian Mission* (1961). Kraemer stated that his reason for not writing the essay was his conviction that "writing theoretical essays time and time again on syncretism as a theological problem for missions has no use whatever" (1961, p. 179). Kraemer saw that the essays did not change mission practice because they remained "theological museum pieces" (p. 179). They were innocuous because the tendency was to treat "theological problems" as theoretical affairs (pp. 179–80). Kraemer explains, "With this tendency I heartily disagree. To me a 'theological problem,' if really of fundamental significance, is an eminently *practical* affair demanding new *decisions* and followed by new *action*" (p. 180). Apparently for Kraemer, the separation between theory and practice was an established fact: "One more article on syncretism as a theological problem for missions will not cause the least change, because theology and spiritual strategy are usually kept neatly separate" (p. 182).

Kraemer viewed theological concepts as not merely matters of intellectual speculation but rather as "the most practical thing in the world" (p. 180). He viewed syncretism as a basic theological problem for *both* missiological thinking and for missionary strategy. However, because the subject was bracketed as a "theological problem" in the proposed essay title, he was of the opinion that no "practical" effect would result. The view that theology was a theoretical affair was entrenched. So it appears today when such practical theologizing done in the course of mission is suspect; because it does not fit within a particular confessional or sectarian system of theology, it is not considered "theology"!

Because of the universal nature of the phenomenon of syncretism and the increasing contact of the Christian faith with non-Christian religions, Kraemer advocated for bands of emic (indigenous) and etic (culturally outside experts) theologians to deal with the problem. These bands of theologians were to do "second phase," fresh theologizing on the basis of the unique problems encountered in each religio-cultural area of the world (1961, pp. 180–81). This second phase of theologizing-as-practice is emphasized when Kraemer states:

> Theology in itself (and that is what the isolated treatment of syncretism as a theological problem for missions often amounts to) is not theology in full but an amputated specimen of theology. Full theology includes expression in action and new forms of life, for the Christian truth, notwithstanding all its exclusiveness, is also all-inclusive. (pp. 181–82)

Fresh theologizing involves both the "dated" nature of theology theory, in terms of its historical-cultural contextual focus, and the demands of the contemporary context with its new issues. The contemporary context of theological reflection calls for a contemporary expression of Christian truth. Actually, it is the first phase of theologizing for the emic theologians, a dynamic biblical process. For Western theologians, it appears as a "second phase" of theologizing because it is done in relation to their own culturally conditioned theological product in Western systematic theology.

Bosch also observes the tentative and imperfect nature of all theology (1975, p. 4). This is the occasion for its dependence on practice. Practice brings theology to face its functional role in the life and mission of the church. In so doing, practice gives theology the occasion for growth in terms of increased insights. Bosch and Kraemer rightly observe that "it is on the frontiers where faith meets unbelief that theological reflection becomes most active" (Bosch, 1975, p. 6). Theology grows from crossing such frontiers. Therefore, mission theology should be characterized by its dynamic and contextual nature and not criticized for this quality.

In elaborating on the possible danger that theology may be regarded as the opponent of practice, or as its opposite, Bosch says that not all theology is "theology" (p. 6). He explains that some theology is not in the formal shape of "conciliar statements" and "ponderous publications." Nevertheless, it has to do with those basic presuppositions and underlying principles that determine the activities of the church in its mission (p. 6). It is clear that Bosch regards the *practice of mission* as "true, living theology," even though this theology does not take a systematized form. However, he states that such theology also must be articulated and not just exist "implicitly" somewhere in the background, like some contemporary mission strategy (p. 7). The pitfall here, as mentioned previously, is the loss of theological orientation and the danger of crass pragmatism, unless the theologian-missionary is working from a biblical theology articulated in the Scriptures. Bosch's discussion about theory and practice, therefore, illustrates the relationship between the two phases of theological reflection—systematic theology and a dynamic, biblical theologizing.

The nature of doing theology this way is often denied because of its apparent non-confessional nature and lack of theological appearance as a formalized theology. However, it should be recognized as a valid and necessary phase of theological reflection. Theology as theory and practice are not to be perceived as mutually exclusive but rather mutually influential and dependent. Both theory and practice are valid phases of theological activity. Systematic theology provides theory, theological presuppositions, and principles that serve to guide missionary practice. These phases close the gap between theory and practice. Dynamic, biblical theologizing provides fresh insights and *prescriptions*, as it reflects on biblical revelation in terms of new contexts and new questions confronting the church in its mission. Practice thereby enriches the whole theological enterprise. It appears that this discussion concerning the tension between systematic theology as a product and biblical theology as a process is extremely relevant for indigenous theologians in the Southern Hemisphere today. In reference to their reaction to the colonial and post-colonial periods of Western missions, there may be the tendency to disparage the Western systematic theology brought by missionaries to such an extent that non-Western theologians "throw out the baby with the bathwater," not recognizing value in a Western contextualized theology (the product) for their biblical theologizing (the process) to achieve their own truly indigenous theology. Kraemer's suggestion above, concerning teams of emic indigenous theologians and etic outside theological experts collaborating in the achievement of indigenous theologies, is relevant.

Bosch's discussion about the relation of theory and practice highlights two theological perspectives that occasion the criticism that church growth mission strategy is theologically deficient. In effect, both perspectives divorce theology from mission practice. One of the perspectives involves church growth missiologists. The other perspective involves the critics themselves. Both perspectives evidence a theological deficiency.

The first "pragmatic" perspective concerns those church growth missiologists who fail to explicitly consider and articulate their mission strategy theologically. Some who espouse church growth principles often fail to articulate their theological presuppositions and methodology. A dangerous dichotomy exists in the thinking of those who take their understanding of mission strategy from the secular term "strategy." For them, strategy is related only to planning and the application of principles in pre-missionary activity, not to the practice of mission. This tends to divorce strategy in its wider application (the practice of mission) from Scripture. Often a secular theory, model (social theory, cultural anthropology, phenomenology of religion), or paradigm is used that controls mission activity without examining its presuppositions in the light of Scripture. Theological work beyond that of proof-texting is necessary in the implementation of secular models in mission strategy. Otherwise, the results will have questionable theological credibility. Also, the potential for an unrestrained influence of the science or the missiologist's worldview on methodology is present. In other words, the pitfall of crass pragmatism is present, even though it is unintentional.

A pragmatic dichotomy of mission theory and practice also occurs with those missiologists who claim to have a theologically oriented mission strategy. In this second perspective, the sectarian issue is in focus. It is the perspective of critics who hold a theological dichotomy because they fail to recognize strategy as a dynamic theological process, practiced in solidarity with theology as a culturally conditioned product (their sectarian systematic theology). Because *their* particular confessional system of theology is considered absolute and perennial, and because it is "dated," focused on another era and its problems, the system is inflexible. It does not lend itself to addressing different contemporary problems, so theologizing outside of that system is considered invalid. However, because of its Western orientation and rationalistic nature, it finds itself not only irrelevant but inappropriate to its non-Western supernaturalistic context. The theological deficiency here involves the dichotomy of theory and practice. Theology is left in the dimension of theory; it is left on the bookshelf. This, in turn, results in distancing theology from the contemporary life and mission of the church. Such a separation tends to contribute to the theological poverty of both systematic theology and mission strategy.

Recognizing Phases of Theologizing

C. Peter Wagner's definition of strategy is of a general nature and is not as restrictive in its application as in the dichotomy above. It is therefore more useful in a theological context: "Strategy is a mutually-agreed means to achieve the ends which have been determined by a particular group. Good strategy will be concerned with broad principles as well as specific tactics, but it will not lose sight of the determined goal" (1971, p. 16). Wagner does not deny the difference between strategy and tactics; they are viewed holistically. There is no rigid dichotomy. This definition can be used to illustrate the different phases of theological activity. "Biblical thinking" that takes place *prior* to mission—theology as a culturally conditioned product (systematic theology)—represents one general phase of theologizing. "Biblical thinking" takes place *during* mission—theology as a dynamic process (fresh biblical theologizing)—represents another phase of theologizing.

In secular usage, "strategy," as distinct from tactics, represents goal-oriented theoretical thinking of a broad scope. It deals with principles, planning, and conceptual action. It is usually done prior to an action. This usage could illustrate a prior phase of theologizing, involving both systematic theology and biblical theology. These provide the theological presuppositions that condition both mission planning and action.

On the other hand, "tactics" are also oriented to goals, but specifically to immediate goals as they relate to the ultimate goal or strategy. Tactics represent thinking of narrower scope, which is situational and more practical in nature. It deals with execution, improvising, and coping in concrete action. It is usually thinking done during engagement of an action and is conditioned by the specific problems of engagement. Tactics are dependent on strategy for the necessary general orientation that ensures their effectiveness in moving toward the ultimate goal. This secular definition of tactics illustrates, somewhat, the nature of the fresh theologizing mentioned previously. It takes place in the context of mission. It represents a necessary continuous phase of theologizing. It involves the dynamic process of theology.

The necessity of recognizing at least two general phases of theological reflection, however, does not derive from the term "strategy." The two phases grow out of the nature of theology as a continuing response of the church to both Scripture and its environment. Both systematic theology and biblical theology (the biblical science, especially when understood as the domain of the biblical historian only) are theological products conditioned by time and culture. Biblical theology, in the sense of the theology *in* the Bible and the Bible's structure of theology, is in a special canonical sense normative. But it is still conditioned by time and culture. Therefore, a dynamic, continuing biblical theologizing must be done. Hermeneutics involves both a historical *and* an interpretive task. Both tasks are necessary in order to apply biblical content to contemporary questions and problems requiring a Christian response. A fresh phase of biblical theologizing is a necessity in every age and every culture.

James Smart points to the early 1960s as the time when a truncated view of biblical theology (the biblical science limited to the historical task only) began once again to include the interpretive-theological task. Smart cites the pressure of the sociocultural needs of the American community and the Vietnam War as the occasion for its emergence (1979, p. 130). Theologians recognized that biblical theology in terms of what Scripture "meant" (the descriptive-historical task) alone was inadequate. The "means" dimension of Scripture (the interpretive-theological task) for contemporary American society was imperative.

Dogmatic theology, however, is clearly conditioned by time and culture. It does not hold the same normative position as biblical theology. It represents the partial, culturally conditioned, and limited statements of the church that are focused on the theological issues of *other* times. In view of this fact, Berkouwer speaks of the need to "reinterpret dogma" (1977, p. 216). This reinterpretation, Berkouwer states, "usually assumes a fundamental distinction: the distinction between form and content, between the formulations of dogma and the truth that is expressed in those formulations" (pp. 216, 218). That distinction is the occasion for the reinterpretation of dogma. Different phases of theological reflection, therefore, are necessary because of the limited and time-bound nature of theological statements in general. A dynamic phase of theologizing is necessary. The need for such dynamic theologizing is much more critical in another cultural context, in which the worldview, value system, and needs that theology must address are diverse.

Berkouwer notes in some detail the Roman Catholic response to "reinterpretation" of dogma: "After all, truth formulated *infallibly* ought to be relevant for all time" (1977, p. 218). But he notes that among Roman Catholics there has been a deep awareness of the historically conditioned nature of the church's dogmatic statements. The activity of reinterpreting dogma within even the Roman Catholic Church, then, is significant evidence for the necessity of a dynamic, continual theologizing. Distinguishing between the unchangeable affirmation (truth) and the changeable representation of truth (its form) represented a hermeneutical challenge for the Roman Catholic Church. They had to recognize different phases of theological work, and it was necessary that the affirmations of the church be reinterpreted in order to address contemporary issues (p. 220).

For the Protestant church, reinterpretation of the confessions of the church from earlier centuries for current theological reflection brought tension. The confessions were obviously time-bound (Berkouwer, 1977, p. 224). The need for such a reinterpretation concerned even the central issues of the faith. Berkouwer discusses in detail how the ancient Christological and Trinitarian formulations are subject to reinterpretation (pp. 226–27, 258). In that discussion, he advocates a non-Cartesian theology, a theology that has for its hermeneutical horizon Scripture rather than a confessional-creedal horizon. Berkouwer advocates a fresh theologizing that has Scripture as its authoritative starting point and controlling orientation in such "reinterpretation" (pp. 233–36, 259–61). Berkouwer points to the nature of theology itself as the reason why "reinterpretation" or fresh theologizing must take place:

> As a matter of fact, theology shows little sign of serene immobility. There is restless searching going on, a groping for ways to understand the gospel more clearly. We should not expect too much from theology; it will at best only give us incomplete knowledge and inadequate understanding. If we forget that theology is always going to be partial, travelling along the way without ever arriving finally, we will be upset by theology's continued movement, and others will be alarmed and disturbed by it, seeing it as a threat to established truth. (pp. 262–63)

Berkouwer affirms the necessity of a continuing theological task, noting that the necessity rests in the incomplete and imperfect nature of all theological reflection (1 Cor. 13:12). Objections to such theologizing often rest in the misconception that dogmatic formulations are somehow absolute and perennial. Those objections result from a failure to recognize the validity of different phases of theological work. The criticism leveled at mission theologizing arises out of this misconception and failure. They are often rooted in a *scholastic view of theology*.

It is helpful at this point also to recognize that the discussion of the reinterpretation of dogma is related to the concept of contextualization. A dogmatic theology needs reinterpretation precisely because it is a *contextualized theology* in a certain time, place, and culture. The act of reinterpretation is a re-contextualization of the Christian faith in contemporary times, under the pressure of the new issues that the ancient statement does not address adequately.

Mission strategy, therefore, involves two phases of theological activity. The first is a theoretical phase involving theological products, representing the presuppositions that support and give strategy theological orientation. Systematic theology gives theological orientation from one's cultural perspective, how a specific people ultimately understand theology in general and God's mission in particular. Biblical theology gives theological orientation from the perspective of what one perceives as the biblical view of God's mission. Cultural perspective is also present here, but the emphasis is on how the biblical writers understood the structure of theology in God's mission. The second phase is a practical phase involving theology of a more immediate, fresh, and contemporary nature. It represents a dynamic process in which biblical revelation is the hermeneutical horizon (as in the biblical theology above). Contextual questions of mission are the focus of theological activity.

Contemporary missiologists and theologians who object to and criticize mission theologizing often do so because of its lack of correspondence to a particular confessional system of theology. Criticism also arises because it often challenges traditional theological affirmations in those systems. While commending the church growth writers for having a sound biblical theology underlying their mission practice, Roger Greenway states:

> Most of church growth missiology's theological bases have been worked out *after* the methodological insights and missions principles were arrived at through field observation and experience. Very often they were defined more in opposition to the arguments raised by opponents of church growth than in relation to a recognized system of theology. (1976, p. 46)

This statement illustrates both the criticism that church growth mission strategy is "pragmatic" in nature and, in terms of the sectarian issue, that it does not appear to be related to a "recognized system of theology." Is not such "after-action" reflection, however, also valid theologizing when done in connection with Scripture? Greenway is positive in his treatment of church growth missiology, but from his Reformed perspective he states that missiology's theology and organization is "seriously deficient" (p. 46).

On the basis of Greenway's admission that sound biblical theology underlies the missiology he criticizes, it appears that the criticism of theological deficiency rests on *how* its theology was attained (the pragmatic nature of the theology). Also, its relation to a system of theology is an issue. One wonders if critics doubt that church growth missiologists *have* theological presuppositions and traditions that condition their approach to the task of mission. Perhaps it is just the kind of nonsectarian theologizing in which they engage that is so objectionable (fresh biblical theologizing).

Obviously, trained missiologists *do* have theological traditions that function as a basis from which they do their theologizing in mission. Furthermore, it is readily admitted that the church growth school is engaged in sound biblical theology. But whatever one decides about these questions of prior theological bases for mission theology, the phenomenon of a theology of mission developing from theological grappling with the contemporary issues of mission, and interacting with the arguments of systematic theologians, is in fact how all theology develops—systematic theology included. The valid, firsthand biblical theologizing done in the context of mission and sharpened by interaction with systematic theologies should not be seen as a "serious deficiency." Rather, it should be viewed as the process of normal theological development that every theology undergoes, mission theology included.

At the writing of this second edition, in light of the new situation in the Southern Hemisphere, there is a critical need today to articulate an evangelical-Pentecostal "biblical theology" to replace the dispensational theology that has influenced evangelicals and Pentecostals for the past one hundred and eighty-five years. It is an unorthodox, pseudo-biblical theology that challenges the basic tenets of Reformation theology (Pomerville, 2014, pp. 25–83, 87–116, 165–78, 205–12, 461–85). I have suggested that a biblical theology focused on the kingdom of God motif in the Bible, such as *Jesus' gospel of the present-dynamic kingdom of God*, which points to the unique experience of the *indwelling Holy Spirit*, should replace dispensational theology's Israel-oriented theology that marginalizes the New Testament. Such a Christ-centered theology, focusing on the "Christ-event" and the events focused around that midpoint of salvation history, would provide a true biblical theology for emic theologians of the churches in the Southern Hemisphere—a real option for working out their own biblical theologies.

How Is Mission Strategy "Pragmatic"?

The thesis of this chapter is that mission strategy is "theologizing." This thesis is reiterated in the statement: "mission strategy is 'biblical' pragmatism." The phrase "biblical pragmatism" emphasizes the dynamic, biblical nature of theology. Mission strategy represents that theologizing in which Scripture functions by providing the church with guidance for its mission in the modern world. In considering mission strategy as biblical pragmatism, therefore, the combination of the two terms aids in illustrating the role of Scripture and the contextual nature of this dynamic theologizing.

In terms of its contribution to evangelicalism, Pentecostalism directly addresses the question, "How is mission strategy pragmatic?" This question draws attention to the dynamic, continuing nature of theology and the necessity of applying Scripture to the contemporary life and ministry of the church. It points to the incarnational nature of theology, to its contextual nature and focus. The question focuses on the second half of the twofold fidelity of theology—fidelity to

cultural context. It has to do with the second hermeneutical task—
the interpretive-theological task. Mission strategy is a continuous,
biblical theologizing whereby contemporary problems of mission
find biblical solutions. Scripture is functional in mission by means
of the interpretive-theological task of hermeneutics.

The Interpretive-Theological Task and the Spirit

The Pentecostal belief that the Holy Spirit continues to work at
the modern end of divine revelation is a chief reason why they are
able to respond so readily to the interpretive-theological task. They
believe that revelation is dynamic and continuing in nature (revelation with a small *r*, the continuing ministry of the Spirit as opposed
to Revelation with a capital *R*, i.e., Scripture). This belief also allows
them to respond positively to the matter of "incarnating" the Christian faith in other cultural contexts. The Holy Spirit, the Supreme
Strategist, is present to guide in that work. A Pentecostal orientation
points to two dimensions of revelation that are crucial for mission
strategy: its *dynamic-continuous nature* and its *incarnational nature*.
Both of these dimensions of revelation are crucial for the hermeneutical task and theology's fidelity to the context of mission.

There are various reasons why the interpretive-theological task
may be neglected, as well as the ministry of the Spirit. While Pentecostalism emphasizes the dynamic nature of Scripture and revelation, Protestant Scholasticism represents a fundamental distortion
of them. Theology, Scripture, and revelation are all transformed
into *static products*. It is at this point especially that mission theology's fidelity to the cultural context is seriously compromised.
Because theology has been contextualized in Western culture, in
its scholastic form the *functional* purpose of Western theology has
been eclipsed. Theology-theory has been separated from theology-
practice. In terms of mission theologizing, this theological orientation represents a fundamental and serious distortion.

D. F. Strauss contended that the doctrine of the witness of the
Spirit (the *testimonium*) was the "Achilles' heel of the Protestant
system," due to the twofold possibility of the perversion of the

doctrine—fanaticism and rationalism (Berkouwer, 1975, p. 64). In the first possibility, the Spirit may be the source of a new revelation that may oppose Scripture. In the second possibility, rationalism, the danger arises from a failure to distinguish between what is from the Spirit and what is from one's own mind working within a particular worldview. In both possibilities, Scripture is pushed to a secondary position. The latter danger and perversion of the doctrine of the *testimonium* became a reality in the post-Reformation period under the influence of the intense rationalism of the Enlightenment and Common Sense philosophy. While not denying the danger of the former perversion, fanaticism, the perversion that is the present handicap of conservative evangelical mission theologizing is rationalism. Ramm states concerning the latter perversion—rationalism—that "a fanatical 'objectivizing' of Scripture can be as detrimental to its proper understanding as a frightful 'subjectivizing'" (1961, p. 99).

Numerous theologians have identified the influence of Protestant Scholasticism in fundamentalism and conservative evangelicalism, especially in their apologetics. In a previous chapter, Ramm was quoted as saying that he found the doctrine of the internal witness of the Spirit to have almost disappeared from evangelical literature and theology (1959, p. 7). The scholastic penchant for rational argumentation supplanted the "witness of the Spirit"—the *testimonium*. Ramm states that the union of word and Spirit is the theological ground for Calvin's theory of the *testimonium* (p. 17). The danger of rationalism is its tendency to conceive of revelation solely as a static product (Revelation with a capital *R)* and not as a dynamic work of the Spirit with Scripture (revelation with a small *r*). The heart of the danger in Protestant Scholasticism is the severe limitation of the "subjective" work of the Holy Spirit with the word at the contemporary end of revelation. Ramm states, "Here [its view of revelation] is the danger of fundamentalism, which turns revelation into court-reporting and does not see it as the divine Person in *conversation* with sinners" (1961, p. 26). I might add, "And does not see it as the divine Person in conversation with *Christians*," limiting the divine speaking to the salvation experience only.

In a discussion about Scripture's authority, Ramm lists three erroneous theories on "certainty": (1) Romanism—the infallible church is the source of certainty; (2) the enthusiasm—certainty rests in the immediate revelation by the Spirit; and (3) the view of the apologist—Scripture's certainty is determined by rational evidences (1959, p. 12). The separation of word from Spirit is involved in all three. The apologists' approach to certainty represents the scholastic distortion of revelation discussed here.

In his book *Fundamentalism,* James Barr states that two streams of tradition feed conservative evangelicalism: (1) Protestant orthodoxies of the seventeenth and eighteenth centuries, with their dogmatism; and (2) Pietism, the deepening of the spiritual life (Keswick convention). The two streams each provide emphasis in different areas in evangelicalism. The first represents the theology; the second, the practical expression of Christianity (Barr, 1978, pp. 188–89). Barr identifies the intellectual leadership of fundamentalism with the Princeton theologians Warfield and the Hodges. These, Barr states, drew their philosophical position from Scottish Common Sense philosophy of Britain and Darby mainstream dispensationalism (p. iv). Barr states, "Fundamentalism distorts and betrays the basic true religious concerns of evangelical Christianity, and it does this especially through its *intellectual apologetic*" (p. v; emphasis mine). He points to the theology of the Hodges and Warfield, scholastic theologians of the post-Reformation period, as those who "moulded the set of ideas we now know as fundamentalism" (p. 262). This view of the influence of the above scholastic theologians on evangelicalism is supported by Jack Rogers and Donald McKim in their book *The Authority and Interpretation of the Bible* (1979), a historical study of the doctrine of Scripture.

Barr sees the "scholastic" stream of tradition in evangelicalism as having an excessive impact on its theological methodology. While he notes that the laity probably follow the pietistic model and influence, theologians and apologists follow the scholastic model. Often, paradoxes arise in conservative evangelicalism, especially in fundamentalism, because of the influence of the two streams of tradition. The warm personal, emotional view of conversion and the devotional nature of the Christian experience are mixed together with a cold intellectual-apologetic approach to doctrine. The excessive impact of reason in theological methodology represents such a paradox. Barr sees the paradox in the fundamentalist view of biblical authority:

> The attempt to support that faith [evangelical] upon an intellectual apologetic is itself from the beginning a sign of abandonment of the inner core of that faith. Evangelical faith is betrayed by the fundamentalist apparatus of argument. For faith it substitutes dependence on rational use of evidence; and in place of the religious functioning of the Bible it takes, as primary guarantee of the authority of scripture, the absence of error, especially in its historical details. (1978, p. 339)

Evangelical methodology, therefore, does not appear to be consistent with evangelical belief and practice. It supplants the fundamental issue of the authority of Scripture and the evangelical's approach to Scripture, faith, in the context of the witness of the Spirit.

The danger of the unconscious mixing of these contrasting streams of tradition is seen in the scholastic priority of reason over faith. Barr states that evangelicals evidence the impact of the Enlightenment in "their craving for intellectual recognition and their flaunting of the rationality and erudition of conservative apologists" (pp. 129–30). He feels that the objectivist, intellectualist attitude is one of the most unattractive features of their literature (p. 130). Perhaps its unattractiveness is due to its inconsistency, in that such rationalistic methodology is not in keeping with faith and the *testimonium* in the evangelical approach to Scripture.

The paradox appears in even greater proportions when Barr notes a tendency toward fundamentalist rationalism in *Pentecostalism*. He states that in view of the central place that "experience," and not orthodoxy, plays with this group, the manifestation of rationalism is even more paradoxical (p. 209). Pentecostalism's whole orientation to the ontic presence of the Holy Spirit, its "God with us" orientation, is threatened by the "scholastic stream" of tradition. It has much more to lose in terms of theology (pneumatology) than other evangelicals if the distorting effect of Scholasticism's rationalistic methodology is not identified. Even more paradoxical for Pentecostals is the continuing influence of dispensational theology that began about the same time, in spite of its denial of the Pentecostal experience on dispensational grounds (Pomerville, 2014, pp.

29–43, 165–68). Any development of Pentecostal theology has to contend with the influence of this "scholastic theological paradigm." The crucial doctrine of revelation is an area that needs fresh attention from a non-Cartesian, biblical, and Pentecostal perspective.

The Interpretive-Theological Task and a Dynamic Concept of Revelation

The functional nature of Scripture and theology points to the dynamic and continuing nature of revelation (revelation with a small *r*). The reason why a dynamic and continuing view of revelation is affirmed here is to call attention to the scholastic distortion of the concept and its importance for the interpretive-theological task. To affirm that revelation is continuing is not a denial that the biblical canon is closed. Nor does it advocate a pneumatic exegesis, the desire for extra-biblical revelation. Nor is it an advocacy for an existential approach to Scripture. Rather, it marks a return to the Reformation view of revelation as dynamic and continuous in nature. In view of the axiom of "word inseparable from Spirit," it marks a reaffirmation of Calvin's view of the *testimonium*. Berkouwer states that the *testimonium* "is not to be isolated to the Spirit's witness to Scripture, [though] both Bavinck and Kuyper rejected this" (1975, p. 45). The *testimonium* is connected with the whole Christian life, pervading the salvation that appears in Christ (John 15:27; 16:8, 13). This view of the *testimonium* affirms that revelation involves a continued divine speaking (revelation with a small *r*). Bernard Ramm states, "As in all instances of revelation and inspiration there is the accompanying inward work of the Holy Spirit—an insight we owe to Calvin's exploration of the witness of the Holy Spirit not only a feature of individual salvation but *as accompanying the giving of special revelation*" (1961, p. 44; emphasis mine). The above theologians, therefore, give a picture of the continuing ministry of the Holy Spirit in connection with the word in the Christian life. Pentecostals, of course, fully subscribe to this view.

Following Luther and Calvin, Ramm holds to a dynamic view of the Word of God (Hebrew *dabar*), stating that Jesus' character is revelation, not just his words. He states that there is a dynamic, ontic dimension to the revelation in Christ (1961, p. 112). Jesus is the "Living Word." Charles Kraft states concerning Christ's claim in John 14:6 ("I am . . . the truth"):

> Personal truth and revelation are not static. A true person will speak truly. But *our understanding of truth (especially in the biblical sense) should not be reduced to a concept of "true information."* . . . As Jesus did the truth, related truly in living the truth, he truly and truth-fully revealed *God*—not simply information about God. We need to learn to *distinguish between such dynamic revelation (and truth) and the information that is inevitably a part but never the whole of either.* (1979, p. 179)

The dynamic dimension of the Holy Spirit cannot be separated from the informational product. Revelation is the ontic (God *with* us) activity of God the Holy Spirit. Ramm especially focuses on the *preaching of the gospel* as the word of God (1961, pp. 116, 118, 149): "So in the preaching of the gospel out of the pages of the New Testament the modality of the incarnation as special revelation is continued; and when men believe this witness by responding to it with saving faith, then Christ comes also to the heart" (p. 116).

Apologetic treatments of the doctrine of revelation have rein-forced a static view of the concept in evangelical literature. This takes place through the use of rational arguments that emphasize the objective nature of revelation. Ramm's book *Special Revelation and the Word of God* (1961) presents numerous arguments in which the static view of revelation is supported. But Ramm does include some balanced statements on the nature of revelation in this book (pp. 158, 160). However, the preponderance of the argumentation is either directed against the view of revelation in liberalism, in neo-orthodoxy, or in Roman Catholicism (pp. 135–36, 139, 142, 152, 164, 173ff.). What often results from an apologetic treatment of the doctrine is a one-sided treatment.

While describing the wide scope of the concept of special revelation in an apologetic-oriented statement, Ramm notes the dynamic dimension of the concept. But the emphasis on the con-tinuing nature of revelation concerns the informational product:

The particular form of the "here-ness" [of revelation] and abiding character of revelation is its conceptual aspect. Certainly the word "revelation" is rich in meaning. God's word to the prophet is revelation; God's act is revelation; the illumination of the Spirit is revelation; the return of Christ is revelation. The concept of revelation in Scripture is too rich to be easily schematized; it is also rich enough to be applied to the conceptual side of revelation. (p. 151)

The concept involves divine speaking, divine action or event, and of course, divine product—the written divine word. But in the apologetic treatment of the doctrine, Ramm consistently represents revelation in its informational mode, arguing for its superiority. A lack of explanation at points that deal with the dynamic nature of revelation also reveals the apologetic treatment (pp. 140–41). The description of the dynamic dimension is obscure in his treatment, with vague references to the Holy Spirit. In the apologetic treatment, therefore, the dynamic dimension is not denied; it is trivialized.

Often in the curious mix of traditions in evangelicalism, especially in the apologetic mode, the influence of Western worldviews and scholastic methodology on theologizing adversely affects the crucial doctrine of revelation. It is generally represented as a static product, as information. Kraft cites the bias of Western worldview as the reason for limiting the concept of revelation to the written mode: "*In keeping with this emphasis of Western culture* [the Western high value on information], *we have both accepted the informationalizing of revelation and often lost our ability to imagine that it could be anything else*" (1961, p. 179). Kraft also notes that together with the Western focus on "knowledge as information" (the noetic view of "knowing" obscuring the ontic "knowing") are the "underlying fear of subjectivity" and the desire to know objectively (1979, p. 183). He points to static orthodox views of revelation as the outcome of Western worldview (pp. 185–86).

Revelation is both information and encounter with the Spirit of God (Ramm, 1961, p. 158). Kraft clarified the issue when he stated that revelation is a divine, continuing activity and not simply the finished product of that activity (1979, pp. 178–85). Any limiting of the concept of revelation to the products of that activity violates the Reformation axiom of "word inseparable from Spirit," as well as the doctrine of the *testimonium*. In a balanced statement Ramm adds, "Revelation is event *and* interpretation, encounter *and* truth, person *and* knowledge" (1961, p. 160). Revelation is activity and this activity leaves a product, special revelation cast into written form. But special revelation is also a "powerful coming of God as well as a concrete coming of God" (p. 21). While space prohibits a further clarification of the issue at this point, using Ramm's previous tack, we may say here that the *concept of revelation is also rich enough to be applied to the dynamic side of revelation and encompass the outward charismatic ministry of the Spirit too* (revelation with a small *r*).

Limiting the concept of revelation seriously affects mission strategy. It presents a picture of revelation in which the activity of the Holy Spirit in his missionary role is obscured. The outward charismatic ministries of the Spirit among God's people are also eclipsed. The factor of the gospel witness being confirmed by "signs following" is also eliminated. Such a serious restricting of the ministry of the Holy Spirit cannot but retard the ongoing mission in the world. This is especially so among the majority of the un-evangelized, those influenced by animism.

The concepts of Scripture and theology are distorted when the dynamic dimension of the Spirit is missing in revelation. The Reformation emphasis on the ontic principle of theology and Scripture's functional nature emphasizes the truth that they have to do with the activity of God in the contemporary moment. The idea that revelation, Scripture, and theology have a dynamic dimension validates contemporary contextualization efforts. Divine activity can be expected in those efforts. This is important for those cultures in which efforts to contextualize the gospel involve power-encounters with the spirit world. The view of Scripture as enlivened by the Spirit when proclaimed, self-authenticating, and sufficient to accomplish its redemptive purpose would encourage and incite evangelistic efforts among animistic-oriented societies. Fear of syncretism would be replaced with the realization that the word of God is living and powerful, a word that has power to transform people and cultures when it is proclaimed with the enablement of the Holy Spirit.

The "real" authority of the Scripture in such societies will never be rationalistic arguments concerning the historical accuracy of a "book," even if it is a holy book (important as the historical nature of the Bible is, methodologically speaking). The supernatural witness of the Holy Spirit in the heart, the demonstration of the word of God in transforming behavior, and the word confirmed with "signs following" could only be adequate authority in those circumstances. Furthermore, in any circumstance, only God is an adequate witness for God. The Christian faith concerns the present activity and rule of the kingdom of God, not merely an intellectual faith. This is the corrective message of Pentecostalism for an Enlightenment-impacted Protestant faith. The history of the church in the Southern Hemisphere in the twenty-first century has confirmed the above claims of dynamic continuing revelation.

6 The Pentecostal and Contemporary Mission Issues

This chapter discusses the activity of God in mission: How God is active in mission today is a key issue in missiological debate. Of course, our response to such a question must come in humility, because of the manifold ways in which God connects with humanity. However, in response to the issue in contemporary mission theology, we may ask: "Is God immediately and primarily involved in revolutionary movements that challenge social and political injustice?" (God-world-church). Or, "Is his activity mediated through the church as it engages in 'Great Commission missions'?" (God-church-world). We can be even more specific. *After the revelation of the gospel of the kingdom of God in Jesus Christ*, "How is God active in the world in which we live *in this particular part of salvation history*?" While we might believe he is active in both ways mentioned above, is there a reason why we might expect God to be *primarily* active in the world today? The various theological responses to these questions bring major issues of contemporary mission theology into focus. Pentecostal theology has much to contribute in resolving this crisis regarding the problematic activity of God in the world.

We should also mention this following "qualifier" to our discussion about God's activity in the world today. Jesus' appearance at the midpoint of salvation history with the gospel of the kingdom of God, involving the gift of the indwelling Spirit, was not merely news that the Messiah had come and everything would continue on as usual in Israel, according to their "Jewish expectations" (as in dispensationalism's Israel-centered theology). No, I'm speaking of a "divine surprise" dawning on Israel of the first century, something the prophets desired to look into but could not, a mystery of Christ that was not made known to other generations (Eph. 3:4–6): the surprise of a universal kingdom of God *arriving prior* to its final consummation at the end of the "last days." This involved the creation of a new people of God—both Jew and Gentile born of the Spirit—indwelt by the Holy Spirit to carry out Christ's mission in the world. To orient ourselves to this momentous "Christ event" at the midpoint in salvation history, along with all of the events following, we must focus on the lofty words of the Apostle Paul in Philippians about Jesus:

> Being found in appearance as a human being, he humbled himself by becoming obedient to death—even death on a cross! Therefore God exalted him to the highest place and gave him the name that is above every name, that at the name of Jesus every knee should bow in heaven and earth and under the earth, and every tongue acknowledge that Jesus Christ is Lord, to the glory of God the Father. (Phil. 2:7b–11)

In Ephesians, when Paul wants to describe the power of the Holy Spirit that dwells *in* Christians because of the "Christ event" at the midpoint of salvation history, the arrival of his "kingdom of God," and Christ's position in heaven after his work of redemption, he refers to:

> [God's] incomparably great power for us who believe. That power is the same as the mighty strength he exerted when he raised Christ from the dead and seated him at his right hand in the heavenly realms far above all rule and authority, power and dominion and every name that can be invoked, not only in the present age but also in the one to come. And God placed all things under his feet and appointed him to be head over everything for the church, which is his body, the fullness of him who fills everything in every way. (Eph. 1:19–23)

Something "new" happened at salvation history's midpoint. In Christ all is *fulfilled*. God's activity in the world would never be the same after this "Christ event." There is a *new paradigm for the activity of God in the world*. Christ has returned to heaven and is enthroned to rule "above all rule and authority, power and dominion," and the power of the Holy Spirit is unleashed in the world to empower the body of Christ for his redemptive mission.

For Pentecostals, therefore, these questions about the activity of God in the world are not a matter of theological debate, but of personal experience with the Holy Spirit, an experience verified by the New Testament and all that it says about the Christ event and its consequences. God has chosen to *mediate* his presence, power, and word in salvation history. Formerly, he sent prophets to speak to his people, as well as in various other ways; but at the midpoint of salvation history, he sent his Son—the incarnate Word—and has spoken through him (Heb. 1:1–2). Jesus Christ then chose disciples and sent them into the world, and then he sent the Holy Spirit to enable them to proclaim the "good news of the kingdom of God." Rather than a somewhat deistic view of God's activities in the world that sees his activities primarily in sociopolitical movements, the Pentecostal perceives God to be immediately and explicitly involved in the world primarily through the activity of the Holy Spirit in what has been called "Great Commission missions"—the proclamation of the good news of Jesus Christ and his kingdom, and discipling the nations through church planting. These *mediated* acts of God at the midpoint of salvation history are in the controlling, authoritative context of Christ's mission in the world.

While they would not deny the sovereign activity of God in the movements of history and his influence in sociopolitical movements among humanity, Pentecostals clearly see God's redemptive activities articulated in the New Testament. God's acts are mediated through the church by the enablement of the Holy Spirit. The church is not only enabled for its mission by the Spirit, but also by his agency (he is a "missionary"-witnessing Spirit). He is the medium through which the Triune God has chosen to manifest his power in redemptive mission. To say this is not to equate the kingdom of God completely with the church or to abandon a Trinitarian view of mission. Rather, it emphasizes the "incarnational means" (the incarnation and the indwelling of the Spirit in the people of God) of God's revelation and mission, and the importance of the church as the vehicle for bringing that reign of God to the hearts of men and women. To say the church, empowered by the Holy Spirit, is active in carrying out God's mission is to point to the true nature of Trinitarian mission.

Scripture is the Pentecostal's primary and authoritative criterion for identifying the activity of God in the world. But that criterion also involves the quickening ministry of the Holy Spirit. The word of God is a dynamic, living word. For Pentecostals, the "heavens are not as brass," and the prophetic voice is not silent as they engage in mission. God's activity in the world is not just theoretical, "muted activity," the work of an "anonymous Christ" in the events of history. The Spirit speaks in the preaching of the written word and through prophecy, tongues, and interpretation of tongues. The latter, revelation with a small *r*, is subordinate to the authoritative written word. Furthermore, the Holy Spirit illumines the proclaimed word and confirms it with the outward charismatic signs of the Spirit. This "executive" of mission continues to minister by guiding the missionary's theological responses to the issues and problems of contemporary mission (dynamic theologizing in mission).

Mission Issues with Pneumatological Gaps

Contemporary mission issues clearly reveal a major problem with pneumatological gaps in mission theology. Mission practice inevitably reflects deficiencies in mission theology (mission theory). The correction comes when contemporary issues force missiologists to examine Scripture afresh. As they do this, the neglected doctrine of the Holy Spirit is repeatedly resurrected in one way or another. It is *that* dimension of Trinitarian mission that is increasingly in focus today—the Holy Spirit's role in God's redemptive mission today. The following description of contemporary mission issues focuses on those issues where pneumatology is neglected. The treatment of these issues is not merely due to the selection of a Pentecostal missiologist. These issues are *representative* issues of contemporary mission theology; they point to a gap in Western theology where the doctrine of the Holy Spirit is neglected.

Chapter 3 described that theological distortion in Western theology and the resulting neglect of the Spirit in the history of mission theology and practice. Generally speaking, the non-experiential view of the Christian faith, the static view of theology and revelation, and the erosion of the sense of the supernatural are all linked to the underdevelopment of pneumatology in Western Christianity.

A predominantly rationalistic, although orthodox, view of the Christian faith has developed. In that view, for all practical purposes, after the conversion experience, God ceases to be actively involved in the affairs of Christians. This position sees God's activity in the world in any other way than in the conversion experience as problematic.

The subjective dimension of the Christian faith is often addressed in pejorative terms in evangelical literature (particularly in dispensationalist literature), as though it is anti-faith in nature. But the subjective spiritual dimension must not be denigrated, because that distorts the fundamental character of the Christian faith. For instance, we do not "spiritualize" when we say Jesus' good news of the kingdom is a kingdom of the heart; it *is* a spiritual kingdom where God the Holy Spirit demonstrates his power. To say that the true people of God are born of the Spirit, both Jew and Gentile, is not "spiritualizing" or "replacement theology"; the true people of God are truly spiritual in nature and are not determined by ancestry (John 1:12–13). Any neglect of the experiential dimension of the faith touches everything else. It impacts negatively on our devotional life and on our theology. In the last analysis, the neglect of the subjective spiritual dimension of Christianity involves our view of the activity of God in Christian experience and our view of God's activity in the world. However, this kind of theological reductionism takes place in dispensational theology, and it negatively impacts mission theory and practice, especially in cultures that emphasize community and their "peoplehood."

Evangelicalism's failure to recognize its theological heritage and the impact of Protestant Scholasticism, especially its "pneumatological hiatus," results in the loss of a major evaluative perspective for viewing Pentecostal movements and the Pentecostal mission phenomenon. For example, in *The Christian World Mission: Today and Tomorrow*, J. Herbert Kane treats the Pentecostal-charismatic movement as a problem when he discusses it under the section entitled, "Continuing Problems." He does not believe that the movement is part of the solution to fill an experiential void in contemporary evangelicalism, a renewal movement filling an enormous theological gap left by scholastic orthodoxy. Kane states that the popularity of the charismatic movement is partly due to the impact of existentialism! He states, "Existentialism in philosophy and theology, with its emphasis on personal experience, has created a climate in which this kind of experience-oriented movement can thrive and grow" (1981, p. 267). Kane misses the fact that both existential theology and the charismatic movement are responses to an overly rationalistic, static-oriented orthodoxy.

To attribute the popularity of the charismatic movement, even in part, to the impact of existential philosophy and theology rather than to a genuine renewal of the Spirit, a valid dimension of the Christian faith, reveals how entrenched static orthodoxy and its rationalistic apologetic is in the Western world. Kane's treatment of the charismatic movement for the most part is objective, and he does mention the great neglect of the Holy Spirit in evangelicalism (1981, pp. 270–72). But he shows no awareness concerning the theological roots of that neglect. Existential theology is a symptom of the neglect; it is not the movement's cause or its crucible. Nor is there any mutual influence connecting the two phenomena, other than the fact that both existential theology and Pentecostalism emphasize "Christian experience." To point out that similarity is no more relevant than to point out that existentialists breathe the same air as Pentecostals! Rather than the view that Pentecostalism is a continuing *problem* in missions, the crucial issue is the nature of God's activity in Western Christianity and the demise of the experiential dimension of the Christian faith.

THE PROBLEMATIC ACTIVITY OF GOD IN MISSIONS

The Western silence on the Spirit in the face of the current issues in mission has created a crisis regarding the doctrine of the providence of God. The fact that both the providence of God and the kingdom of God are problematic in contemporary mission theology is symptomatic. They provide a major theological context for discussing contemporary mission issues.

"The Kingdom" and God's Activity

The theme of the kingdom of God has emerged as a source from which theological responses to mission problems are being made. Some of the problems addressed by this theme are the nature of the church's mission, social justice, poverty, religious renewal, and the contextualization of the Christian faith in the varied cultures of the developing world. But the kingdom theme is given various interpretations in mission theology. The question arises, "How is God's reign manifested in mission today?" The kingdom of God theme directly addresses the issue of the manifold activity of God in the world today; the theme *should* be "center stage." It has a theological affinity with the doctrine of the providence of God, which concerns God and Christ's all-inclusive presence and rule in the world "behind the scenes." The mission problems mentioned above all concern how God is active in contemporary mission. The Pentecostal's view of the kingdom of God represents a unique biblical paradigm in modern Christianity for the approach to and solution of these problems. If it is true that the kingdom theme is a significant biblical dimension for the solution of these problems, then it is reasonable to assume that the neglect of this theme would result in mission problems with significant pneumatological gaps. In other words, if the kingdom is "hidden" in any way from contemporary evangelicalism, it must not only retard mission but also inevitably result in mission problems where a deficiency in pneumatology is endemic.

In his article "Preaching the Kingdom of God," I. Howard Marshall finds the contemporary "silence" on the kingdom of God rather surprising, because New Testament scholars universally agree that the theme is central to the Gospels and the teaching of Jesus Christ. Marshall attributes this silence to the lack of expectancy among contemporary Christians and their loss of belief in divine intervention in history. He also cites the difficulty of defining the concept because of its "already" and "not yet" references in the New Testament (1977, p. 212).

In C. Peter Wagner's *Church Growth and the Whole Gospel*, he mentions that the "kingdom idea" was resurrected in evangelicalism shortly after World War II. He discusses the irony involved in the fact that the kingdom of God was central in Jesus' preaching and teaching but is seldom mentioned in evangelical circles. Wagner attributes this to distortions arising from the "social gospel," dispensationalism, and cultic-apocalypticism—all of which provided a false justification for the kingdom's neglect in evangelicalism (1981, pp. 2–3). Another possible reason for its neglect in contemporary evangelicalism is the theme's pneumatological implications. To help clarify this, Wagner identifies two categories of "signs" of the kingdom of God:

> Category A: Social signs or signs applied to a general class of people. These include (1) preaching good news to the poor, (2) proclaiming release to the captives, (3) liberating the oppressed, and (4) instituting the Year of Jubilee ("acceptable year of the Lord").
>
> Category B: Personal signs or signs applied to specific individuals. These include (1) restoring sight to blind people, (2) casting out demons and evil spirits, (3) healing sick people, (4) making lame people walk, (5) cleansing lepers, (6) restoring hearing to deaf people, and (7) raising the dead. (p. 16)

Category B signs are easily identified with a Pentecostal expression of the Christian Faith. They involve the outward charismatic ministry of the Holy Spirit. Evangelicals may have avoided the kingdom theme, and to an extent their social obligations, because type A signs are linked with the "social gospel" of liberal Christianity. But they could have also neglected that central theme of Jesus' ministry because of the type B signs that characterize and support Pentecostal theology. Without a doubt, the kingdom of God theme emphasizes two greatly neglected areas in conservative evangelicalism—the social and pneumatological implications of the gospel. Pentecostals neglect the former area with other evangelicals. Of course, the latter refers specifically to the outward charismatic nature of pneumatology. It is that "hidden dimension" of the kingdom of God in evangelicalism (or their failure to consider it valid activity of God today, type B signs) that brings the Pentecostal contribution to contemporary mission into focus.

The frequent mention of the kingdom of God theme and its biblical and theological articulation throughout this study indicates of religion by explaining its tenacity in history. The motif is expressed in the following ways: "religion is the projection of man surrounded by the powers of nature," or "theology is anthropology," or "religion is the opiate of the masses," and so on (Berkouwer, 1952, pp. 19–20). Berkouwer's third motif, the catastrophic, is especially relevant for a discussion of the crisis in connection with contemporary mission theology. It simply has to do with the catastrophic terrors and sufferings of humanity, and the deplorable conditions under which the majority of the human race exists in the modern world. The doctrine of providence must address how God is active in such a world. In turn, mission theology must articulate how God is active in carrying out his mission today, and also what the church's response should be in such a world.

The catastrophe motif and the resulting crisis of providence became prominent in mission circles as the leaders of the younger developing world churches became more involved in the worldwide missionary movement. When they began to tell of their struggles with poverty and social injustice, especially in ecumenical circles, this struggle of part of the worldwide church became the focus of mission theology. The history of the International Missionary Council (IMC) after World War II reveals a growing consciousness on the part of the worldwide missionary movement of the deplorable conditions in some of these emerging nations. The agenda of the IMC began to show an increased concern for the social, economic, and racial injustices taking place in the world. This attention to the socioeconomic and political dimensions of the church's mission challenged mission theology to be relevant to a new emerging world. A valid aspect of the church's mission in the world was coming into focus, and mission theology needed to address that dimension of the church's mission in the new world.

The crisis concerning the activity of God in the world became acute, however, when the conditions of the developing world began to dominate the agenda of mission thinking. In other words, the crisis in the context of mission—poverty, violence, and oppression—began to impact excessively on mission theologizing. These issues themselves became the hermeneutical horizon for mission theologizing. The world, it was said, sets the agenda for mission its importance for the development of pneumatology and mission theology. The link between the kingdom of God theme and pneumatology is the good news of the kingdom of God (the kingdom that Jesus proclaimed was "present") and it involves the twofold gospel truth: (1) Christ's redemptive death, plus (2) the *gift of the Holy Spirit*. Our belief is that the biblical theme of the kingdom of God represents the theological underpinnings of Pentecostal theology. The kingdom of God represents the dynamic power and reign of God in the world. The kingdom in its biblical sense designates God's supernatural breaking into history in the person of Jesus Christ; he came declaring that the kingdom of God had arrived (Luke 11:20). The kingdom is synonymous with the activity of God; it is a more pregnant expression for the rule of God himself and his power released in the world. In the new age of the Spirit, the New Testament shows that God's power and activity among people involves the Third Person of the Godhead, the Holy Spirit. The coming of the new age is characterized by a new full dimension of the Spirit of God (John 1:33; 3:34). That work of the Spirit among believers involves both an inward life-source dimension and an outward charismatic dimension (Grassi, 1978, pp. 7–8; Montague, 1976, pp. 32, 366). The outward charismatic dimension of the Holy Spirit's ministry is identified in the New Testament with the concept of the kingdom (Luke 24:49; Acts 1:3–8; 2:4). The kingdom of God refers to the *Holy Spirit's mediated activity in and through the church in its mission to the world.*

A Crisis in the Doctrine of the Providence of God

G. C. Berkouwer devotes a chapter to this crisis in the doctrine of the providence of God in his *Studies in Dogmatics: The Providence of God* (1952). He cites three motifs that occasioned the doctrine's demise in the Western world: the scientific, the projection, and the catastrophic (p. 17). The first motif, the scientific, has appeared repeatedly in this study. It is primarily cultural and has eroded the sense of the supernatural in the Western world. The second motif, projection, is the most radical. It has been used by Marx, Feuerbach, Nietzsche, and Freud to dispose of the truth-character

(God-world-church). The "Great Commission," the proclamation
of the gospel, was swallowed up in social justice and other social
concerns. In a sense, the "catastrophic" nature of the context of
mission and its pressing needs eclipsed confidence in the activity of
God through Scripture, the true hermeneutical horizon for mission
theology. In the last analysis, the methodological shift of horizons
from Scripture to the "world" constituted a compromise in biblical
authority. God's "speaking from the world" became the norm rather
than God's speaking from Scripture. This phenomenon brings to
mind the previously cited historic "ebbs of the Spirit" in salvation
history. A diminishing sense of the active presence of God resulted
in an increased attention to more objective revelation (in this case,
the written word). God's active redemptive presence appeared to
subside, so a deistic-providential emphasis replaced it.

The crisis of providence in contemporary mission, however,
involves more than an eclipse of the activity of God as mediated
by Scripture. God is said not only to speak from the world, but his
immediate activity is also found in revolutionary movements in
the world. The eclipse of the mediated activity of God through the
church (God-church-world) through the ministry of the Holy Spirit
becomes complete. We must now discover where God is active in the
world and join him in order to participate in God's mission (Bassham,
1979, p. 68). For many, it was no longer clear where God was working in his redemptive mission. The catastrophic needs of the context
of mission, in some circles, led to an abandonment of the mediated
activity of God in mission (God-church-world) for a search for his
immediate activity in those catastrophic contextual events.

The crisis in the doctrine of the providence of God, therefore,
provides the basis for some crucial missiological issues. What *is*
mission? Is it a search for God's presence in sociopolitical movements and an alignment with those movements? What then is the
role of the church? What is the role of Scripture? What of the "Great
Commission" mission, the church motivated by the Spirit and sent
into the world to proclaim God's salvation from sin? What about
evangelism? In *The World Council of Churches and the Demise of
Evangelism*, Harvey Hoekstra speaks of a reconceptualization of
mission in conciliar theology after the integration of the IMC with

the World Council of Churches (WCC). "New mission" was then characterized by the above crisis about the manner of God's activity in the world. It gave humanization as the primary emphasis of mission. Hoekstra shows how this "new mission" resulted in the demise of evangelism and Great Commission mission in the history of the WCC (1979, pp. 12, 21, 26–27, 69).

The methodological error arising out of "the crisis in providence" was the forfeiture of Scripture as the authoritative starting point for mission theology. Some at the Third Assembly of the WCC at New Delhi in 1961 recognized the danger of a theological methodology that started from the context of mission. Bassham states that some of the participants saw a "basic methodological difficulty . . . in this way of approaching mission theology" (1979, p. 68). Bassham states further that they thought the idea of participating in God's mission in the world

> ran too much risk of breaking away from the necessary controls (theological, liturgical, and canonical) that the Church has painfully developed in the course of its history. . . . The method of searching for God's presence in contemporary situations runs the danger of assuming a "second source of revelation" (in "the world") uncontrolled by the theological criteria provided by the given revelation of Christ. (pp. 68–69)

The redefinition of mission is directly related to the conciliar "contextual" hermeneutic. In the quest for relevancy, mission theologizing was excessively impacted by its context, resulting in a compromise of biblical authority. This compromise affected the very agenda of mission itself. The redefinition of mission is directly related to the crisis in the nature of the activity of God in mission. Bassham states:

> This new understanding of mission radically changed the traditional view of God and his relationship to the world. No longer was mission accomplished primarily through the church: the new emphasis stressed that God's primary relationship is to the world and it is the world, and not the church, that is the focus of God's plan. The value of this insight, as stated and developed, tended to overlook completely the meaning and importance of God's covenant with his people and the call to "the obedience of faith for the sake of his name among all the nations" (Rom. 1:5). (p. 69)

The new pattern of God-world-church now replaced the classical mission pattern of God-church-world (p. 69). Under the pressure of the catastrophic context of mission and a faulty hermeneutic, what began as an effort to discover the true, holistic nature of the church's mission led to a fatal redefinition of "mission." That redefinition excluded the Great Commission as the meaning of mission for the contemporary world.

The idea of *missions* (plural)—as the church empowered and sent into the world to make Jesus Christ known as Lord and Savior, persuading men and women to become his disciples and responsible members of his church—was replaced by the idea that "the church is mission." In the contemporary world that "mission" means improving the human condition. Everything the church is called to do is mission. The capitulation to the pressures of the context of mission is evident in that the very goal of mission itself is considered negotiable. A tactical matter concerning the emphasis of mission is allowed to alter basic mission theory. The compromise in biblical authority allowed such a strategic error. However, if the theme of the kingdom of God was taken seriously, this deviation from the church's mission would not have taken place, because Jesus' gospel of the kingdom of God refers to *both* social justice and the proclamation of the gospel (Luke 4:18–19). Lesslie Newbigin states concerning the two terms "mission" and "missions":

> Any progress in thought and action depends on being able to discern and state *both* the relation between things *and* the distinction between things. Or to put it another way, it depends upon being capable of looking at one thing at a time without thereby falling into the illusion of thinking that it is the only thing that exists. (1960, p. 23)

Newbigin gave a prophetic warning during the period when the integration of the IMC and WCC was being discussed:

> Now it is my plea that if ecumenicity is not to mean Christianity without its cutting edge, one of our needs today is to identify and distinguish the specific foreign missionary task within the total Mission of the Church understood in ecumenical terms. (p. 23)

A failure to differentiate between "mission" and "missions" in conciliar theologies of mission *has* taken the cutting edge off of the Christian faith. Broadening mission to include everything the church should do without discrimination resulted in a practical reduction of the concept of mission. That which especially should not be neglected, the narrower view of mission—the Great Commission—is neglected. This has been documented in the subsequent history of the WCC's Committee on World Mission and Evangelism (CWME) (Hoekstra, 1979; Johnston, 1978).

MISSIO DEI AND "NEW MISSION"

Therefore, one of the most fundamental and crucial issues of contemporary mission emerges from the context of the problematic activity of God in the world—the nature of the church's mission. The theological springboard for the redefinition of mission is the *missio Dei* (mission of God) concept. The idea itself does not provide a basis for the redefinition of mission as "new mission." But its use by conciliar missiologists represents a deviation from its original meaning in contemporary discussion, as well as a deviation from its traditional use in Roman Catholic missiology. In fact, in its emergence in Protestant mission circles at the meeting of the IMC at Willingen, Germany, in 1952, it pointed to a solution to the crisis about the activity of God in the world. *Missio Dei* arose in connection with a discussion of the Trinitarian view of mission (Rosin, 1972, pp. 6–7). That view specifically involves the principle of "delegated" mission and the roles of the Son and the Spirit in commissioning the church in mission. But the concept's modification and interpretation by some conciliar missiologists reflects the crisis with regard to the problematic activity of God in mission.

H. H. Rosin did a critical literary study of the *missio Dei* concept in order to determine its original meaning and function in Protestant missiological discussion (*"Missio Dei"*: an examination of the origin, contents, and function of the term in Protestant missiological discussion, 1972). His study supports the contention that the phrase *missio Dei* originally referred to the Trinitarian view of mission. Rosin shows that the concept was subsequently used by conciliar missiologists to support their "new mission," in which social justice and other social concerns were their goal. They contended that the immediate activity of God in the movements of liberation was the manner of God's activity in the contemporary world of mission.

Georg F. Vicedom's *Mission of God* (1965) brought the phrase *missio Dei* into popular use in Protestant missionary circles. Vicedom placed the origin of the phrase at the Willingen Conference of the IMC in 1952 (p. 5). Rosin states that Vicedom must have obtained the Latin term from Karl Hartenstein's conference report in *Mission zwischen Gestern und Morgen,* because the phrase does not occur in the printed Willingen documents, only the idea (1972, p. 6). For Vicedom, the phrase *missio Dei* clearly had Trinitarian content and belonged with Trinitarian theology and terminology (p. 9). The Willingen Conference centered on the Trinitarian basis of the missionary enterprise, emphasizing the source of mission as the Triune God and the primacy of the activity of the Godhead in mission (pp. 9–10).

Missio Dei in the Trinitarian sense describes God as the protagonist of mission (he sends), but also as the One who is sent. The Son is sent (the incarnation), and the Holy Spirit is sent (Pentecost) (Rosin, 1972, pp. 14–15). The idea of "delegation" is prominent, therefore, along with incarnation in the Trinitarian view. The Son is sent (Gal. 4:4–6), the Holy Spirit is sent (John 14:16), and the disciples are sent (John 17:18). Nowhere in the Trinitarian understanding of mission is the church eliminated because mission originates in God, or because it is to be understood primarily as the activity of God. Rosin states that consideration of the thought "God has a mission" does not take away from the sovereignty of God: "God himself—in Christ, through the holy Spirit, with the participation of the Church—is totally engaged and involved in a world where he rules in 'judgment and redemption' " (p. 18). The church also has a mission, because it is commissioned and sent into the world by Christ and empowered by the Holy Spirit for the task (pp. 17, 21).

Vicedom complained that the phrase *missio Dei* underwent a modification and interpretation in the hands of some conciliar missiologists. Their treatment of the concept resulted in a deviation from its original meaning. From the Trinitarian usage, denoting what God was doing mediately through the church in the proclamation of the gospel, the phrase was used to accent what was happening in historical development (Recker, 1977, p. 186). John V. Taylor somewhat prophetically noted the danger of the misuse of *missio Dei*, which is meant to establish the divine initiative, when used so vaguely that it includes the whole action of God throughout time and space, as though, if he chose, God might have accomplished the renewal of man without Jesus Christ (Rosin, 1972, p. 34). Such a vague use also has resulted in bypassing the instrumentality of the church in mission. In the attempt to describe the contemporary immediate activity of God among humanity, his mediated activity through the church was neglected. Rosin shows the danger of taking the concept *out of its salvation history context*, with regard to the definition of mission:

> By extending the concept *"missio Dei"* limitlessly (defined as "the history" or the "dynamic revolutionary events" or the "sum total of all the good that is being done") the term loses its original meaning entirely and comes finally to signify everything except what it literally means: *God's (special) "mission."* For this after all indicates an action, which does not point indiscriminately to all kinds of happenings in the world, but only to one incomprehensible event, namely that God, the creator of all things submerged himself in his own world as a stranger . . . who in this world pursues a very special, hidden road in order to liberate it. (1972, p. 34)

The limitless use of the term *affects adversely the crucial midpoint event of salvation history*: the incarnation, crucifixion, and resurrection of Christ, which is the heart of the missionary message. The primacy of evangelism in the concept of mission is thereby eclipsed, and the role of the church in mission is trivialized. Proponents of such a use of *missio Dei* say, "Mission is God's or Christ's but not ours." It is proposed that mission is to be found in the anonymous immediate activity of God in the history of humanity's struggles for human dignity and justice, not in the contemporary proclamation of the gospel.

The crux of understanding the *missio Dei* issue is the ability to differentiate between God's immediate activity and his mediated activity in the world. When this is done, the misuse of the concept in the support for "new mission" is evident. The twofold view of the activity of God is simply not a matter of either/or. Newbigin's counsel with regard to "mission" and "missions" also applies to God's manifold activity in the world. One must discern and state *both* the relation between things *and* the distinction between them. One must be capable of looking at one thing at a time without falling into the illusion of thinking it is the only thing that exists. Rosin mentions that this "illusion" is the case with conciliar discussions on mission, and he says this in terms of the problematic activity of God in mission. He states concerning the 1963 CWME Meeting in Mexico City:

> The discussion raised a theological issue which remained unresolved. Debate returned again and again to the relationship between God's action in and through the Church and everything God is doing in the world apparently independently of the Christian community. Can a distinction be drawn between God's *providential action* and God's *redeeming action*? If the restoration and reconciliation of human life is being achieved by the action of God through secular agencies, what is the place and significance of faith? If the Church is to be wholly involved in the world and its history what is the true nature of its separateness? (1972, p. 26; emphasis mine)

The question about whether a distinction can be drawn between God's providential activity and God's redeeming activity must be answered in the affirmative *methodologically*. The critical question is not whether all of the activity of God in the world is one or not, as Recker states (1977, p. 186). Of course, that historical activity of God is one *in essence* with his redemptive activity. But the problem concerning God's activity in mission is its *recognition by men and women*; it is an epistemological issue, not one concerning the ontological nature of the activity. The question concerns how the activity of God may be discerned and differentiated in mission theology. The issue does not concern theological speculation primarily but an eminently practical matter: how God is involved among men and women in his redemptive activity.

A further reason why there must be a differentiation made between God's providential activity in history and his redemptive activity is the *revelational nature* of the latter. Because God's redemptive activity is revelational activity, it necessarily requires the response of faith. It could therefore be hidden activity. The biblical description of God's activity necessarily separates God's providential activity in history from his mediated redemptive activity—not in essence but necessarily for human observers. A parallel discussion, one involving primarily methodology, concerns the nature of general history and salvation history. Some theologians use the German terms *Historie* and *Geschichte* to differentiate between the providential activity of God in history and his redemptive activity respectively. Methodologically speaking, in terms of historical-critical methodology, salvation history is not completely unveiled by such methods. The reason is that salvation history is not only *historical* in nature, but is also *revelational* in nature, having to do with the Spirit. The inadequacy of the historical-critical method is due to its inability to plumb the depths of the supernatural dimensions of the *acts of God* in history. A fundamental question is, "What kind of activity do we find in the New Testament?" Its primary focus is on the revealed, mediated activity of God through Christ and his kingdom in the hearts of men and women—the presence and power of the Holy Spirit mediated through the church in the world.

Therefore, a reason for differentiating between God's providential activity and his redemptive activity is that in the latter God has chosen to act mediately through human agency. This choice sets apart God's redemptive activity. The mediated nature of God's redemptive activity is in keeping with the nature of divine revelation itself—it is *incarnational*. God co-opts men and women to represent him, condescending to speak through them (Recker, 1977, p. 192). This biblical picture of God's use of human agency in his redemptive purpose conflicts with the *ordo salutis* of "new mission": God-world-church. In its Trinitarian sense, Samuel Volbeda affirms human agency in divine mission:

> Even a slight acquaintance with Scripture will indicate that the idea of sending and being sent is one of the fundamental categories of

Scripture. Revelation itself is mediated by God's sending such as He chooses to use in its communication and effectuation. . . .

God—Revelation—Missionaries—People

Without missions, revelation would never come home. God always picks out some men and sends them. (Recker, 1977, pp. 194–95)

By God's choice, therefore, mission is characterized as mediated divine activity. By means of the enabling power of the Holy Spirit, the church engages in missions. This affirms the formula of God-church-world.

The somewhat extended treatment of the concept *missio Dei* here is warranted because it is the "Trojan horse," as Rosin puts it, by which the "walls" of the traditional Trinitarian theology of mission were breached. But the distortion of the concept and its use as a vehicle for "new mission" are not the only reasons for discussing it. The concept illustrates the crisis in Western mission theology about the activity of God in the world, especially in the catastrophic developing world. That crisis of God's activity in the world establishes a *major context* for understanding contemporary mission issues; it represents a basic common denominator for contemporary mission problems. They have a crucial *pneumatological* dimension.

One could ask how such a major theological shift could take place in an area as fundamental as the church's mission. Of course, the reasons are numerous. Was it the catastrophic nature of the needs of the church in the developing world? Certainly the methodological or hermeneutical error contributed to the shift from the Great Commission to the nebulous, limitless use of *missio Dei*. At least these matters can be understood from the viewpoint of developing world theologians. The contextualization phenomenon itself is an explanation for the shift from their perspective. For them, theologizing in mission represented an effort to make theology relevant to a new set of needs. In so doing they emphasized the need for a more holistic view of mission. Certainly the neglect of the socioeconomic dimension of mission in the West was a contributing factor, even though the resulting mission theology neglected, and in some conciliar theologies omitted, the evangelistic mandate. The excessive impact of the context of mission on the content of mission theology, however, took place in the absence of biblical authority. This arbiter and check to the pull of context in theologizing was not present, due to the use of a faulty hermeneutic: Scripture was not the authoritative starting point for theologizing.

But one could ask, "If there were a strong conviction as to God's redemptive activity through the preaching of the gospel, and an equally firm conviction concerning the mediated, transforming activity of God in the church, would such a shift have taken place?" If there were a firm belief in, and experience of, the charismatic activity of God the Holy Spirit in worship and mission, would there be such an intensive search for his presence elsewhere? Would not the Holy Spirit, a "missionary" Spirit who also "sheds the love of God in our hearts," give an emphasis to both an outreach involving the preaching of Christ and his salvation, *and* one involving social justice and concern for the poor? Would there be the limitless idea of *missio Dei*, a view of the undifferentiated activity of God in the world? Under the circumstances of a dynamic experience with the redemptive activity of God, could a shift from a Trinitarian, Great Commission mission to "new mission" take place? Does not the shift itself point to a spiritual malaise? Could it not represent a theologizing in mission that is due to the participants' contemporary experience of the Spirit being in an ebb stage?

The crisis of providence and the emergence of *missio Dei* as an alternative to the mediated redemptive activity of God through the church indicates an underlying pneumatological hiatus in conciliar theology. Perhaps since the activity of God was so problematic, was of such an esoteric nature, the notion of discovering his activity elsewhere was not so strange under the circumstances. Since the signs of the kingdom in terms of the redemptive activity of God the Holy Spirit (category *B* signs) were so obscure, theologizing gravitated toward an emphasis on the more *objective* signs of God's activity in history. This would be the case, especially, in view of the catastrophic needs of the context of mission in the developing world. On the part of Western theologians, the shift could also be explained by a desire to show solidarity with the younger churches of the developing world.

In the brief discussion of the problematic activity of God and the *missio Dei* concept, a number of significant mission issues have emerged. Chief among them is the nature of mission itself; its holistic nature, encompassing both the evangelistic and cultural mandates as being problematic. The limitless use of *missio Dei* calls the church's role in mission into question. It also brings into focus the problem of discerning whether Scripture sets forth a priority of mission activity among all the good works the church could do in the world. The conciliar theologies of mission emphasize the neglected issue of ecumenism. Theological method in mission strategy is also an issue arising from the pressing needs of the mission context of the developing world. The issue of contextualization, with its pitfalls, is evident. The practical nature of mission strategy (mission theologizing) brings the theological issue of biblical authority into the arena of contemporary mission issues. The phenomenon of independency movements in the developing world, furthermore, is an issue that has been in focus repeatedly in the wider context of this study. At times, these movements were in focus in connection with the contextualization issue, with the indigenous nature of the church. At other times, they arose directly in connection with the deficiency in Western pneumatology (e.g., their causation). Such movements must be viewed as a challenge to our pneumatology. They also would come under the "major context of mission problems"—the problematic activity of God in the world. The movements present a challenge to Western notions of orthodoxy and call for a practical, cross-cultural view of orthodoxy (Watney, 1982, p. 2). The African Independent Church Movement brings the question of the unity and diversity of the body of Christ in its international dimensions into focus. This issue of ecumenism also has an important pneumatological dimension.

Finally, in view of the crisis in the manner of God's activity in mission and the confessed Trinitarian basis of mission, the Holy Spirit's role in mission appears as an issue. Those theologies of mission focusing on the undifferentiated use of *missio Dei*, which also utilize the kingdom theme but yet fail to articulate the role of the Holy Spirit, point to the pneumatological hiatus in contemporary mission theology. However, Jesus' emphasis on the kingdom and both the

New Testament and Pentecostal perspectives on the kingdom bring pneumatology into the arena of mission problems. In a real sense, the Pentecostal-charismatic movement in the Southern Hemisphere at the beginning of the twenty-first century until the present day has provided an answer to the now somewhat naive question, "How is God active in the world today?" For Pentecostal Christians in the Southern Hemisphere the question is moot, but the above theological discussion is not moot; the danger of redefining the mission of the church in some cases still exists in the Global South, because of the intense interest in liberation theology. The Pentecostal nature of the Christian faith there has not solved all the issues connected with *missio Dei*, but the "renewal" of the redemptive activity of God through Christ's good news of the kingdom of God, the power of the Holy Spirit in his church, greatly helps to avoid the errors spoken of above. They have a powerful example of how God is working in their world through their Pentecostal experience.

In summary, the identification of a major theological context of contemporary mission issues—pneumatology—has gone a long way toward their solution. In the past, the catastrophic circumstances of the context of mission in the developing world brought the whole church to realize that a holistic view of mission was needed for twentieth-century mission. However, the hermeneutical error that arose in response to those needs, and the ill-conceived view of *missio Dei* used to support "new mission," resulted in a compromise of the heart of "God's special mission"—the Great Commission mission, the declaration of the gospel of the kingdom of God to the world. The Pentecostal movement is a chief source from which to emphasize God's special mission, as mediated by the activity of God the Holy Spirit through the agency of the church. As a "people of the Spirit," Pentecostals represent a source for dispelling the confusion concerning the activity of God in the world of mission. By means of the kingdom motif, which has been prominent throughout this study, this biblical motif is used again in the next chapter to provide a Pentecostal perspective for mission theology.

7 The Pentecostal and the Kingdom of God

This chapter summarizes the Pentecostal contribution to contemporary mission theology by giving Pentecostal perspectives on contemporary mission issues. The kingdom of God motif provides a biblical perspective that is needed to approach the problems of contemporary mission. The motif is inseparably related to pneumatology, so a Pentecostal perspective also emerges. Therefore, it is also instrumental in bringing new insights to a major context of contemporary mission issues—the problematic activity of God in mission. The kingdom motif helps to clarify the Holy Spirit's role for a Trinitarian view of mission. The issues of the holistic nature of the missionary enterprise, its priority, and the role of the church in mission are addressed by the kingdom motif in a significant way. The kingdom motif brings into view a major issue of contemporary mission—the poor. This social issue can be examined, therefore, from the perspective of a major biblical theme.

THE KINGDOM WITHOUT THE SPIRIT?

In chapter 6, the discussion of *missio Dei* illustrated a failure to distinguish between God's immediate providential activity in the world and his mediated redemptive activity. This resulted in a mission emphasis in which the cultural mandate or social justice and other social concerns dominated. Any approach to mission that neglects the mediated redemptive activity of God, the Great Commission mission, contrasts starkly with the Pentecostal perspective of mission founded on the biblical concept of the kingdom of God. Jesus' specific mention of the poor in his proclamation of the gospel of the kingdom of God indicates a holistic mission that includes both the "evangelistic mandate" and "the cultural mandate" (both category *A* and *B* signs of the kingdom). The kingdom motif emphasizes the dynamic, evidential experience of the Spirit—the mediated activity of God through the church. Pentecostalism provides insights into this experiential dimension of the Christian faith; in this sense it functions as the "third corner" of Christianity.

With respect to the mission of the church, the kingdom idea's scope is clearly comprehensive in Scripture. It concerns both the evangelistic mandate (the narrow view of mission—evangelism or the Great Commission mission) and the cultural mandate (the wider view of mission—the social dimension). The latter mandate is the primary emphasis of most conciliar theologies of mission, and the former points to the area of Pentecostal emphasis and contribution. The cultural mandate also functions as a challenge to Pentecostalism's inadequate biblical response to the wider mission of the church.

The kingdom perspective puts contemporary mission problems in a biblical framework from which fresh theologizing can provide solutions. But curiously, the kingdom theme is often used in theologizing about mission without articulating the role of the Holy Spirit; such a use indicates a lack of understanding regarding the gospel of the kingdom of God. Instead the kingdom theme is often used to support the wider view of mission by emphasizing the immediate providential activity of God in social and political movements. The need to specify that activity in terms of the Holy Spirit does not appear to be crucial in such cases. The concept of *missio Dei*, used improperly in its undifferentiated sense, puts the emphasis on the activity of God the Father. However, a biblical theology, the gospel of the kingdom of God, requires a description of the role of the Third Person of the Trinity for a true Trinitarian view of mission. The description of his role brings the holistic nature of mission into focus, and it points to the biblical priority of mission.

When the kingdom theme is treated apart from the role of the Holy Spirit, mission theology is severely impaired, even distorted. The published documents of the 1980 World Council of Churches' Committee on World Mission and Evangelism (CWME) Meeting at Melbourne, Australia, reveals the typical silence on the ministry and role of the Holy Spirit in conciliar theologies of mission. One would expect that a conference on evangelism and mission gathered to discuss the mission perspectives, with the theme "Thy Kingdom Come," would have much to say about the Holy Spirit's role in mission. But the scarcity of pneumatology in the conference documents is curious.

In the plenary presentations, only Ernst Käsemann broached the subject, due to his treatment of the New Testament concept of the kingdom in its eschatological context. While Käsemann mentions the signs of the kingdom in terms of the outward ministry of the Holy Spirit *in the New Testament* (category *B* signs), most of his *contemporary* applications of the concept concern the social and political dimensions of the kingdom (category *A* signs) (1980, pp. 64–66). Apparently for Käsemann, the signs of the kingdom today only involve the preaching of the gospel, ecumenical openness, and social justice (p. 70). The latter two signs of the kingdom were typical of the focus of the whole conference.

The section reports make scattered references to the Holy Spirit, but only about his inward work in regeneration, revelation, and strengthening the believer (pp. 194–96). When mission in the wider sense (social justice) is linked with the kingdom theme, emphasizing the undifferentiated activity of God, the result is relative silence on the work of the Holy Spirit. The kingdom concept, therefore, is no guarantee that the missionary role of the Spirit and a holistic view of mission will be considered. Since the concept of the kingdom is comprehensive, one may choose to only emphasize one aspect of God's activity, either his immediate providential activity or his mediated pneumatic activity. The limitless use of *missio Dei* under the alleged purpose of attaining a holistic view of mission appears to function as a smokescreen for an obvious bias for pursuing social justice and other social concerns as the goal of mission. But the crucial question is, "Does the New Testament indicate a priority for mission?" If biblical authority means anything, then this question must be answered.

Even evangelical approaches to the kingdom theme can neglect the role of the Holy Spirit for a number of reasons. George Eldon Ladd's otherwise excellent survey of the kingdom of God theme in

The Presence of the Future (1974) is an illustration. He is unusually silent on the role of the Holy Spirit. His thesis chiefly concerns the truth that the kingdom of God is the dynamic, redemptive activity of God himself in history. But his chief omission is *how* God acts and works in history apart from Jesus Christ himself. Ladd's silence on the Holy Spirit is counterproductive to his purpose of showing that the kingdom breaks through into contemporary history in the person and mission of Jesus Christ (1974, p. xi). Ladd does not describe the kingdom concept as God's activity in the world by means of the Holy Spirit's dynamic ministry, both in and independent of the church. Various terms are used for the kingdom: "God's rule and reign," "a dynamic power at work," "the nature of God's present activity," "God's redemptive working in history," "God's supernatural breaking into history in the person of Jesus," "a new realm of blessing foretold by the prophets," Jesus himself or his words, and the messengers of the gospel themselves (pp. 139, 142, 167–68, 171–72, 189, 204–5, 256). In what appears to be an almost studied manner he avoids the mention of the Third Person of the Trinity. In certain obvious pneumatological contexts, references to the Holy Spirit are missing. Although such terms as "power," "signs," "exorcisms," and "healings" are mentioned, they are not related to pneumatology (p. 183). The topic "The Kingdom: Supernatural" is discussed without a single reference to the Holy Spirit (pp. 188–94).

Perhaps the fact that the Christological context of the kingdom is consistently in focus in Ladd's treatment is the reason for the omission. But given the fact that Ladd primarily confines his treatment of the kingdom to the Old Testament, the ministry of Christ, and the mission of the Twelve and the Seventy pre-Pentecost, his silence on the Spirit is still conspicuous. In the solitary reference to Pentecost, when the kingdom's powers were said to be no longer limited to Jesus and his close disciples, pneumatology is even avoided! The coming of the kingdom to all believers is spoken of as "Jesus returning in the Spirit" (John 14:16–18) and believers being "delivered from the dominion of darkness and transferred into the kingdom of Christ" (Col. 1:13). The only mention of the Third Person of the Godhead is a reference to Romans 14:17 (Ladd, 1974, pp. 272–73). The lone paragraph and an "aside" reference involving one

sentence represents an incredible paucity of references to the Spirit
in a biblical study of the kingdom of God (p. 271). The pneumatological hiatus is conspicuous when Ladd treats "The Ethics of
the Kingdom" in chapter 12. The subjects of righteousness apart
from law, the ethical demands of the reign of God, sanctification,
and the inner spiritual life and renewal are treated under the kingdom theme without even mentioning the enablement of the Holy
Spirit. The Third Person of the Trinity appears to be intentionally
avoided in his book when he deals with biblical texts articulating
the ministry of the Holy Spirit (p. 298). Is this an example of a latent
christomonism in evangelical theology?

The neglect of the Spirit in discussions of the kingdom theme
in exegetical studies of Jesus' preaching in the Gospels may be due
to several causes. A failure to recognize *the kingdom as Jesus uses
it—to describe the gospel in the New Testament*—and a *failure to
recognize a major transition in salvation history itself* in connection
with the gospel are common reasons why the Spirit is neglected.

A Reinterpretation of the Kingdom?

In his article "The Concept of the Kingdom of God in the
Preaching of the Apostles," Donald E. Macomber observes that in
the book of Acts the preaching of the kingdom and the preaching
of the gospel were one and the same. He explains, however, "In
the progress of doctrine in the New Testament, the term 'kingdom of God' is, in Acts dropping out for the term 'gospel'" (1958,
p. 356). In various New Testament references to the term "kingdom,"
Macomber shows that the concept is linked with the *preaching of
the gospel and the name of Jesus Christ* (pp. 356–58). Granted that
preaching the kingdom and preaching the gospel are the same thing
(p. 359), the disciples' use of the two terms does not indicate a reinterpretation. I. Howard Marshall agrees concerning this reinterpretation of the kingdom notion when he says, "What these changes in
terminology indicated was . . . a realization that the saving action
of God was to be unpacked in terms of the work of Christ, in his
ministry, death and resurrection" (1977, p. 213). He states further,

"The person in whom the kingdom was revealed replaced the kingdom in Christian preaching" (p. 213). Is this another example of christomonism by evangelicals? Furthermore, Jesus "unpacked" the kingdom concept in terms of the *Holy Spirit*. How could a term he defines as the gospel, the good news of the kingdom of God, be neglected by his disciples?

Jesus prepared the disciples for a "reinterpretation" of the kingdom by his own interpretation, but that reinterpretation concerned Jesus' correction of the disciples' expectation about the kingdom from a Jewish perspective. This happened just after his resurrection and just prior to Pentecost (Acts 1:1–8). Jesus spoke to the disciples about the kingdom of God over the period of forty days (Acts 1:3). The disciples were expecting the coming of the kingdom on Jesus' own word, but they thought an earthly Jewish kingdom would be set up by their Messiah. Furthermore, they were instructed to wait for the promise in Jerusalem. After all, did not Jesus say in Luke 24:49, "I am going to send you what my Father has promised; but stay in the city until you have been clothed with power from on high"? However, they thought this promise of the kingdom meant they would be enthroned to judge the twelve tribes in an earthly Jewish kingdom. Jesus disregarded these expectations and spoke to the disciples concerning the power of the Holy Spirit in the context of their mission (Acts 1:8).

Saying there was a "reinterpretation" of the kingdom in order to connect it with the gospel is an unnecessary tack in understanding the kingdom motif in the New Testament. The very notion of reinterpreting the kingdom speaks to the loss of pneumatological awareness among evangelicals due to Protestant Scholastic theology's influence. In the attempt to bring the powerful "Spirit-dimension" of the gospel back into evangelical thought, the idea of the reinterpretation of the kingdom emerged among evangelicals, latching on to the terms used by the disciples in their preaching. However, the gift of the Spirit with its outward charismatic ministry was *always* an integral part of the gospel of the kingdom. The apostles did not "reinterpret" the kingdom. Jesus had taught his disciples about the power of the kingdom; it was central in his teaching to the disciples, and he defined it throughout his ministry.

Jesus arrived "preaching the *good news of the kingdom* . . . healing every disease and sickness among the people." In this description of Jesus' preaching, Matthew notes the accompanying power of the Spirit as part and parcel of the gospel (Matt. 4:17, 23–24). Jesus called the good news the good news of *the kingdom*, with the term "kingdom" referring unequivocally to the *twofold* nature of the gospel: (1) the redemptive death of Jesus on the cross for sin, and (2) the gift of the Spirit. After his resurrection, Jesus did not reinterpret anything for his apostles; his Jewish disciples had a wrong concept of the kingdom of God from Judaism, which he *corrected* in his post-resurrection forty-day seminar on the kingdom (Acts 1:3b–8). When, expecting an earthly Jewish kingdom, they asked Jesus if he "at *this time* was going to restore the kingdom to Israel" (Acts 1:6), he told them that it was not for them to know the times or dates the Father had set by his own authority; but he said they would "receive power when the Holy Spirit comes" to be witnesses for him. In effect, at that time, he was saying that they would receive a "kingdom of the heart," the powerful indwelling presence of the Holy Spirit (Acts 1:8; 2:4). Their false expectations concerning an earthly Jewish kingdom immediately arriving would not be changed in their cultural consciousness until they *experienced* the powerful coming of the "kingdom" at Pentecost, and then under the guidance of the Spirit they began to understand the kingdom.

Instead of just using the expression "kingdom motif," as if it is disconnected from the gospel, it should be considered as part and parcel of Jesus' gospel of the kingdom of God. Concerning the different terms used "gospel" or "kingdom," in Acts the apostles *assumed* the powerful dimension of the Spirit when they preached the gospel, and Luke *assumed* it in writing his history of the early church. They knew the "gospel" was the "gospel of the kingdom of God." Even so, the gift of the Spirit is often mentioned along with Jesus' cross, or the power of the Spirit is manifest in an outward visible way when they speak of the gospel (Acts 2:17–25; 3:6–16; 5:30–32; 7:51–52; 8:32–39 [alternate reading of vs. 39, "the Spirit of the Lord suddenly took Philip away and the Spirit fell on the eunuch"]; 10:38–40, 44–46; 11:16–17; 20:25–29; 28:23, 31).

After Pentecost, the redemptive activity of God is mediated primarily through the preaching of the gospel and the manifest power of the Holy Spirit in Jesus' name. The church empowered by the Spirit demonstrates the kingdom's presence and power by the preaching of the gospel—Jesus' redemptive death for sin, which was confirmed by signs and wonders (Mark 16:15–17, 20). It is in this saving activity of God the Holy Spirit, through the agency of the church, that the priority of mission is found. The priority of proclaiming the gospel, the Great Commission mission, dominates the church's mission in the book of Acts. Scripture *does* put emphasis on the evangelistic mandate, God's "special" mission.

Recognizing a Salvation History Transition

While it may not have been so evident to the disciples before Pentecost, it should be clear for the modern reader today that Acts 1:4–8 contains a pneumatological statement. Because of the Pentecost event and Jesus' lead in explaining the kingdom as the Holy Spirit's power in the Christian working through the church (not as an earthly Jewish kingdom), we must understand the kingdom in terms of the Spirit. Jesus' interpretation of the kingdom clearly linked the ministry of the Holy Spirit with the church's mission. Montague states, "What is important [in the Acts 1:1–8 passage] is the present world mission of the church impelled by the Holy Spirit. In Acts the fact that the Kingdom has begun is manifested on earth by the activity of the Spirit" (1976, p. 273).

The prominence of the Holy Spirit's presence and role in Acts 1:8 points to the passage's transitional nature for salvation history. The age of the Spirit was dawning for the church. In Jesus' answer to the disciples' kingdom question, the matter of the coming kingdom's consummation (its "not yet" dimension; Acts 1:11) is subordinated to the presence of the kingdom and the imperative of mission in the "time between the times" (its "already" dimension; Acts 1:8). It is so throughout the New Testament. The understanding of the kingdom concept, in terms of pneumatology in the transition of salvation history, points to centrifugal mission in the power of the Holy Spirit. The Pentecost event (Acts 2) is a pivotal point in salvation history. Boer states:

> At Pentecost a distinct period in the divine economy of redemption was introduced, the characteristic feature of which is the presence of the Holy Spirit. We may therefore say that after Creation and Incarnation the outpouring of the Spirit is the third great work of God. (1961, p. 66)

There is no doubt that what Boer says here about the "third great work of God" is true, especially when we consider that the gift of the Spirit is part and parcel of the gospel of the kingdom of God. We take what Boer is saying above as meaning that the gift of the Spirit, his continuous indwelling presence in Christians, is a unique event in all of salvation history. The *new* covenant in distinction from the old is in the gift of the indwelling Spirit of God in Christians (born of the Spirit, baptized in the Spirit, empowered by the Spirit)—or in other words, Jesus' gospel of the kingdom of God.

Recognizing that a transition in salvation history took place in Acts 1:1–8 allows us to understand the kingdom concept in terms of pneumatology. Pentecost means the church is not only confronted with the *fact* of the Holy Spirit's presence, but also with the *power* of his presence, and the *effects* of his presence, and that the new people of God are from that point forward are continuously indwelt by the Holy Spirit. The power and effects of his presence in Acts are primarily concerned with the witness of the church. Boer states concerning this "coming of the kingdom with power":

> The being filled with the Spirit at Pentecost manifested itself in *irrepressible speaking* about the great works of God that came forth from the human spirit wholly seized by the divine Spirit. Pentecost momentarily placed in sharp and dramatic relief that the Church that had come into being in her New Testament form is a speaking, proclaiming Church and that she addresses all men and all nations with her message. (1961, p. 102)

In effect, therefore, Pentecost confirms that the *kingdom* equals the proclamation of the *gospel*. The New Testament church's understanding of the gospel of the kingdom of God emphasizes the evangelistic mandate's priority in its mission. Jesus' interpretation of the kingdom also points in this direction. The kingdom in pneumatological terms has to do with the witness of the church in the Spirit's power and the universalization of mission, in the inclusion of Gentiles, under his direction (Acts 8:4–8, 12, 14–17; 10:1–46; 11:15–17; 13:13).

Pentecost represented the renewal of the Spirit of prophecy, a tremendous flow of the Spirit after its ebb in salvation history. Boer states further about Pentecost, "If we ask, what is the 'meaning' of the Spirit, we must answer: it consists in this that he is the Gift of speaking about the mighty acts of God" (1961, p. 103). Boer refers to the Apostle Peter's quotation in his sermon to indicate what this gift of speaking means for the church: "This is what was spoken by the prophet Joel: 'In the last days, God says, I will pour out my Spirit on all people. Your sons and daughters will *prophesy*'" (Acts 2:16–17; emphasis mine). He notes that there are two types of speaking that occur at Pentecost: speaking in other tongues under the enablement of the Spirit, which was accompanied with signs; and the preaching of the gospel by Peter under the same enablement. Boer states concerning these two forms of witness:

> The difference between the two types of speaking can perhaps best be so described: *The speaking with other tongues dramatically demonstrated the witnessing character of the Church; Peter's sermon set the pattern through which that witnessing character finds normal and continuing expression.* (p. 103)

It is noteworthy that Peter's sermon at Pentecost gave prominence to both the redemptive death of Jesus and the gift of the Spirit—the twofold gospel of the kingdom.

Boer interprets Pentecost in a salvation history context, emphasizing the priority of the proclamation of the gospel in the church's mission in the "time between the times." Not only is the priority of mission established by this interpretation but also the instrumentality of the church. The focus on the ministry of the Spirit in the new age, therefore, brings attention to the *mediated redemptive activity of God through the fulfillment of the Great Commission mission.*

He notes that both of the above "speakings" of the church establish the "central task" of the church. That task is to witness to the great works of God in the power of the Spirit in the "last days." Boer sees the proclamation of the gospel and the outpouring of the Spirit as signs of the end (1961, p. 103). Therefore, both the preaching of the gospel and the outpouring of the Spirit are "signs of the kingdom." They represent two major dimensions of the Holy Spirit's ministry in the age of the Spirit: his life-giving ministry through the word, and his charismatic ministry in connection with that word.

While Boer holds that the speaking in tongues is a "passing sign," Montague sees such category B signs as typical of the messianic age. Following the summary description of the primitive church in Acts 2:42–47 (where both category A and B signs of the kingdom are mentioned), Montague notes that Luke's first recorded event is the healing of the cripple at the Beautiful Gate (Acts 3:1–10):

> This cure is important not only in that it gives Peter another opportunity to preach Jesus Christ (3:11–26) but also because it is a sign typical of the messianic age (Isa 35:3, 6) and moreover typical of the new life of the resurrection already experienced here and now (4:2). Significantly, though the Holy Spirit is not expressly mentioned in the Speech, Jesus is portrayed as the prophet raised up and acting through the apostles (3:22, 26). The man is healed *in the name of Jesus Christ* (3:6, 16). It seems to be a consistent pattern for the Acts that while the charismatic gifts of tongues and prophecy are attributed to the Holy Spirit . . . cures and exorcisms are attributed to the name of Jesus. (1976, p. 289).

We should remember that to preach in the name of *Christ*, to preach *Jesus Christ*, or to preach in *Jesus' name* are references to preaching his gospel of the kingdom of God.

While there are passages of Scripture that may be interpreted to show that Christ is at work in human history, showing solidarity with the oppressed and needy, Scripture plainly states how Christ is active in contemporary mission. The Great Commission passages contain crucial statements concerning the church's mission in the world. Matthew's and Mark's accounts specifically mention the presence of Christ as the church engages in God's "special" redemptive mission. This is not an anonymous presence; it is in connection with the two signs of the messianic age—the preaching of the gospel and the charismatic activity that accompanies this proclamation (Matt. 28:18–20; Mark 16:15–20; Luke 24:47; John 20:21, 31). Christ confirms the former by the latter (Mark 16:20).

The Kingdom and the Poor

When the issue of the poor in contemporary mission theology is linked with the kingdom theme, the transition in salvation history in Acts 1:8 is prominent. The biblical references to the poor are tied to this new age of the Spirit in the exegetical framework of salvation history. When John the Baptist was in prison, he sent his disciples to Jesus to confirm that he was the one who was to come. Jesus replied, "Go back and report to John what you have seen and heard: The blind receive sight, the lame walk, those who have leprosy are cleansed, the deaf hear, the dead are raised, and the good news is proclaimed to the poor. Blessed is anyone who does not stumble on account of me" (Luke 7:22–23). By the addition of the last phrase, it appears that "the poor" are those who are receptive to the gospel, along with the other persons mentioned in the verse who respond in faith to Jesus; therefore, it is not just a reference to their economic status. The poor are also specifically mentioned in the beginning of his ministry in Nazareth: "The Spirit of the Lord is on me, because he has anointed me to proclaim good news to the poor. He has sent me to proclaim freedom for the prisoners and recovery of sight for the blind, to set the oppressed free, to proclaim the year of the Lord's favor" (Luke 4:18–19). In both passages, the poor are specifically mentioned as those targeted for the proclamation of the good news (of the kingdom of God). Jesus sought those who were responsive to his ministry; he associated with and looked for those who would respond in faith (Pomerville, 2010, pp. 101–28).

The solidarity of Pentecostalism with the poor is often noted, and Pentecostalism's phenomenal growth is frequently attributed to its ties with the poor and the working classes. However, it is clear that such solidarity with the poor is not due to overt mission strategy. At the Melbourne meeting of the World Council of Churches' CWME, Joaquim Beato stated:

Pentecostalism today is, without any doubt, the most dynamic Protestant group, and it has experienced remarkable growth. In spite of
signs of "aging" in some of their groups, it is the only group with close
ties with the poor and the working classes, and it is the one which has
absorbed the cultural characteristics of the lower classes. It does not
seem to me, however, that this fact is considered by the Pentecostals
as of value in itself, nor that it is the result of a conscious strategy.
(CWME, 1980, p. 95)

As a group, Pentecostals do not generally show a concern for
social issues. In fact, the case is quite the opposite. Neglect in this
area is often noted about Pentecostalism (Wagner, 1973, pp. 137–38).
It is no longer true that Pentecostals in general are only from "the
other side of the tracks." Pentecostals are also frequently numbered
among the middle class overseas. Ever since the neo-Pentecostal
movement and Catholic charismatic renewal, this is all the more
the case. Is it true that Pentecostals have a greater percentage of the
poor in their ranks than any other Christian group overseas? Do
they have greater ties with the poor and, therefore, greater growth?
The solidarity of Pentecostalism with the poor is somewhat paradoxical in the modern mission discussion, especially in view of the
intense interest concerning mission and the poor. We might ask,
"If Pentecostalism's ties with the poor are not due to their mission
strategy, or because they particularly value social concern for that
group of society, then why do they have such solidarity with them?"

When theological reasons are sought for phenomenal Pentecostal growth, an alleged preference of God for the poor is emphasized.
God's favor for the poor is supposed to be demonstrated by the
rapid growth of the gospel among them around the world (Wagner,
1981, p. 31). A common text used by both evangelical and conciliar
missiologists (to support God's alleged preference for the poor) is
Jesus' quotation of the prophet Isaiah at Nazareth (Luke 4:18–19).
The question of interpretation immediately emerges about the emphasis of the Luke passage, as well as other New Testament passages
that are supposed to support the position that God has a preference
for the poor. But is God's preferential favor demonstrated in these
passages, or does the key to Pentecostal growth rest with the poor
themselves, with their ready response to the gospel (Matt. 5:3)?

Somehow Pentecostals, the poor, and phenomenal growth are all linked together. The view of mission and the gospel that narrows down to focus on this economically deprived group is often treated in connection with the kingdom motif in conciliar theology (CWME, 1980, p. 171). Conciliar theologians interpret Luke 4:18–19 to refer to the socioeconomic poor; it is said to be a reference to the cultural mandate (social justice and other social concerns). We are cautioned that the passage should not be "spiritualized," that it is a reference to the literal poor and oppressed. But the meaning of the Luke 4 text is confused when the "literal" interpretation versus the "spiritual" interpretation question is asked. *Both* interpretations may be suggested; the literal poor do have the gospel proclaimed to them. But this does not settle the question of the passage's intended emphasis.

It is at this point where Wagner's two types of kingdom signs emerge in his discussion of Luke 4:18–19 (type *A* social signs and type *B* personal charismatic signs; 1981, p. 16). The twofold sign of the kingdom shows that both interpretations are possible in Luke 4:18–19. A critical question, therefore, is: "What was the intended meaning of the passage when it was spoken and written in its historical context?" The literal poor *are* addressed in the passage; the Spirit was upon Jesus to proclaim the good news to them. But are the poor set apart here because of their socioeconomic status? Or are they mentioned because they represent the increased focus of the gospel in the new age, to the class of people *who were ready to respond to the gospel in that age?*

The emphasis of Jesus' statement in the Luke 4:18–19 passage refers to a new period dawning in salvation history. The parallel passages in the Synoptic Gospels support this:

> After John was put in prison, Jesus went into Galilee, proclaiming the good news of God. "The time has come," he said. "The kingdom of God is near. Repent and believe the good news!" (Mark 1:14–15)

> "Repent, for the kingdom of heaven is near." (Matt. 4:17)

That the poor represent *an enlargement of the gospel focus in the new age* is indicated by the transition from the ministry of John the

Baptist to that of Jesus ("After John was put in prison"). The references to "the time has come" and "the kingdom of God [heaven] is near" also point to this. Both Matthew and Luke make the salvation history transition clear (Matt. 7:28; 11:1–13; Luke 16:16). Luke states: "The Law and the Prophets were proclaimed until John. Since that time, the good news of the kingdom of God is being preached, and everyone is forcing his way into it" (Luke 16:16). The significance of the poor is *their affective disposition* that allows them entrance into the kingdom through *repentance and faith*, not their socio-economic class.

In view of the salvation history context of Luke 4:18–19 and the twofold sign of the kingdom in the passage, it should be interpreted as a reference to the evangelistic mandate. The passage refers to God's "special" mission, the universal proclamation of the gospel offered in the new age on the basis of repentance and faith. The proclamation of this good news even involved "violent responses of faith" as people pressed into the kingdom, seeing it as the "treasure hidden in a field," as a "pearl of great price" (Matt. 13:44–45). The context of the kingdom and the poor in the other crucial references in the New Testament also support this interpretation.

The *real* question is not whether the statement concerning the poor in the New Testament *may be* used by way of an interpretive application (the second hermeneutical task) to emphasize the church's responsibility to the poor. This would be a valid use and extrapolation of the Luke 4:18–19 text. Nor is the question about whether God is concerned with the poor; this is obvious throughout Scripture, especially in all of the references to the poor in Proverbs and the Old Testament injunction to "love your neighbor as yourself."

The first question must be to ask whether the cultural mandate was *the intended meaning* of the statements when they were made in their historical context (the descriptive-historical task). Are all of the statements concerning the poor in the New Testament direct references to the cultural mandate? Or must they be differentiated in terms of groups? Is their meaning that God had, and has, preference for this socioeconomic group? Or do these crucial references to the poor (those in the context of the kingdom) represent people who are particularly responsive to the gospel? In other words, what *is* the emphasis of the New Testament concerning the poor? But first, a word about the position that God has *preference* for the poor.

The idea that God has a preference for the poor approaches a theological absurdity, especially in the context of the New Testament. God is biased? Can one say this without a reference to the response of faith? Only a view of the poor as synonymous with the true, elect people of God, in an extreme Calvinistic sense, would avoid the absurdity (see Ridderbos, 1962, p. 192). But even that view emphasizes the spiritual nature of the relationship between God and his people: "The special relation to God that was first applied to the totality of Israel is now restricted (and extended) to those who respond to the preaching of the Kingdom with faith and repentance" (Ridderbos, 1962, p. 198).

In *Rich Christians in an Age of Hunger: A Biblical Study*, Ronald Sider states:

> The poor are the only group specifically singled out as recipients of Jesus' gospel. Certainly the gospel he proclaimed was for all, but he was particularly concerned that the poor realize that his good news was for them. (1977, p. 66)

Sider takes Luke 4:18–19 to refer to the socioeconomic poor as a group that receives special concern from God and the ministry of Jesus. But at the outset, the question should be asked: Did Jesus have a preferential concern for the poor, or were they not in fact those who readily recognized the great treasure that was being offered to them?

Sider notes that the preaching of the gospel to the poor was also the mission of Jesus. But due to the focus of his book, he emphasizes what he considers to be an *equally important* mission of releasing literal captives and liberating the socially oppressed (pp. 66, 231). He refers to Jesus' healing the sick and blind in his ministry, according to Luke 4:18–19, but he does not give any New Testament examples where literal social captives and oppressed are set at liberty. Does the lack of such New Testament references point to the primary nature of Christ's kingdom as portrayed in the Gospels (it is not of this world, not a political kingdom—John 18:36)? Does this lack have a bearing on the interpretation of Luke 4:18–19? Is the obvious meaning "spiritual" with reference to the oppressed and the prisoners? The New Testament is replete with exorcisms and deliverances from demon possession, but political and social deliverances are few and are clearly not the thrust of the gospel of the kingdom of God. Whether Christians, led by the Spirit, may choose to engage in movements with that purpose is another thing.

Sider quotes numerous Old Testament references in support of God's special concern for the poor. But even these contain references to the affective disposition of the poor in their response to God, or to the negative affective disposition of the rich and wicked who oppress the poor (1977, pp. 67, 72–74). However, Sider's treatment does not emphasize this crucial dimension. When the affective dimension is not emphasized in viewing the rich, they are often unjustly stereotyped. The "rich bad guys/poor good guys" dichotomy is not helpful for deciding the "poor issue" in the New Testament. While consistently maintaining God's preference for the poor (pp. 66–68, 70–71, 82), Sider is forced to admit that God in reality *does not have preference for the poor* (pp. 73, 83–84). The apparent contradiction emerges from the forced nature of the exegesis and the theological absurdity involved with such a contention. Sider does, however, make an excellent case for God's judgment on those who oppress the poor. The neglect, mistreatment, and oppression of the poor are all clearly condemned by Scripture; ministry to the poor is clearly a Christian duty (pp. 59–85).

The key to understanding the references to the poor in the New Testament is not God's preferential favor, but the response of faith on the part of the poor. The crucial New Testament passages concerning the poor (those in the context of the kingdom motif) refer to persons who are *receptive* to the gospel message. The Luke 4:18–19 passage quoted above is somewhat typical in that it contains the characteristic twofold sign of the kingdom in the new age: the preaching of the gospel and the charismatic signs of the Spirit. The parallel passage in Matthew 4:12–17 and the reference in Luke 4:43 specifically mention the preaching of the good news of the kingdom of God. The mention of the poor at the beginning of the ministry of Jesus in the Synoptic Gospels comes at a crucial point in salvation history. The reference to "the poor" as the recipients of the gospel is a sign of the messianic age, because it refers to the universalization of salvation in the new age (Luke 7:22; cf. Matt. 11:11–13).

In Luke's Gospel, the consistent themes accompanying issues of the kingdom and the poor are: (1) the universal proclamation of the gospel (Luke 4:18–19, 43; 7:22; 13:29–31; 14:15–24; 16:16; cf. Acts 1:8); and (2) the charismatic signs of the Spirit's power (Luke 4:18–19, 31–43; 8:1–2; 9:2, 11; 10:18; 11:20; 13:32). These signs of the kingdom accompany the crucial "poor" references and are in keeping with what was previously stated about the interpretation of the kingdom. At times, the kingdom theme is more explicit and frequent in the parallel passages of Matthew's Gospel. Also, there are numerous references and incidents referring to the category *B* charismatic signs of the kingdom interspersed between the verses listed above.

The "poor," therefore, are consistently linked with the universal proclamation of the gospel in the new age. As a group, their significance is not that they represent a particular socioeconomic class, but that they represent "common humanity." The poor represent the enlarged audience to whom the gospel message is now directly addressed in the new period of salvation history. There are references to the socioeconomic poor in Luke (10:30–37; 11:41; 12:32; 14:13; 18:22), but these references do not dominate the Gospel or the teaching of Jesus, as do the crucial references in connection with the kingdom motif. The "salvation history" poor, as the recipients of the gospel message in the new age, are characterized not by their material poverty but by their receptivity to the gospel message (Luke 6:20, 24–25; 8:9–15; 9:2–6; 10:8–11, 21–22; 14:15–21).

Luke 14 is instructive for telling the difference between "socioeconomic poor" references and "salvation history poor" references. In Luke 14:1–14, the socioeconomic poor as an economic class are in view (14:13). But even in this case, Jesus uses the poor to illustrate the importance of humility in the kingdom of God (14:7–11; Matt. 5:3). The passage, however, is a clear reference to the Christian duty to the socioeconomic poor. But the second reference to the poor, in Luke 14:15–24, is entirely different in its thrust and meaning. The parable of the Great Banquet in the second passage refers to the "salvation history poor." It is occasioned by the statement, "Blessed is the man who will eat at the feast in the kingdom of God" (14:15). The reference to the poor here is connected with the kingdom of God. The point of the parable is not the socioeconomic status of those who finally attend the banquet. It is that *the poor respond to the invitation*, while those who were invited did not respond (Luke 14:21–24). The opening up of the banquet to all, regardless of class, is emphasized (14:23). The parable is like the parable of the vineyard and the tenants (Mark 12:1–11) in that it alludes to the general Jewish rejection of the kingdom that is the occasion of offering the kingdom to the Gentiles. The parable illustrates the universalization of the gospel and the responsiveness of the poor.

The key to the "Pentecostal paradigm" *(Pentecostals—the poor—phenomenal growth)* is the receptivity of the poor to the gospel of the kingdom of God. Furthermore, rather than a *narrowing* of the focus of mission to a socioeconomic group, the crucial New Testament references concerning the poor refer to a *widening* of the focus of mission in salvation history, referring to the universalization of the gospel (Matt. 11:11–13). These crucial statements about the poor do not focus on a "preferential group" or on an economic category; the New Testament message as a whole opposes this idea. Rather, the gospel is universally proclaimed without respect for persons or classes. It is offered without discrimination on the condition of "repentance and faith," whether to rich or poor. The "poor issue" concerns the central theme of the New Testament—the faithful response of men and women to the grace of God revealed in the gospel (Eph. 2:8). The context of the majority of statements concerning the poor in the New Testament (the crucial kingdom references) is the evangelistic mandate, not the cultural mandate. The church growth school's admonition to seek the responsive in evangelism is founded on this principle of the gospel of the kingdom of God.

The idea that God prefers the poor, and the use of New Testament passages concerning the poor as proof-texts to support that position, illustrate the pitfall of the contextualization of theology among the catastrophic circumstances in the Southern Hemisphere. The excessive impact of the sometimes catastrophic context of mission on the content of mission theology distorts the New Testament teaching on the poor. However, in the horrific catastrophic circumstances of mission in the Southern Hemisphere, through the preaching of the gospel of the kingdom of God, the poor are delivered from the cruelty of those circumstances and are ushered into the church, under the umbrella of God's grace and mercy in Jesus Christ.

The significance of the poor, therefore, in connection with the kingdom, is that they are ready to respond to the gospel because of their humility and probable positive affective disposition toward repentance and faith—the crucial prerequisites for entrance into the kingdom. The crucial "salvation history poor" references in the New Testament must be differentiated from the "socioeconomic poor" references. They refer to different mandates. Those references accompanying the kingdom motif make up the group that dominates the teaching of Jesus.

A third theme that would logically accompany the kingdom and the poor, besides the preaching of the gospel and the charismatic confirming signs of the Spirit, would be the *required faith response* to that message. Receptivity to the gospel is the consistent theme accompanying the kingdom motif and the poor in Luke's Gospel. The *faith issue* is clearly the immediate context of the crucial Luke 4:18–19 passage also; the unbelief of the Nazarenes is the context of this passage, as well as the widow of Zarephath story. Also, the Pharisees are contrasted with the common people in Luke. The common people were responsive to the gospel, but the Pharisees and experts of the law were typical of Israel's rejection of the kingdom:

> "I tell you, among those born of women there is no one greater than John; yet the one who is least in the kingdom of God is greater than he." (All the people, even the tax collectors, when they heard Jesus' words, acknowledged that God's way was right, because they had been baptized by John. But the Pharisees and experts in the law rejected God's purpose for themselves, because they had not been baptized by John.) (Luke 7:28–30)

The salvation history transition is evident in this passage, as well as the "principle of the poor"—the necessity of repentance and faith. The Pharisees are also consistently condemned because of their suppression of the knowledge of God, for being obstacles in the widening of God's purpose to humanity and rejecting the gospel (Luke 11:37–52; 14:1–14; 20:45–47).

The answer to the question asked previously about the nature of the New Testament teaching concerning the poor is twofold. The references to the socioeconomic poor teach the Christian duty to help the poor. These are references to the cultural mandate. However, the references that dominate the New Testament are those that are connected with the kingdom motif and refer to the evangelistic mandate. The "kingdom and poor" theme is consistently accompanied by the twofold sign of the kingdom: the proclamation of the gospel and the charismatic signs of the Spirit's power. The poor are representative of those who respond to the good news in repentance and faith. These "kingdom and poor" references represent the broadening of mission in salvation history and illustrate the basis upon which the good news of the present kingdom of God may be received—repentance and faith. God is no respecter of persons (Acts 10:34–35). The faith of the centurion foreshadows the age of the universalization of the gospel that would follow the period of Jewish particularization (Luke 7:1–10). Of course, with hindsight today we look at the unusual expansion of the Pentecostal Christianity in the catastrophic circumstances of the poor in the Southern Hemisphere, and we see a demonstration of the point about the receptivity of the poor to the gospel of the kingdom of God.

The early church grasped the good news as the good news of the kingdom, and in their proclamation of that gospel they emphasized the narrow view of mission. This role of the church cannot be trivialized. For the kingdom is known by the dynamic activity of Christ in the church as it proclaims his name in the power of the Holy Spirit. This view of the resurrected Christ working with the contemporary church points to the need for a clarification of roles in a Trinitarian view of mission.

THE KINGDOM AND TRINITARIAN MISSION

Both the concept of the kingdom and that of Trinitarian mission have significant pneumatological "gaps" in Protestant discussions about mission. The description and importance of the role of the Holy Spirit is usually wanting in the evangelical use of these concepts. Previously, our study of Ladd's view of the kingdom illustrated how the name "Holy Spirit" is studiously avoided. In contrast to his view, the term "kingdom" is often substituted for "Holy Spirit" when describing some aspect of the Spirit's ministry in mission (Shenk, 1979, pp. 24–26). Although the kingdom may be identified as "a concept of the acting God," a discussion of both the kingdom and the nature of mission itself can take place with only a few references to the Holy Spirit sprinkled here and there (p. 23). Usually, references to the Spirit are connected with Jesus' ministry, or they are confined to the first century. This may not be intentional, but a "silence on the Holy Spirit" results when the kingdom concept is not unpacked in terms of the full ministry of the Spirit. Also, the Trinitarian view of mission needs to be understood in the same way; the role of the Holy Spirit must be identified and articulated in a full-blown Trinitarian mission theology.

Often, when Pentecostals claim the Spirit is neglected among evangelicals, it is said that their interest is doctrinaire. Or they are charged with overemphasizing the Spirit in sort of a "monism of the Holy Spirit." Bernard Ramm notes that "the standard objection of historic Christianity and Reformed theology to all forms of enthusiasm, fanaticism and Pentecostalism" is that they "build a temple where Scripture permits only a tent" (1959, p. 30). Pentecostals, however, are not alone in their apparent overemphasis of a particular person of the Godhead. Both Roman Catholicism and various Protestant denominations also do this (Spiceland, 1980, p. 144).

Also, it is understandable that Pentecostalism, a renewal movement, emphasizes and brings to the attention of Christianity that neglected reality of the Holy Spirit in Christian experience. As previously stated, this represents their contribution as the "third corner" of Christianity. Evangelicals usually emphasize the ministry of the Spirit in uplifting Christ. But Ramm asks whether the doctrine of the Trinity does not dictate a "Trinity-consciousness," a consciousness of all three persons of the Godhead (1959, p. 28). Then he asks a question that shows there may be further biblical reason for the Pentecostal emphasis on the Holy Spirit. He suggests a reason beyond pneumatology's historic neglect and the particular Pentecostal doctrinal emphasis—that there may be a christomonism in evangelicalism. Ramm asks if it is true that Scripture teaches that Christian consciousness must be "Christ-consciousness" and not "Spirit-consciousness" (p. 29). The previous discussion about the kingdom concept clearly mentioned both the activity of God the Son and God the Holy Spirit in the church as it engages in mission. The contemporary silence on God the Holy Spirit's role in that mission has contributed greatly to the underdevelopment of Trinitarian theology.

As a by-product of Christology, the Holy Spirit's specific Trinitarian role has historically been left undeveloped (Bray, 1980, pp. 58–59). This may also be the reason for the intense reaction we feel concerning Ramm's suggestion about the Christian's "Christ-consciousness" rather than a "Spirit-consciousness" regardless of its accuracy. The historic Christological controversies and the undeveloped nature of pneumatology have helped to promote what appears to be an excessive Christ-consciousness. There is no doubt concerning Christology being crucial in those controversies concerning the Trinity in theology in general. But we must avoid pitting Christology's importance over against pneumatology. Rather, the various roles of the persons of the Godhead must be identified in terms of their role and work in the church and mission.

The Trinitarian controversies clearly affirm the equality of the persons of the Godhead. But the church fathers also maintained that the persons of the Godhead were distinct though inseparable. And the same held true for their work. Speaking of the Cappadocians, Bray states:

> To them it was clear that the work of each person was the common work of all three, without however detracting from the specific aspects attributed to each one. Thus, it was the Son, not the Father nor the Spirit, who suffered in a human body on the cross . . . and the Spirit not the Father nor the Son who descended on the Apostles at Pentecost . . . the fullness of God was present and active in both great typical works in a way which the human mind can perceive yet never fully understand. (1980, p. 58)

It is a theological necessity to distinguish the various persons of the Godhead, as well as their particular work in the church. To do so does not mean that we are slipping into the errors of modalism, subordinationism, or tritheism. Spiceland supports this view when he says, "The Trinitarian formulations were an attempt to express and preserve the threefold experience of God in Christ through the Spirit" (1980, p. 149). He states further: "The entire apparatus of technical language about the Trinity results from the attempt . . . of the Christian Fathers to make sense of Christian life" (pp. 149–50). The particular area of Christian life we must understand here is the experience of the Holy Spirit in the context of the church's mission. The contemporary silence on the Third Person of the Godhead in mission reflects the need for the Holy Spirit to be emphasized in order to make sense of mission and to avoid a practical subordinationism of the Third Person of the Trinity. Perhaps during these times of the "three waves" of Pentecostal-charismatic renewal in the world, it is an occasion for Pentecostals to make the contribution of stating the true role of the Holy Spirit in missions.

Missio Dei, the Silence, and the Issues

The switch from the Trinitarian use of *missio Dei* to its limitless use (God's providential activity in historic events) not only reveals a pneumatological hiatus in Western theology, but it is also a means for perpetuating the silence on the Third Person of the Trinity for the Christian mission. It does so in that the misuse of the term results in a non-Trinitarian emphasis, specifically a mistaken view of the role of God the Father in mission. He is viewed as originating, owning, and carrying out this mission in the contemporary world to the point of detracting from the roles of the other persons of the Godhead. God the Son's role is often confined to the first century, the crucial midpoint of salvation history (Nababan, 1980, pp. 3–4). Or Christ becomes an anonymous presence in revolutionary movements in contemporary times. God the Holy Spirit's role in mission is seldom articulated. In Roland Allen's words, this is a "neglect of one whole hemisphere" of pneumatology (and Trinitarian theology), a crucial one for mission.

Along with a non-Trinitarian use of *missio Dei* is the character-istic paucity of pneumatology in the Christian mission. J. Verkuyl's *Contemporary Missiology: An Introduction* reveals this use of *missio Dei* and neglect of the Holy Spirit in mission theology. The brevity of the references to the Holy Spirit in his missionary role at crucial points of Verkuyl's theology is conspicuous (1978, pp. 105, 108, 111, 145–46). The attempt to discern where the powers of the kingdom are at work today, especially in liberation movements, betrays a loss of appreciation for the Holy Spirit's missionary role and ministry in contemporary mission. This is shown by the tendency to speak of the activity of God entirely as providential in a socioeconomic context. In this view, the signs of the kingdom are typically social (category *A* signs). In Verkuyl's mission theology there are no clear references to the biblical signs of the Spirit (category *B* signs). These are either used figuratively or they are interpreted in social terms. Often in Verkuyl's work a "cognitive leap" is made from healing in the New Testament, due to the power and agency of the Holy Spirit, to medical missions (pp. 202, 212–13).

Therefore, the aspect of mission as "the self-revelation of the triune God in the Son *and in the Holy Spirit*" is neglected (Ander-sen, 1955, p. 60). This is the case in theologies of mission where the distorted view of *missio Dei* is influential. It is clear in Verkuyl's mission theology that the use of the kingdom motif does not guar-antee a full description of pneumatology. To do so would topple the whole idea of *missio Dei* in its misconstrued form. Connecting the kingdom motif to the gospel of the kingdom of God avoids the vulnerability of the motif when it stands alone.

A by-product of the neglect of the Holy Spirit in most conciliar theologies of mission is a neglect of evangelism. As previously men-tioned, "new mission's" sociopolitical context, its hermeneutical horizon, is the dominating principle of conciliar theology. It lends itself to interpreting mission as social justice, other social concerns, and the creation of a new world order (Hoekstra, 1979, p. 12). Part of this anthropocentric mission theology is the rejection of everything that tends to be "propaganda," that is, proclamation-persuasion mission (McGavran, 1977, p. 48; Hoekendijk, 1977, pp. 48–49). *Kerygma* is held to mean the proclamation that *shalom* has come;

this *shalom* is lived in community *(koinonia)* and demonstrated in humble service *(diakonia)*. The three are considered comprehensive "evangelism" (McGavran, 1977, pp. 50–51; Hoekendijk, 1977, p. 50). Along with the unhappy redefinition of mission, there is also an ill-conceived redefinition of evangelism.

While Verkuyl does emphasize both the evangelistic mandate and the cultural mandate, advocating a holistic view of mission, the evangelistic cutting edge of mission is blunted by his view of *missio Dei* and the kingdom. Taking the goal of mission *(missio Dei)* to be the kingdom of God (1978, p. 197), mission becomes everything God intends for the world (pp. 200–201). There are no priorities of mission, for they change with the context of history and the changing needs of people (p. 203). In other words, the world sets the agenda for mission; the previously mentioned hermeneutical error, therefore, is also illustrated in Verkuyl's work.

The one-sided use of both *missio Dei* and the kingdom motif has perpetuated the eclipse of the Holy Spirit's role in mission. This in turn has eclipsed the area of mission in which he is central— the fulfillment of the Great Commission mission. The neglect of the mediated activity of God the Holy Spirit in mission has also called into question the instrumentality of the church by blurring the distinction between the church and the world. In their rejection of "church-centrism," conciliar theologies state that God is not primarily related to the world by means of the church. Rather, they state that God's primary relationship is to the world; it is the focus of God's plan (Hoekstra, 1979, p. 75). The church, they say, is only instrumental in God's plan; it is defined as function, not essence. It is this view that the church is not in essence any different from the world to which the Frankfurt Declaration addressed itself: *"We therefore oppose* the view that the church, as the fellowship of Jesus, is simply a part of the world. The contrast between the church and the world is not merely a distinction in function and in knowledge of salvation; rather, it is an essential difference in nature" (McGavran, 1977, p. 291). The misuse of *missio Dei* trivializes the church's nature and role in mission and thereby denigrates the Holy Spirit's work in the creation of that community and in his missionary role in connection with it.

The emphasis that the church *is* mission, and that primarily God the Father "does" mission *(missio Dei)* amounts to a capitulation to "Christian presence" and service, replacing conversion-focused mission. Through secular work and involvement in social issues and politics, the church is said to be in dialogue with the world. As people join together with God in his mission in these diverse ways, there is unity in the church. All of these modes of mission are conceived to be valid mission structures (Bassham, 1979, p. 71). *Missio Dei,* the "silence on the Holy Spirit," and the neglect of evangelism are all related in the paradigm of "new mission." The failure to identify and articulate the role of the Holy Spirit in mission and the failure to unpack the kingdom concept in terms of pneumatology are fundamental to the shape of this "new mission."

The Holy Spirit's Role in Mission

What is the Holy Spirit's role in mission, and how does that role affect the issues of contemporary mission theology? These questions emerge from the discussion concerning the misuse of the *missio Dei* concept in contemporary mission theology. A Trinitarian view of mission must articulate the activity of the Third Person of the Godhead. The biblical nature of mission cannot be completely brought into focus, nor can it be adequately stated, apart from a description of the Holy Spirit's role. Mission cannot be derived or defined from the church's task in a world of great need. It must have its source in the Father, Son, and Holy Spirit—the Trinitarian view of mission as set forth in Scripture. The recovery and further development of a Trinitarian view of mission, in biblical perspective, must come to grips with this contemporary pneumatological silence. How is mission the self-revelation of the Triune God in the Son *and in the Holy Spirit*? What specifically is the role of the Third Person of the Trinity? Does this question detract from the previously mentioned activity of the *resurrected Christ* in mission? Does it merely reflect the Pentecostal bias coming through, a provincial or doctrinaire interest?

Bernard Ramm addressed these questions when he said that Pentecostalism was frequently charged with attempting to "build a temple where Scripture permits only a tent." But in view of the pneumatological hiatus in Western theology and the resulting missiological dilemmas, we might question whether a "tent" is either sufficient for contemporary mission theology or for a truly biblical theology like that suggested previously—the theology of the gospel of the kingdom of God. All of the points of our discussion, and the New Testament itself, indicate that a "temple" is a more appropriate metaphor for the missionary ministry of the Spirit today. The previous discussion concerning the true meaning of the kingdom concept according to both Jesus and the early church supports this contention, because the gospel as Jesus described it is the gospel of the kingdom of God; it is not a sidebar in Scripture. Therefore, Pentecostal theology is not provincial or doctrinaire in centering its attention on the Acts of the Apostles and the prominence of the Holy Spirit's work in that early history of the church.

Roland Allen states that "it is in the revelation of the Holy Spirit as a missionary Spirit that the [book of] Acts stands alone in the New Testament" (1960, p. 21). This missionary role of the Spirit can be observed elsewhere in the New Testament (especially in the "Trinitarian" passages concerning the divine Paraclete: John 14:16, 26; 15:26; 16:7; 17). But the story of the new creation of the Spirit, the church, and its mission in the first century is central in revealing the continuing role of the Spirit. Allen speaks of how crucial the book of Acts is in this regard:

> In the Acts it [the missionary role of the Spirit] is the one prominent feature. It is asserted, it is taken for granted, from the first page to the last . . . it is necessary to any true apprehension of the Holy Spirit and his work that we should understand it and realize it . . . if we ignore it . . . we lose sight of the perfection of the Spirit. Our view is necessarily one-sided, our understanding of the past is robbed of its true foundations, *our conception of our present duty is incomplete*, and our hope for the future is rendered doubtful and indistinct. (p. 21; emphasis mine)

Succinctly, Allen describes the evangelical view of pneumatology today. George Peters also speaks of the crucial role of Acts in providing a picture of this dimension of the Spirit's ministry in the church:

The superintendence of the Holy Spirit in missions is evident from the Book of Acts. Here it is also evident that the Holy Spirit was not only resident in but also President of the early church. When this happens there is a mighty all-out horizontal push in world evangelism. (1972, p. 304)

As executive of the Godhead in this age of the Spirit, the Holy Spirit is also the Supreme Strategist of world mission (p. 305). Vicedom states that it is through the sending of the Spirit that missionaries receive their power and their authority; it is through the Spirit that missions are linked with the *missio Dei* (1965, p. 70). Vicedom states that the Holy Spirit continues the mission God began in his Son until Jesus himself returns and terminates that mission (p. 56). Ramm also states that the Holy Spirit is the executive of the Godhead in the church age, and as such he makes concrete and real the will of the Father and the Son (1959, p. 30). The Son is the mediator and content of revelation, but "what the Son mediates is realized within the creature by the executive of the Trinity, the Holy Spirit" (p. 31). The designation "executive of the Godhead" points to the Spirit's missionary role in the economy of salvation history.

The Holy Spirit is also Lord (2 Cor. 3:17). As initiator, motivator, and superintendent of mission, he is the Lord of the Harvest (Matt. 9:37–38). The word *harvest* is often used in the Bible to express spiritual readiness (Matt. 9:37–38; John 4:35). Making men and women ready to receive the gospel is the work of the Spirit (John 16:8). Sending laborers into the harvest is also the work of the Spirit (Matt. 9:38; Acts 13:2, 4). The Holy Spirit is the inner motivation and dynamic of the church's mission. It is his harvest, and he is its Lord. This missionary role of the Spirit is clearest in the book of Acts where we read of his motivating, empowering, and supervising the mission of the early church (Acts 8:29; 13:2, 4; 15:28; 16:6, 7, 10; 20:28).

The dimensions of the missionary role of the Spirit are especially clear when we consider the significance of Pentecost for salvation history. An examination of the role of Pentecost in the initiation and universalization of mission reveals the Holy Spirit's central role after the earthly ministry of Christ. Jesus himself spoke of the executive role that the Holy Spirit would have with the church. He spoke of the coming of *another Paraclete* (John 14:16).

The Holy Spirit was to be Christ's advocate; he was to stand in for Christ. He would empower the church and direct it in its mission as Jesus did when he was with them. In John 15:26, the Holy Spirit is given the name "Paraclete" again. Twice in that verse, the Spirit is spoken of as being sent from the Father: "When the Counselor [Paraclete] comes, whom I will send to you from the Father, the Spirit of truth who goes out from the Father, he will testify about me" (John 15:26). The double mention of the Paraclete coming from the Father denotes the *mission* of the Spirit. The Holy Spirit has a mission as executive of the Godhead. He himself, as well as the people whom he empowers and sends in mission, bears witness to Christ (John 15:27).

The Holy Spirit's role in his universal mission is illustrated in Acts by the Pentecostal event and in his breaking through Jewish particularism. The Spirit was the One who opened the door to the expansion of the church among the Gentiles. Oscar Cullmann explains the theological context of the universalizing ministry of the Spirit in terms of salvation history. He sees God's redemptive focus as contracting and expanding in salvation history according to the principle of election and representation. God begins the redemptive purpose in creation and expands to humanity: it contracts to Abram and expands to Israel, contracts to the remnant, and finally contracts to the faithful Servant of the Lord—the Messiah. Christ's incarnation is the midpoint of salvation history, and from this midpoint, there is an expanding movement in the redemptive purpose of God. The previous movement from creation to its midpoint (creation—humanity—Israel—remnant—Messiah) is primarily conceived as a *contracting* movement in salvation history. On the other side of the midpoint (Messiah—apostles—church—humanity), there is an *expanding* movement in salvation history. Christ is the midpoint of a "bow tie-like" progression in the movement of salvation history (Cullmann, 1964, p. 78). It is in this expanding movement of salvation history, in the age of the Spirit, that the Holy Spirit has a prominent role and work. A chief work of the Spirit in "the time between the times" is the universal witness of the gospel.

The Spirit's primary role in his universal mission is demonstrated in the early chapters of Acts. This is especially so in the

Spirit's dealing with the Apostle Peter in chapters 10 through 11, when the Spirit instructs him to make no distinction between Jew and Gentile in the offering of the gospel (Acts 11:11–14). The decisive event that validated the Gentile mission, for both Peter and the early church, was the outpouring of the Spirit in Pentecostal fashion on the uncircumcised Gentiles (Acts 10:44–48; 11:15–17; 15:8–9). After this crucial work of the Spirit in breaking through cultural barriers, the mission of the church spread to the Gentile world. The Spirit in each instance was initiating his mission and causing it to expand in ever-widening circles.

Pentecost, therefore, had epochal meaning; it marked an end of the age of Jewish national particularism and the return of God's redemptive purpose to the nations. The ethnic diversity brought about by the primeval confusion of languages was reversed at Pentecost. Through the miracle of languages, God began to restore the unity of all races that was lost at Babel. Pentecost was both a symbol of that unifying work of God and the actual beginning of the unification of the human race. Beyond Acts, however, the Epistles also show the Holy Spirit to be the agent who universalizes mission. The Spirit has a primary role in accomplishing what Paul speaks of as the "mystery," the eschatological union of Christ with the Jews and Gentiles in his body, the universal church (Rom. 11:25–26; 16:25–26; Eph. 1:3–6, 8–11; 5:32; Col. 1:26–27; 1 Tim. 3:16). The mystery is spoken of in eschatological and universal terms. The concept of mystery has three emphases that condition it in nearly all of its expressions in the New Testament: its eschatological setting, its Christ-centeredness, and its universalistic reference (Boer, 1961, p. 153). Pentecost is of significance for the "mystery," because through the Spirit's work all are baptized into one body, whether Jew or Greek (1 Cor. 12:13; Eph. 2:18, 22).

At Pentecost, the revelation of the mystery first took place (the predominance of Gentile proselytes in the "Court of the Gentiles" who responded to Peter's message). The Spirit reveals this mystery to God's apostles, prophets, and saints (Eph. 3:5; Col. 1:26); the indwelling Holy Spirit enables them to proclaim it (Eph. 3:8–9; 6:19; Col. 1:29; 4:3). It was the *Spirit who was the agent of this restoration of unity.* The role of the Spirit in his mission, breaking through the barriers that separate people, points to the importance of pneumatology for ecumenism. A full-blown Trinitarian view of mission is an ecumenical touchstone (Rosin, 1972, p. 11).

In summary, a Trinitarian view of mission in biblical and salvation history perspective gives the Holy Spirit a primary role in contemporary mission. As executive of the Godhead, he is "Lord of the Harvest." This perspective focuses on the centrality of the church as the agent of mission. But the church is not to be characterized primarily by its instrumentality. It is the new creation of the Holy Spirit and endued with his power, a called-out people who belong to God and who carry out his mission in the world. The missionary role of the Spirit, in biblical perspective, is related inseparably with the indwelling, empowering, and sending of the church to fulfill the Great Commission mission. This sending, God's special mission, is characterized by the preaching (followed by signs) of the gospel of the kingdom of God in the power of the Spirit.

EPILOGUE (2015)

One of the striking differences about the second edition of *The Third Force* is that in 2015, thirty years after the first edition was written, there appears to be confusion among classical Pentecostals about the proliferation of Pentecostalism, especially regarding its variety of expressions in the cultures of the Southern Hemisphere. This variety is mind-boggling, and I suspect this is part of the reason for the confusion. It has led some classical Pentecostals to despair that Pentecostalism can no longer be identified. The "name game" that missionaries and missiologists both in the Northern and Southern Hemispheres engage in to describe the Pentecostal-charismatic movement in a variety of cultural contexts is an indication of this confusion.

At the time of writing the first edition in 1985, before the explosive "third wave" of Pentecostal renewal in the Southern Hemisphere, there was also confusion—but it was on the part of *evangelicals* who were concerned about the growth of Pentecostalism and its expressions in non-Western cultures. Pentecostal missionaries with whom I worked during the second wave, in the 1970s and 80s, did not show the concern about the expansion and variety of Pentecostalism on the "mission field" that Pentecostal missions literature reveals today. To the contrary, we hoped and looked for such successful growth of the Pentecostal faith in non-Western cultures; there was no concern that someone not belonging to our group was casting out demons in Jesus' name (Luke 9:49–50). I suspect there is a certain amount of paternalism involved in this "concern" toward the growth of Pentecostalism in the non-Western world, but there could also be other reasons for the anxiety about the diversity of Pentecostalism.

A major reason for this concern is the focus of scholarship today in the social sciences and in the phenomenology of religion on the diversity of Pentecostalism in that part of the world. The progress of those sciences, and their application in understanding Pentecostalism and its phenomenal grown by both Western and non-Western Pentecostals, has outpaced the development of a global Pentecostal theology. This is in spite of excellent theologizing by some indigenous Pentecostal theologians who have contextualized the Christian faith in their own cultures. This activity is a sign of hope. Nevertheless, the development of *a Pentecostal biblical theology in the West* has not kept up with the development of scholarship in other fields, and the application of their sciences to the growth of Pentecostalism, in gaining insights for the effective expansion of the church.

However, the concern about being able to identify "Pentecostals" in the various cultures and styles of worship in the Southern Hemisphere will not be assuaged by academic scholarship in the social sciences. For some classical Pentecostals, this will only add to the anxiety, as illustrated previously with the mission strategy of the "church growth school." Applications of the social sciences to mission must be guided by the theological core of Pentecostal movements; this requires a *Pentecostal-oriented biblical theology*. A Western systematic theology influenced by scholastic theology is ill prepared for this task.

The scientific approaches to the movements have and will continue to provide helpful information on the growth of Pentecostalism. However, concern will no doubt remain about these Pentecostal movements in the non-Western world that seem out of control because they do not look like classical Pentecostalism in the West or operate within the confines set by Pentecostalism in the West. In approaching the goal of achieving a Pentecostal-oriented biblical theology, my suggestion has been that, first, we should view these Pentecostal-charismatic movements as "renewals" of the gospel of the kingdom of God taking place in differing cultural contexts. But the next step must be taken to develop a Pentecostal-oriented biblical theology. Pentecostal movements should be measured and identified on the basis of a biblical foundation; it is not necessary to give new movements of the Spirit new names and engage in endless classification according to the standards of Western classical Pentecostalism. Rather, they should be evaluated on the basis of a Pentecostal-oriented biblical theology. By this I do not refer to finding biblical references for a theological position held, or a doctrine that is felt to be paramount in order to qualify a Pentecostal movement as a valid. Rather, evaluation should start on the basis of a system or pattern of theology found in the Bible—such as Jesus' theology of the gospel of the kingdom of God. In other words, fresh theologizing must be done with Scripture as our hermeneutical horizon in evaluating the movements. Evaluations from the social sciences or phenomenology of religion should be guided by a biblical theology.

One of the reasons why I was comfortable writing a second edition of the *Third Force in Missions*, a thirty-year-old book, was the theological focus of the first edition on the "kingdom of God." It connected the Pentecost experience of the Spirit to the biblical theme of the kingdom of God; I knew that this core New Testament emphasis would never change and would always be relevant to the Christian mission. I knew the second edition would give me the chance to expand the kingdom of God theme, to show that it was indeed the foundation for a Pentecostal theology.

To use this terminology from the New Testament is not just a convenient way to explain the "full gospel." It is to introduce *the theology of the gospel of the kingdom of God* as a basis for a Pentecostal biblical theology that would also yield substantial results in the exploration of the theme in the Old Testament. Using this terminology from the New Testament is to say that Jesus' gospel of the kingdom of God was *twofold* (Matt. 4:23); the good news of the kingdom is inseparable from the power and rule of the Holy Spirit in Christians. At a transitional moment in salvation history, John the Baptist introduced Jesus as the one who would "baptize in the Holy Spirit" (Matt. 3:1–2; Luke 3:16, 18; John 1:15–16, 29–34). These introductions of the Baptist in the Gospels do not specifically mention the redemptive death of Jesus; John only made a figurative reference to Jesus as the Lamb of God who takes away the sin of the world (John 1:29). In his announcing the coming of Jesus and the good news at this transitional moment in salvation history (the midpoint), the Baptist focused on the Holy Spirit in connection with the coming of Jesus—he saw the Spirit come upon Jesus, and he said Jesus would baptize with the Spirit.

It was in respect to this sense of the Spirit coming at the midpoint of salvation history, with his unique inner work of dwelling in Christians, that Harry Boer stated that *Pentecost was the third great work of God in salvation history*. Along with Jesus' incarnation and the work of the Spirit in *creation*, the gift of the indwelling Spirit of God (a new people of God "born of the Spirit," "baptized in the Spirit," and empowered by the Spirit) is what marks Jesus' message of the kingdom as unique in salvation history; it marks the arrival of Jesus' *kingdom of the heart*.

The revelation of Jesus Christ as Savior and Lord through his redemptive death on the cross at the midpoint of salvation history and *the gift of the Spirit* is the gospel of the kingdom. To say the gospel is twofold, pointing to the distinct inward work of the Spirit, his indwelling Christians in salvation history, is not to disparage any of the efforts to explain the benefits of the gospel in terms of a threefold, fourfold, or fivefold gospel. These efforts are important in pointing out the richness of the gospel that Jesus brought. But to note that the gospel is *twofold*—the redemptive sacrifice of Jesus on the cross and the gift of the Spirit—is embedded in Jesus' teaching about the kingdom of God and its arrival in salvation history. We use the term "the gospel of the kingdom of God" to focus on the language of the new covenant, Jesus' description of the gospel as a manifestation of the kingdom, as well as to focus on it as a foundation for a Pentecostal-oriented biblical theology.

A major reason why the development of a Pentecostal-oriented biblical theology has not been forthcoming is the hindrance and diversion that dispensational theology has had among classical Pentecostals. A theology of the gospel of the kingdom of God in the New Testament readily connects with the Pentecostal experience and the importance of the mediated role of the Holy Spirit in the church's mission in the world. On the other hand, Darby-oriented dispensational theology (which is "dispensationally silent" on the Holy Spirit) denies the Pentecostal experience outright and marginalizes the New Testament and the church in its mission. It is most important to note that it removes Jesus Christ, and his *present* gospel of the kingdom of God, from his central and rightful place at the midpoint in salvation history. All of this is forfeited by the theological system that centers on the nation of Israel, an Israel-centered theology, and a future Jewish kingdom. Pentecostals have espoused this "Pentecostal self-contradiction" now for over a century.

Part of its sustaining existence is due to Pentecostals using the theology as an "ad hoc" theology, mainly to articulate a premillennial view of the end times. Often, this is done while maintaining basic Reformation theology, inserting the biblical basis for the Pentecostal experience and Reformation tenets in fresh theologizing. In this case, however, the biblical theology product achieved has very little to do with classical dispensational theology. At times, this kind of fresh theologizing is done without realizing what the *system* of dispensational theology does to Reformation theology (Pomerville, 2014, pp. 25–56).

Dispensational theology is a major reason for the confusion among Pentecostals today regarding the diversity of Pentecostalism in the world. It does not afford any insights into Pentecostal movements; it denies them. If we depend on it for evaluation of Pentecostal movements, for a sense of who the "people of God" are, and for what the church should be doing today in the world, then its unorthodox theological notions only add to the confusion. In my view, there is no greater task for classical Pentecostals in the Western world today than to develop a Pentecostal-oriented biblical theology to replace dispensational theology. This "leaven of the Pharisees" is a deadly message for Pentecostal movements in the Southern Hemisphere; it should no longer be exported.

As for concern about Pentecostal-charismatic movements in that part of the world, Jesus said the message of the kingdom is like leaven: it has tremendous ability to expand and permeate (Matt. 13:33), like a mustard seed has great potential for growth (Matt. 13:31–32); it is like a seed that, when received by "good soil," produces a crop disproportionate to what was sown (Matt. 13:18–23). Jesus' kingdom manifests itself in this way, because the Lord of the Harvest, the Holy Spirit, enables the kingdom message to have this power and effect in the world. This is not an occasion for concern but for faith. Those *renewals of the gospel of the kingdom* in the Southern Hemisphere will be the "first force" for the church's mission in reaching the world and in hastening Jesus' coming again. With joy, we will then experience his future kingdom.

APPENDIX

HISTORIC REFORMED VIEW OF SCRIPTURE

Approach to Scripture: Non-Cartesian; Scripture is the first principle. Emphasis: the priority of faith and the function of Scripture, with a focus on the work of the Holy Spirit, in connection with the written word of God. The self-revelation of God, due to his transcendence and incomprehensibility.

Nature of Scripture: Christocentric, dynamic, holistic view of the word of God—the incarnate Word, the written word, and the proclaimed word. Scripture is a historical account of the acts and words of God. Inspiration: both the divine and human dimensions of Scripture are held in biblical tension, due to the incarnational model of divine communication and the principle of accommodation. Scripture is "from God."

Purpose of Scripture: To bring persons to salvation and give guidance for the Christian life.

REFORMED SCHOLASTIC VIEW OF SCRIPTURE

Approach to Scripture: Cartesian; the categories of the mind; Aristotelian philosophy. Human reason is the first principle. Emphasis: the priority of reason and the form of Scripture; focus on the text and its precision. The activity of humans in their use of reason to understand God's revelation. Reason is held to be analogous with truth as it is in the mind of God.

Nature of Scripture: The word of God is static in nature, being synonymous with the written word; it consists of propositional statements. Scripture is the "quarry" for systematic theology. Inspiration: the divine dimension of Scripture is emphasized; the human dimension is ignored or virtually denied. Authors of Scripture are as "penmen"; the historical-cultural context of Scripture is not in focus.

Purpose of Scripture: To provide inerrant information on all branches of learning and a unified system of knowledge; the objective completeness of Scripture is stressed.

HISTORIC REFORMED VIEW OF SCRIPTURE

Authority of Scripture: Authority is in the context of faith and inner testimony of the Holy Spirit; there is no separation between word and Spirit. The authority of God's written word is God himself. Scripture is self-authenticating. God authenticates Scripture. Authority is functional in nature, the ability of Scripture to accomplish its redemptive purpose. "Certainty" is a matter of faith.

Role of the Holy Spirit: His role extends from the authors of Scripture to the hearers and interpreters of the word. The present inward work of the Spirit in the believer is emphasized.

Clarity of Scripture: Those things necessary to be known, believed, and observed for salvation are plain and clear in Scripture.

REFORMED SCHOLASTIC VIEW OF SCRIPTURE

Authority of Scripture: Authority is in the context of reason, the accuracy of the written text of Scripture; internal and external evidence, logical, rational arguments for its divinity prove its authority. Authority is abstract in nature. Humans authenticate Scripture; rationalistic inerrancy is the guarantee for the divinity of Scripture.

Role of the Holy Spirit: His role is confined to the original authors of Scripture, according to Princeton theologians; his work at that end of revelation is emphasized.

Clarity of Scripture: The clarity of Scripture rests on logic rather than on its self-authentication; every subject on which it speaks is clear and to be defended (Pomerville, 1980, pp. 96–97).

REFERENCES

BOOKS

Allen, R. (1960). *The Ministry of the Spirit.* Grand Rapids: Wm. B. Eerdmans.

Andersen, W. (1955). *Towards a Theology of Mission: A Study of the Encounter between the Missionary Enterprise and the Church and Its Theology.* London: SCM Press.

Anderson, A. H. (2013). *To the Ends of the Earth: Pentecostalism and the Transformation of World Christianity.* New York: Oxford University Press.

Anderson, G. H. (Ed.). (1961). *The Theology of the Christian Mission.* London: SCM Press.

Atter, G. (1962). *The Third Force.* Peterborough: The College Press.

Barr, J. (1978). *Fundamentalism.* Philadelphia: The Westminster Press.

Barrett, D. B. (1968). *Schism and Renewal in Africa.* Nairobi: Oxford University Press.

Bartleman, F. (1980). *Azusa Street.* Plainfield: Logos International.

Bassham, R. C. (1979). *Mission Theology, 1948–1975: Years of Worldwide Creative Tension—Ecumenical, Evangelical, and Roman Catholic.* Pasadena: William Carey Library.

Bavinck, J. H. (1960). *Introduction to the Science of Missions.* Grand Rapids: Baker Book House.

Berkouwer, G. C. (1952). *The Providence of God: Studies in Dogmatics.* Grand Rapids: Wm. B. Eerdmans.

Berkouwer, G. C. (1975). *Holy Scripture: Studies in Dogmatics.* Grand Rapids: Wm. B. Eerdmans.

Berkouwer, G. C. (1977). *A Half Century of Theology: Movements and Motives.* Grand Rapids: Wm. B. Eerdmans.

Blauw, J. (1962). *The Missionary Nature of the Church: A Survey of the Biblical Theology of Mission.* London: McGraw-Hill.

Bloch-Hoell, N. (1964). *The Pentecostal Movement: Its Origin, Development, and Distinctive Character.* Oslo: Universitetsforlaget.

Bloesch, D. G. (1973). *The Evangelical Renaissance.* Grand Rapids: Wm. B. Eerdmans.

Boer, H. (1961). *Pentecost and Missions.* Grand Rapids: Wm. B. Eerdmans.

Bosch, D. J. (1975). *Theology of Mission: Missiology and Science of Religion (B.Th.).* Pretoria: University of South Africa.

Bosch, D. J. (1980). *Witness to the World: The Christian Mission in Theological Perspective.* London: Marshall, Morgan & Scott.

Bray, G. L. (1980). The Patristic Dogma. In P. Toon & J. D. Spiceland (Eds.), *One God in Trinity: An Analysis of the Primary Dogma of Christianity.* Westchester: Cornerstone Books.

Bright, J. (1953). *The Kingdom of God: The Biblical Concept and Its Meaning for the Church.* New York: Abingdon Press.

Bromiley, G. (1958). Church Doctrine of Inspiration. In C. F. H. Henry (Ed.), *Revelation and the Bible.* Grand Rapids: Baker Book House.

Brumback, C. (1961). *Suddenly . . . From Heaven: A History of the Assemblies of God.* Springfield: Gospel Publishing House.

Bruner, F. D. (1970). *A Theology of the Holy Spirit: The Pentecostal Experience and the New Testament Witness.* Grand Rapids: Wm. B. Eerdmans.

Burgess, S. M. & van der Maas, E. M. (Eds.). (2003). *The New International Dictionary of Pentecostal Charismatic Movements.* Grand Rapids: Zondervan.

Christenson, L. (1975). Pentecostalism's Forgotten Forerunner. In V. Synan (Ed.), *Aspects of Pentecostal-Charismatic Origins.* Plainfield: Logos.

Committee on World Mission and Evangelism. (1980). Section Reports. *Your Kingdom Come: Missions Perspectives Report on the World Conference on Mission and Evangelism, Melbourne, Australia, 12–25 May 1980.* Geneva: CWME WCC.

Conn, H. M. (Ed.). (1976). *Theological Perspectives on Church Growth*. Nutley: Presbyterian and Reformed.

Cullmann, O. (1964). *Christ and Time: The Primitive Christian Conception of Time and History*. (F. V. Filson, Trans.). Philadelphia: The Westminster Press.

Dayton, D. W. (1976). *Discovering the Evangelical Heritage*. Grand Rapids: Wm. B. Eerdmans.

Dayton, E. R. & Fraser, D. A. (1980). *Planning Strategies for World Evangelization*. Grand Rapids: Wm. B. Eerdmans.

Dunn, J. D. G. (1970). *Baptism in the Holy Spirit*. London: SCM Press.

Faupel, D. W. (1972). *The American Pentecostal Movement: A Bibliographical Essay*. Franklin Springs: The Society for Pentecostal Studies.

Fee, G. (1976). Hermeneutics and Historical Precedent—A Major Problem in Pentecostal Hermeneutics. In R. P. Spittler (Ed.), *Perspectives on the New Pentecostalism*. Grand Rapids: Baker Book House.

Filson, F. (1950). *The New Testament against Its Environment*. London: SCM Press.

Frodsham, S. H. (1946). *With Signs Following: The Story of the Pentecostal Revival in the Twentieth Century*. Springfield: Gospel Publishing House.

Gause, R. H. (1976). Issues in Pentecostalism. In R. P. Spittler (Ed.), *Perspectives on the New Pentecostalism*. Grand Rapids: Baker Book House.

Gaxiola, J. (1970). *La Serpiente y La Paloma*. Pasadena: William Carey Library.

Gee, D. (1949). *The Pentecostal Movement*. London: Elim Publishing Company.

Gordon, A. J. (1964). *The Ministry of the Spirit*. Minneapolis: Bethany Fellowship.

Grassi, J. (1978). *The Secret of the Apostle Paul*. New York: Orbis Books.

Green, M. (1975). *I Believe in the Holy Spirit*. Grand Rapids: Wm. B. Eerdmans.

Greenway, R. S. (1976). Winnable People. In H. M. Conn (Ed.). *Theological Perspectives on Church Growth*. Nutley: Presbyterian and Reformed.

Hesselgrave, D. J. (1978a). *Dynamic Religious Movements: Case Studies of Rapidly Growing Religious Movements around the World.* Grand Rapids: Baker Book House.

Hesselgrave, D. J. (Ed.). (1978b). *Theology and Mission: Papers Given at Trinity Consultation No. 1.* Grand Rapids: Baker Book House.

Hodges, M. L. (1957). *Build My Church.* Springfield: Gospel Publishing House.

Hodges, M. L. (1977a). *A Theology of the Church and Its Mission.* Springfield: Gospel Publishing House.

Hodges, M. L. (1977b). A Pentecostal's View of Mission Strategy. In D. McGavran (Ed.), *The Conciliar-Evangelical Debate: The Crucial Documents 1964–1976.* Pasadena: William Carey Library.

Hoekendijk, J. C. (1977). The Call to Evangelism. In D. McGavran (Ed.), *The Conciliar-Evangelical Debate: The Crucial Documents 1964–1976.* Pasadena: William Carey Library.

Hoekstra, H. T. (1979). *The World Council of Churches and the Demise of Evangelism.* Wheaton: Tyndale House.

Hollenweger, W. J. (1972). *The Pentecostals: The Charismatic Movement in the Churches.* Minneapolis: Augsburg.

Holy Bible. (1978). *New International Version.* Grand Rapids: Zondervan Bible Publishers.

Holy Bible. (2005). *Today's New International Version. International Bible Society.*

Horton, R. (1979). Ritual Man in Africa. In W. A. Lessa & E. Z. Vogt (Eds.), *Reader in Comparative Religion: An Anthropological Approach.* New York: Harper & Row.

Hummel, C. E. (1978). *Fire in the Fireplace: Contemporary Charismatic Renewal.* Downers Grove: InterVarsity Press.

Inch, M. A. (1978). *The Evangelical Challenge.* Philadelphia: The Westminster Press.

Jenkins, P. (2002). *The Next Christendom: The Coming of Global Christianity.* New York: Oxford University Press.

Johnston, A. P. (1978). *The Battle for World Evangelism.* Wheaton: Tyndale House.

Käsemann, E. (1980). The Eschatological Royal Reign of God. In *Your Kingdom Come: Missions Perspectives Report on the World*

Conference on Mission and Evangelism, Melbourne, Australia 12–25 May 1980. Geneva: CWME WCC.

Kane, J. H. (1974). *Christian Missions in Biblical Perspective.* Grand Rapids: Baker Book House.

Kane, J. H. (1981). *The Christian World Mission: Today and Tomorrow.* Grand Rapids: Baker Book House.

Kauffmann, Y. (1972). *The Religion of Israel.* New York: Schocken Books.

Kraemer, H. (1961). Syncretism as a Theological Problem for Missions. In G. H. Anderson (Ed.), *The Theology of the Christian Mission.* London: SCM Press.

Kraft, C. H. (1979). *Christianity in Culture: A Study in Dynamic Biblical Theologizing in Cross-Cultural Perspective.* Maryknoll: Orbis Books.

Ladd, G. E. (1974). *The Presence of the Future: The Eschatology of Biblical Realism.* Grand Rapids: Wm. B. Eerdmans.

Latourette, K. S. (1967). *A History of the Expansion of Christianity: Three Centuries of Advance* (Vol. 3). Grand Rapids: Zondervan.

Latourette, K. S. (1969). *A History of the Expansion of Christianity: The First Five Centuries* (Vol. 1). Grand Rapids: Zondervan.

Lindsell, H. (1949). *An Evangelical Theology of Mission.* Grand Rapids: Zondervan.

Linton, R. (1979). Nativistic Movements. In W. A. Lessa & E. Z. Vogt (Eds.), *Reader in Comparative Religion: An Anthropological Approach.* New York: Harper & Row.

MacDonald, W. G. (1964). *Glossolalia in the New Testament.* Springfield: Gospel Publishing House.

Margull, H.-J. (1960). The Awakening of Protestant Missions. In *History's Lessons for Tomorrow's Mission: Milestones in the History of Missionary Thinking.* Geneva: World Student Christian Federation.

Marty, M. (1975). Pentecostalism in the Context of American Piety and Practice. In V. Synan (Ed.), *Aspects of Pentecostal-Charismatic Origins.* Plainfield: Logos International.

McDonnell, K. (1976). Classical Pentecostal/Roman Catholic Dialogue: Hopes and Possibilities. In R. P. Spittler (Ed.), *Perspectives on the New Pentecostalism.* Grand Rapids: Baker Book House.

McDonnell, K. (1980). *Presence, Power, Praise: Documents on the Charismatic Renewal* (Vol. 3). Collegeville: The Liturgical Press.

McGavran, D. A. (Ed.). (1977). *The Conciliar-Evangelical Debate: The Crucial Documents 1964–1976.* Pasadena: William Carey Library.

McGavran, D. A., Huegel, J., & Taylor, J. (1963). *Church Growth in Mexico.* Grand Rapids: Wm. B. Eerdmans.

McIntire, C. T. (Ed.). (1977). *God, History and Historians: An Anthology of Modern Christian Views of History.* New York: Oxford University Press.

McNeill, J. T. (Ed.). (1960). *Calvin: Institutes of the Christian Religion (Vol. 20).* (F. L. Battles, Trans.). Philadelphia: The Westminster Press.

McQuilkin, J. R. (1973). *How Biblical is the Church Growth Movement?* Chicago: Moody Press.

Menzies, W. W. (1971). *Anointed to Serve: The Story of the Assemblies of God.* Springfield: Gospel Publishing House.

Menzies, W. W. (1975). The Non-Wesleyan Origins of the Pentecostal Movement. In V. Synan (Ed.), *Aspects of Pentecostal-Charismatic Origins.* Plainfield: Logos International.

Menzies, W. W. (1979). The Holy Spirit in Christian Theology. In K. Kantzer (Ed.), *Perspectives in Evangelical Theology.* Grand Rapids: Baker Book House.

Montague, G. T. (1976). *The Holy Spirit: Growth of a Biblical Tradition.* New York: Paulist Press.

Montgomery, J. (1967). *New Testament Fire in the Philippines.* Manila: FEBC Marshburn Press.

Nababan, S. (1980). Your Kingdom Come. In *Your Kingdom Come: Missions Perspectives Report on the World Conference on Mission and Evangelism, Melbourne, Australia 12–25 May 1980.* Geneva: CWME, WCC.

Needleman, J. & Baker, G. (Eds). (1978). *Understanding the New Religions.* New York: Seabury Press.

Neill, S. (1964). *History of Christian Mission.* Middlesex: Hazell Watson & Viney.

Newbigin, L. (1954). *The Household of God.* New York: Friendship Press.

Oosterwal, G. (1973). *Modern Messianic Movements*. Elkhart: Institute of Mennonite Studies.

Oosthuizen, G. C. (1968). *Post-Christianity in Africa: A Theological and Anthropological Study*. Grand Rapids: Wm. B. Eerdmans.

Palmer, D. C. (1973). *Explosion of People Evangelism*. Chicago: Moody Press.

Peel, J. D. Y. (1968). *Aladura: A Religious Movement among the Yoruba*. London: Oxford University Press.

Peters, G. W. (1972). *A Biblical Theology of Missions*. Chicago: Moody Press.

Peters, G. W. (1973). *Indonesian Revival: Focus on Timor*. Grand Rapids: Zondervan.

Piepkorn, A. C. (1979). *Profiles in Belief: The Religious Bodies of the United States and Canada* (Vol. 2). San Francisco: Harper & Row.

Pinnock, C. H. (1976). The New Pentecostalism: Reflections of an Evangelical Observer. In R. P. Spittler (Ed.), *Perspectives on the New Pentecostalism*. Grand Rapids: Baker Book House.

Pomerville, P. A. (2009). *Culture Blind Evangelicals and the Good News of the Kingdom of God*. North Charlestown: Booksurge.

Pomerville, P. A. (2010). *Rediscovering the Gospel*. Seattle: Createspace.

Pomerville, P. A. (2014). *The New Testament Case against Christian Zionism: A Christian View of the Israeli-Palestinian Conflict*. Seattle: Createspace.

Quebedeaux, R. (1974). *The Young Evangelicals*. New York: Harper & Row.

Quebedeaux, R. (1978). *The Worldly Evangelicals*. San Francisco: Harper & Row.

Ramm, B. (1959). *The Witness of the Spirit: An Essay on the Contemporary Relevance of the Internal Witness of the Holy Spirit*. Grand Rapids: Wm. B. Eerdmans.

Ramm, B. (1961). *Special Revelation and the Word of God*. Grand Rapids: Wm. B. Eerdmans.

Ramm, B. (1973). *The Evangelical Heritage*. Waco: Word Book Publishers.

Ramm, B. (1977). Is "Scripture Alone" the Essence of Christianity? In J. Rogers (Ed.), *Biblical Authority*. Waco: Word Book Publishers.

Ranaghan, K. & Ranaghan, D. (1969). *Catholic Pentecostals.* New York: Paulist Press.

Read, W. (1965). *New Patterns of Church Growth in Brazil.* Grand Rapids: Wm. B. Eerdmans.

Read, W., Monterroso, V. M., & Johnson, H. A. (1969). *Latin American Church Growth.* Grand Rapids: Wm. B. Eerdmans.

Ridderbos, H. (1962). *The Coming of the Kingdom.* Philadelphia: Presbyterian and Reformed.

Rogers, J. (1966). *Scripture in the Westminster Confession: A Problem of Historical Interpretation for American Presbyterianism.* (N. V. Kampen & J. H. Kok, Eds.). Grand Rapids: Wm. B. Eerdmans.

Rogers, J. (Ed.). (1977). *Biblical Authority.* Waco: Word Book Publishers.

Rogers, J. B. & McKim, D. K. (1979). *The Authority and Interpretation of the Bible.* San Francisco: Harper & Row.

Shenk, W. R. (Ed.). (1980). *Mission Focus: Current Issues.* Scottsdale: Herald Press.

Sider, R. J. (1977). *Rich Christians in an Age of Hunger: A Biblical Study.* Downers Grove: InterVarsity Press.

Smart, J. D. (1979). *The Past, Present and Future of Biblical Theology.* Philadelphia: The Westminster Press.

Smith, E. C. (1970). *God's Miracles: Indonesian Church Growth.* Pasadena: William Carey Library.

Spiceland, J. D. (1980). Process Theology. In P. Toon & J. D. Spiceland (Eds.), *One God in Trinity: An Analysis of the Primary Dogma of Christianity.* Westchester: Cornerstone Books.

Stott, J. R. W. & Coote, R. (Eds.). (1980). *Down to Earth: Studies in Christianity and Culture.* Grand Rapids: Wm. B. Eerdmans.

Sundkler, B. G. M. (1948). *Bantu Prophets in South Africa* (1st ed.). London: Lutterworth.

Sundkler, B. G. M. (1961). *Bantu Prophets in South Africa* (2nd ed.). London: Oxford University Press.

Synan, V. (1971). *The Holiness-Pentecostal Movement in the United States.* Grand Rapids: Wm. B. Eerdmans.

Synan, V. (1980). Frank Bartleman and Azusa Street. In *Azusa Street.* Plainfield: Logos International.

Synan, V. & Yong, A. (Eds.). (2016). *Global Renewal Christianity: Spirit-Empowered Movements Past, Present, and Future* (Vol. 1). Lake Mary: Charisma House Book Group.

Tan-Chow, M. L. (2007). *Pentecostal Theology for the Twenty-First Century: Engaging with Multi-Faith Singapore.* Aldershot: Ashgate.

Taylor, J. V. (1969). Selfhood: Presence or Persona? In P. Beyerhaus & C. F. Hallencrentz (Eds.), *The Church Crossing Frontiers.* Uppsala: Almquist & Wiksells.

Thielicke, H. (1974). *The Evangelical Faith* (Vol. 1). Grand Rapids: Wm. B. Eerdmans.

Verkuyl, J. (1978). *Contemporary Missiology: An Introduction.* Grand Rapids: Wm. B. Eerdmans.

Vicedom, G. F. (1965). *The Mission of God: An Introduction to a Theology of Mission* (G. A. Thiele & D. Hilgendorf, Trans.). St. Louis: Concordia.

Wagner, C. P. (1971). *Frontiers in Missionary Strategy.* Chicago: Moody Press.

Wagner, C. P. (1973). *Look Out! The Pentecostals Are Coming.* Carol Stream: Creation House.

Wagner, C. P. (1981). *Church Growth and the Whole Gospel: A Biblical Mandate.* San Francisco: Harper & Row.

Wagner, C. P. & Dayton, E. R. (Eds.). (1978). *Unreached Peoples '79.* Elgin: David C. Cook.

Wallace. A. F. C. (1979). Revitalization Movements. In W. A. Lessa & E. Z. Vogt (Eds.), *Reader in Comparative Religion: An Anthropological Approach.* New York: Harper & Row.

Warren, M. (1976). *I Believe in the Great Commission.* Grand Rapids: Wm. B. Eerdmans.

Webber, R., & Bloesch, D. (Eds.). (1978). *The Orthodox Evangelicals.* Nashville: Thomas Nelson.

Winter, R. (1970). *The Twenty-Five Unbelievable Years, 1945–1969.* New York: Harper & Row.

Yong, A. (2005). *The Spirit Poured out on All Flesh: Pentecostalism and the Possibility of a Global Theology.* Grand Rapids: Baker Academic.

Encyclopedias

Barrett, D. B. (1978). African Christianity. In P. D. Meagher, T. C. O'Brien, & C. M. Aherne (Eds.), *Encyclopedic Dictionary of Religion*. Washington, DC: Corpus Publications.

Barrett, D. B. (Ed.). (1982). *World Christian Encyclopedia: A Comparative Study of Churches and Religions in the Modern World AD 1900–2000*. Nairobi: Oxford University Press.

McClintock, J. & Strong, J. (1880). *Cyclopedia of Biblical, Theological, and Ecclesiastical Literature* (Vol. 9). Grand Rapids: Baker Book House.

Articles

Barrett, D. B. & Johnson, T. (2001). World Christian Trends: AD 2001 Reality Check: 50 New Facts and Figures about Trends and Issues concerning Empirical Global Christianity Today. Pasadena: William Carey Library.

Center for the Study of Global Christianity. (2013). Christianity in Its Global Context 1970–2020: Society, Religion, and Mission. South Hamilton: Gordon-Conwell Theological Seminary.

Center for the Study of Global Christianity. (2014). Status of Global Mission, 2014, in the Context of AD 1800–2050. South Hamilton: Gordon-Conwell Theological Seminary.

Hodges, M. L. (1970). My Spirit upon All Flesh. *Paraclete, 4*(4), 3–6.

Hollenweger, W. J. (1980). Charismatic Renewal in the Third World: Implications for Mission. *Occasional Bulletin, 4*(2), 68–74.

Hughes, R. H. (1998, November 15). Pentecostal World Growth at 19 Million a Year. *Christianity Today, 42*(13).

Hurst, D. V. (1968). The Evidence Points to the Evidence. *Paraclete, 2*(1), 22–30.

Johnson, T. M., Crossing, P. F., & Jangsun Ryu, B. (2004). Looking Forward: An Overview of World Evangelization. In *A Special Report for Lausanne Forum of World Evangelization*. Center for the Study of Global Christianity. South Hamilton: Gordon-Conwell Theological Seminary.

Johnson, T. M. (2007, January). Global Table 5: Status of global mission, presence and activities, AD 1800–2025. In Status of Global Mission 2007: Annual Update. *International Bulletin of Missionary Research, 31*(1), 8.

Johnson, T. M., Zurlo, G. A., Hickman, A. W., & Crossing, P. F. (2015, January). Christianity 2015: Religious Diversity and Personal Contact. *International Bulletin of Missionary Research, 39*(1).

Kantzer, K. (1980, February 22). The Charismatics among Us. *Christianity Today, 24*(4), 24–29.

Loewen, J. A. (1976). Mission Churches, Independent Churches, and Felt Needs in Africa. *Missiology* (4), 405–525.

Macomber, D. E. (1958). The Concept of the Kingdom of God in the Preaching of the Apostles. *Gordon Review* (4), 72–76.

Marshall, I. H. (1977). Preaching the Kingdom of God. *Expository Times, 89*(1), 211–14.

Meyer, B. (2004). Christianity in Africa: From African Independent Churches to Pentecostal-Charismatic Churches. Research Center Religion and Society: University of Amsterdam.

Newbigin, L. (1960, August 1). From "Mission" to "Missions." *Christianity Today*, 23.

Niklaus, R. L. (1982). Brazil: Pentecostal Invasion. *Evangelical Missions Quarterly, 18*(2), 117–18.

Patheos Library. (2015, July 13). African Pentecostals.

Pew Research Center. (2006, October 5). Overviews of Latin America, Africa, and Asia. In Spirit and Power: A 10-Country Survey of Pentecostals.

Pew Research Center. (2014, November 13). Religion in Latin America: Widespread Change in a Historically Catholic Region.

Recker, R. (1977). The Concept of the *Missio Dei* and Instruction in Mission at Calvin Seminary. *Calvin Theological Journal, 2*(2), 181–98.

Roebeck, C. M. (2011). The Status of Global Pentecostalism: An Overview. Global Christian Forum.

Sengwe, N. (1981). Identity Crisis in the African Church. *Evangelical Missions Quarterly, 17*(2), 91–99.

Shenk, W. R. (1979). Church Growth and God's Kingdom. *Mission Focus, 7*(2), 21–26.

Stetzer, E. (2011, December 22). The Pew Forum Releases New Research on Global Christianity. *Christianity Today.* www.christianitytoday.com.

Suico, F. (2005). Pentecostalism and Social Change. *Asian Journal of Pentecostal Studies* (8), 2.

Turner, H. W. (1963). African Prophet Movements. *Hibbert Journal,* 62(242), 112–16.

Van Dusen, H. P. (1955, August 17). Caribbean Holiday. *Christian Century, 72,* 946–47.

Van Dusen, H. P. (1958, June 9). The Third Force in Christendom. *Life,* 113–24.

Wasdel, D. (1980, January/February). HUP: A Defense against Anxiety. *Global Church Growth Bulletin,* 1–3.

Weigel, G. (2015, February 25). World Christianity by the Numbers. *Journal of Religion and Public Life.*

Woodward, K. L. (1982, April 26). The Split-Up Evangelicals. *Newsweek,* 88–91.

Unpublished Reports

Avery, Jr., A. W. (1969). African Independency: A Study of the Phenomenon of Independency and the Lessons to Be Learned from It for Greater Church Growth in Africa. Master's Thesis, School of World Mission, Fuller Theological Seminary, Pasadena, California.

Branner, J. K. (1975). Roland Allen, Donald McGavran and Church Growth. Th.M. Thesis, School of World Mission, Fuller Theological Seminary, Pasadena, California.

Chant, B. (1981). Australian Pentecostalism. Unley, Australia: House of Tabor, 1–3.

Conn, H. M. (1977). The Homogeneous Unit Principle: Some Background Perspectives. Unpublished manuscript, Westminster Theological Seminary, Philadelphia, Pennsylvania.

Division of Foreign Missions. (1981). Official Statistics: Assemblies of God. Springfield: Division of Foreign Missions, 1–8.

Hodges, M. L. (1974). MSS 535 Pentecostal Movement in Missions. Unpublished mimeographed class notes, Assemblies of God Graduate School, Springfield, Missouri.

Menzies, W. W. (1978). A Taxonomy of Pentecostal-Charismatic Theologies. Unpublished address given November 30, 1978, at the Annual Meeting of the Society for Pentecostal Studies.

Padilla, C. R. (1977). The Unity of the Church and the Homogeneous Unit Principle. Pasadena: Pasadena HUP Consultations.

Pomerville, P. A. (1980). A Case Study in the Contextualization of Theology: A Critique of the Reformed View of Scripture in the Post-Reformation Period. Master's Thesis, Seattle Pacific University, Seattle, Washington.

Rosin, H. H. (1972). "*Missio Dei*": an examination of the origin, contents, and function of the term in Protestant missiological discussion." Unpublished paper from the Interuniversitair Instituut voor Missiologie en Oecumenica, Leiden, Netherlands.

Sandidge, J. L. (1976). The Origin and Development of the Catholic Charismatic Movement in Belgium. Unpublished Master's Thesis, Leuven, Katholieke Universiteit Leuven, Belgium.

Watney, P. (1982). Positive Missiological Assessment of an African Independent Church. PhD dissertation proposal for the School of World Mission, Fuller Theological Seminary, Pasadena, California.

CORRESPONDENCE/INTERVIEWS

Durasoff, S. (1982, February 18). Missionary Evangelist to Eastern Europe. Correspondence.

Harrison, D. (1981, April 25). Assemblies of God Missionary to Brazil. Interview.

Seleky, T. E. (1982, March 2). Far East Advanced School of Theology, Manila, Philippines. Correspondence.

INDEX